Awakenings

Awakenings

Complete New Poetry, Language and Writing Skills for Leaving Certificate

Ordinary Level

John G. Fahy and **Anne Gormley**

Gill & Macmillan

Gill & Macmillan Ltd
Goldenbridge
Dublin 8
with associated companies throughout the world
www.gillmacmillan.ie

© John G. Fahy and Anne Gormley 1999
0 7171 2399 5

Print origination and design by
Niamh Lehane Design Consultant
Colour Reproduction by Typeform Repro Ltd, Dublin.

The paper used in this book is made from the wood pulp of managed forests. For every tree felled, at least one tree is planted, thereby renewing natural resources.

Contents

Poetry
John G. Fahy

Part 1: Prescribed Poems

1. Fleur Adcock	For Heidi with Blue Hair	1
2. W. H. Auden	Funeral Blues	4
3. Elizabeth Bishop	The Fish	7
	The Prodigal	11
	Filling Station	13
4. William Blake	A Poison Tree	17
5. Eavan Boland	Child of Our Time	19
	This Moment	22
6. Emily Dickinson	'Hope' is the thing with feathers	24
	A narrow Fellow in the Grass	26
7. Paul Durcan	Going Home to Mayo, Winter 1949	31
8. Robert Graves	Hedges Freaked with Snow	35
9. Michael Hartnett	Death of an Irishwoman	37
10. Séamus Heaney	The Forge	39
	Mossbawn: (1) Sunlight	42
	A Constable Calls	45
11. John Hewitt	The Green Shoot	48
12. John Keats	La Belle Dame sans Merci	51
	To Autumn	55
13. Philip Larkin	At Grass	60
	The Explosion	64
	Cut Grass	67
14. Michael Longley	Badger	69
	Wounds	72
15. John Montague	The Cage	77
16. Eiléan Ní Chuilleanáin	Swineherd	81
17. Siegfried Sassoon	Everyone Sang	83
18. William Shakespeare	Shall I compare thee	87
	Let me not to the marriage of true minds	88
	Fear no more the heat o' the sun	91
19. Percy Bysshe Shelley	Ozymandias	93
20. Stevie Smith	Deeply Morbid	96
21. Pauline Stainer	Sighting the Slave Ship	101
22. Richard Wilbur	The Pardon	104
23. Judith Wright	Request to a Year	108
24. William Butler Yeats	An Irish Airman Foresees His Death	111

Biographical Information on the Poets   115

Part 2: Unseen Poetry   144

Language and Writing Skills

Anne Gormley

Part 1: **Comprehension**   **193**

        Structure and form   194
        Style and language   194
        Descriptive writing   202
        Methods of answering comprehension questions   207
        Vocabulary for comprehension   208

Part 2: **English Grammar**   **211**

        Parts of speech   211
        Sentences and phrases   214
        Punctuation   214

Part 3: **The English Composition**   217

        Pre-composition writing   217
        Features of a good composition   219
        The language of narration   222
        The language of argument   225
        The language of information   227
        The language of persuasion   235
        Exercises   236

The work on each poet is arranged in four sections:
—The poet
—The poem
—Explorations
—A critical commentary

ACKNOWLEDGMENTS

For permission to reproduce copyright material, grateful acknowledgment is made to the following:

Poems (including recordings on CD)

Oxford University Press for 'For Heidi with Blue Hair' (text and recording) and 'The Telephone Call' by Fleur Adcock;

Farrar, Strauss and Giroux Inc. for poems by Elizabeth Bishop from *The Complete Poems 1927–1979* by Elizabeth Bishop, copyright © 1979, 1983 by Alice Helen Methfessel (texts and recordings);

Carcanet Press for poems by Eavan Boland from her *Collected Poems* (texts and recordings), for 'Hedges Freaked with Snow' from *Complete Poems* by Robert Graves (text and recording) and for 'Request to a Year' from *Collected Poems* by Judith Wright (text and recording);

Harvard University Press for poems by Emily Dickinson, reprinted by permission of the publishers and the trustees of Amherst College from *The Poems of Emily Dickinson*, Thomas H. Johnson, ed., Cambridge, Mass: The Belknap Press of Harvard University Press, copyright © 1951, 1955, 1979, 1983 by The President and fellows of Harvard College (texts and recordings);

Paul Durcan for 'Going Home to Mayo, Winter 1945' (text and recording); 'Backside to the Wind' and 'Wife who Smashed Television Gets Jail';

Michael Hartnett for 'Death of an Irish Woman' (text and recording);

Faber and Faber Ltd for poems by Séamus Heaney (texts and recordings); for 'The Explosion' and 'Cut Grass' by Philip Larkin (texts and recordings); for 'Ravens' by Ted Hughes; 'Funeral Blues' by W.H. Auden (recording: Curtis Brown Ltd.); 'Morning Song' by Sylvia Plath; 'The Pardon' by Richard Wilbur (recording: Harcourt, Bruce and Co.) and 'Anseo' by Paul Muldoon;

The Blackstaff Press for 'The Green Shoot' by John Hewitt (text and recording);

Marvell Press for 'At Grass' by Philip Larkin (text and recording);

Michael Longley and Lucas Alexander Whitley Ltd for poems by Michael Longley (texts and recordings);

The Gallery Press for 'The Cage' from *The Collected Poems* by John Montague (1995) (text and recording); 'Swineherd' from *The Second Voyage* by Eiléan Ní Chuilleanáin (1986) (text and recording); 'Seed' from *The Man who was Marked by Winter* by Paula Meehan (1991); 'Claudy' from *Poems 1956–1986* by James Simmons; 'Minding Ruth' by Aidan Mathews; 'My Mother' by Medbh McGuckian and for 'The Meadow' from *News of the World* (1988) by Peter Fallon;

George Sassoon and Barbara Levy Literary Agency for 'Everyone Sang' by Siegfried Sassoon (© Siegfried Sassoon by permission of George Sassoon) (text and recording);

Cambridge University Press and Professor G. Blakemore Evans for the following from *New Cambridge Shakespeare: The Sonnets* edited by G. Blakemore Evans (1996): No's 18 and 116,

Cymbeline Act IV Scene ii ('Fear no more the heat o' the sun') (texts and recordings);

James MacGibbon for 'Deeply Morbid' from *The Collected Poems of Stevie Smith* (Penguin Twentieth Century Classics) (text and recording);

Bloodaxe Books for 'Sighting the Slave Ship' by Pauline Stainer (1992) (text and recording);

A.P. Watt and Michael B. Yeats for 'An Irish Airman Foresees His Death' (text and recording), 'No Second Troy', 'Under Bare Ben Bulben's Head', 'Down by the Salley Gardens' and 'He Wishes for the Cloths of Heaven' by W.B. Yeats;

Sheil Land Associates for 'A Blessing' by James Wright;

Dermot Bolger for 'Leinster Street' from *Taking my Letters Back: New and Selected Poems* (New Island Books, 1998);

Rita Ann Higgins for 'Sunny Side Plucked' and 'Anything is Better than Emptying Bins';

Noel Monahan for 'Christmas in the West' from *Snow Fire* (Salmon Publishing);

John Johnson Ltd for 'Dawn Walkers' by Jenny Joseph;

Thomas Kinsella for 'Mirror in February' and 'Death Bed';

Brendan Kennelly for 'Dream of a Black Fox';

Don Byrne for 'Driving Home with Donal, 4';

David Higham Associates for 'Theme for English B' from *The Collected Poems of Langston Hughes*, for 'Prayer Before Birth' from *Collected Poems* by Louis MacNeice, for 'One Flesh' from *Collected Poems* by Elizabeth Jennings and for 'Harvest Hymn' from *Collected Poems* by John Betjeman;

Jonathan Cape Ltd for 'Hearts and Flowers' by Roger McGough;

Peter Fallon Literary Agent for 'Inniskeen Road: July Evening' and 'Innocence' by Patrick Kavanagh;

Derek Mahon for 'Northwind: Portrush';

Chronicle Books for 'Oranges' from *New and Selected Poems* by Gary Soto;

John F. Deane for 'Penance';

R. Dardis Clarke, 21 Pleasants Street, Dublin 8 for 'The Planter's Daughter' and 'The Redemptorist' by Austin Clarke;

The Author and Rogers, Coleridge & White Ltd for 'Portrait of a Young Girl Raped at a Suburban Party' from *Notes to a Hurrying Man* by Brian Patten, copyright © Brian Patten 1969;

Michael O'Loughlin for 'The Smile';

Sterling, Lord Literisic Inc. for 'Unknown Girl in the Maternity Ward' by Anne Sexton;

Keith Douglas for 'Vergissmeinicht';

Michael Smith for 'A Visit to the Village';

Peters, Fraser & Dunlop for 'When I was Fifteen' by Michael Rosen;

The co-operation of all who took part in the recording of poems for the CD is gratefully acknowledged as is the assistance of Poetry Ireland.

Illustrations

Picture Research: Anne Marie Ehrlich

P.1   Fleur Adcock — Camera Press;
P.4   W.H. Auden — Mark Gerson;
P.7   Elizabeth Bishop standing with bicycle in Key West — photo: Lloyd Frankenberg/Special Collections, Vassar College Libraries, Poughkeepsie, New York;
P.15   'Interior with Calder Mobile' painting by Elizabeth Bishop (whereabouts unknown) reproduced from *Changing Hats: Elizabeth Bishop Paintings*, edited with an introduction by William Benton, published by Farrar, Strauss, Giroux (New York 1996) — reproduced with permission of the publishers, copyright © 1996 by Alice Helen Methfessel;
P.17   William Blake (artist: Thomas Phillips, 1770–1845) — National Portrait Gallery, London;
P.19   Eavan Boland — The Irish Times;
P.24   Emily Dickinson — Amherst College Library;
P.31   Paul Durcan — Universal Pictorial Press;
P.35   Robert Graves — Hulton Getty;
P.37   Michael Hartnett — Radio Telefís Éireann;
P.39   Séamus Heaney — Radio Telefís Éireann;
P.48   John Hewitt — Victor Patterson;
P.51   John Keats (artist: Joseph Severn 1793–1879) — National Portrait Gallery, London;
P52   'La Belle Dame Sans Merci' (oil painting by Sir Frank Dicksee) — Bridgeman Art Library/City of Bristol Museum and Art Gallery;
P.56   'The Cornfield 1826' (artist: John Constable) — National Gallery, London/E.T. Archive;
P.60   Philip Larkin — Camera Press;
P.61   'Hyperion' at stud — Popperfoto;
P.66   Coal Miners — Popperfoto;
P.69   Michael Longley — photo by Leon McAuley;
P.73   Royal Irish Rifles at the Somme, July 1916 — Imperial War Museum London;
P.77   John Montague — Peter Fallon/The Gallery Press;
P.81   Eiléan Ní Chuilleanáin — Macdara Woods;
P.83   Siegfried Sassoon — Hulton Getty;
P.85   William Shakespeare (artist: John Taylor d.1651) — National Portrait Gallery, London;
P.86   (left) Henry Wriothesley, 3rd Earl of Southampton (artist unknown) — National Portrait Gallery London;
P.86   (right) Anne Leighton, Lady St John c.1615 (Larkin) — Bridgeman Art Library;
P.93   Percy Bysshe Shelley (artist: Amelia Curran, d.1847) — National Portrait Gallery, London;
P.96   Stevie Smith — Camera Press;
P.101 Pauline Stainer — Bloodaxe Books;
P.104 Richard Wilbur — Faber and Faber Ltd;
P.108 Judith Wright — Coward of Canberra/Carcanet Press;
P.111 W.B. Yeats — National Library of Ireland;

The publishers have made every effort to trace copyright holders but if they have inadvertently overlooked any, they will be pleased to make the necessary arrangements at the first opportunity.

AWAKENINGS CD

Contents

Track 1:   Introduction

Track 2:   Fleur Adcock - *For Heidi with Blue Hair*

Track 3:   W.H. Auden - *Funeral Blues*

Track 4:   Elizabeth Bishop - *The Fish*

Track 5:   Elizabeth Bishop - *The Prodigal*

Track 6:   Elizabeth Bishop - *Filling Station*

Track 7:   William Blake - *A Poison Tree*

Track 8:   Eavan Boland - *Child of Our Time*

Track 9:   Eavan Boland - *This Moment*

Track 10: Emily Dickinson - *'Hope' is the thing with feathers*

Track 11: Emily Dickinson - *A narrow Fellow in the Grass*

Track 12: Paul Durcan - *Going Home to Mayo, Winter 1949*

Track 13: Robert Graves - *Hedges Freaked with Snow*

Track 14: Michael Hartnett - *Death of an Irishwoman*

Track 15: Séamus Heaney - *The Forge*

Track 16: Séamus Heaney - *Mossbawn: (1) Sunlight*

Track 17: Séamus Heaney - *A Constable Calls*

Track 18: John Hewitt - *The Green Shoot*

Track 19: John Keats - *La Belle Dame sans Merci*

Track 20: John Keats - *To Autumn*

Track 21: Philip Larkin - *At Grass*

Track 22: Philip Larkin - *The Explosion*

Track 23: Philip Larkin - *Cut Grass*

Track 24: Michael Longley - *Badger*

Track 25: Michael Longley - *Wounds*

Track 26: John Montague - *The Cage*

Track 27: Eiléan Ní Chuilleanáin - *Swineherd*

Track 28: Siegfried Sassoon - *Everyone Sang*

Track 29: William Shakespeare - *Shall I compare thee*

Track 30: William Shakespeare - *Let me not to the marriage of true minds*

Track 31: William Shakespeare - *Fear no more the heat o' the sun*

Track 32: Percy Bysshe Shelley - *Ozymandias*

Track 33: Stevie Smith - *Deeply Morbid*

Track 34: Pauline Stainer - *Sighting the Slave Ship*

Track 35: Richard Wilbur - *The Pardon*

Track 36: Judith Wright - *Request to a Year*

Track 37: William Butler Yeats - *An Irish Airman Foresees his Death*

1
Prescribed Poems

1 *Fleur Adcock* (born 1934)

Fleur Adcock was born in New Zealand and lived there at various times but has spent much of her life in England. Her volumes of poetry include *The Eye of the Hurricane* (1964), *Tigers* (1967), *High Tide in the Garden* (1971), *The Inner Harbour* (1979), *The Incident Book* (1986), and *Time Zones* (1991). She is considered one of the foremost feminist poets of the age, famous for her 'anti-erotic' style of love poems. 'For Heidi with Blue Hair' is taken from *The Incident Book* and is dedicated to her god-daughter, Heidi Jackson. (For fuller information see page 115.)

For Heidi with Blue Hair

When you dyed your hair blue
(or, at least, ultramarine
for the clipped sides, with a crest
of jet-black spikes on top)
you were sent home from school   5

because, as the headmistress put it,
although dyed hair was not
specifically forbidden, yours
was, apart from anything else,
not done in the school colours.

Tears in the kitchen, telephone-calls   10
to school from your freedom-loving father:
'She's not a punk in her behaviour;
it's just a style.' (You wiped your eyes,
also not in a school colour.)

'She discussed it with me first—   15
we checked the rules.' 'And anyway, Dad,
it cost twenty-five dollars.
Tell them it won't wash out—
not even if I wanted to try.'

It would have been unfair to mention   20
your mother's death, but that
shimmered behind the arguments.
The school had nothing else against you;
the teachers twittered and gave in.

Next day your black friend had hers done   25
in grey, white and flaxen yellow—
the school colours precisely:
an act of solidarity, a witty
tease. The battle was already won.

Explorations

First reading

1. What details of the story stand out? What in particular do you notice on a first reading?
2. Visualise the scene in the kitchen. What details do you notice? How do you hear the voices? Comment on the tones of voice, or say the words aloud as you imagine them.
3. Read the second stanza aloud as you imagine the headmistress would say it. How would you describe the tone? What kind of person do you think she is? Explain.
4. What kind of person do you think the father is?

Second reading

5. Why do you think Heidi dyed her hair?
6. Why did Heidi's black friend have hers done? Explore the last stanza for clues.
7. 'It would have been unfair to mention | your mother's death, but that | shimmered behind the arguments.' What do you imagine people were thinking? Write out the thoughts that the father, or the headmistress or the teachers, might have had. What might Heidi herself have thought? Comment on the word 'shimmer'.
8. What kind of school do you suppose it was? Comment on the school's attitude and outlook as revealed in the poem. Do you think it was strict, 'stuffy', 'posh', reasonable, or what? Read the entire poem again before committing yourself.
9. Do you think the poem accurately reflects the demand for conformity found in school life? Do you find it true? Explain.

Third reading

10. Would you consider the father's attitude usual or unusual for a parent? Explain.
11. What truths about the life of a teenager do you find in this poem?
12. Do you think the poem is humorous? Mention *two* ways in which this humour is created. Is this note of humour maintained all the way through?
13. Make notes on the main themes and issues you find dealt with in the poem.

A Critical Commentary

Issues

This poem deals with adolescent assertiveness and the right to choose one's own dress code, hair style, and so on. These issues often become symbolic of individual freedoms and rights in the conflict between the teenager and authority, whether school or home. This conflict between youth culture and school culture has been elevated to the status of a 'battle' in this poem.

On a broader scale we might view the poem as demonstrating the conflict between different outlooks, attitudes, or philosophies—liberalism versus the need to conform. The more relaxed tolerance of the father is pitted against the rather snooty conformism of the school. But the school is not really very authoritarian, as the teachers give in, probably taking the home background into account.

Tone

For the most part, the poem is written in humorous or mock-serious tone. The humour is brought about through the contrast between the formality of the language and the relative insignificance of the event. Examine, for instance, the formal expression and complex structure of the language in the headmistress's telephone call (stanza 2). There is also a sense of the ridiculous in the witty, repartee-style comment 'you wiped your eyes, I also not in a school colour.' The rebellious, trend-setting ending adds to the sense of mischief and lets us see where the poet's sympathies lie: with the teenager and in support of the subversive. The exuberant colours add to the lightness of atmosphere here.

The one bleak note sounded concerns the reference to the mother's death, 'that shimmered behind the arguments.' 'Shimmered' suggests a vague, ill-defined, ghost-like presence and captures well the background thoughts on the mother's death, which nobody has had the courage to formulate into words. Would this be happening if her mother was alive? Should we indulge this child a bit because of her loss?

Capturing character

Adcock is particularly good at evoking the essence of characters in a spare yet effective way. The kind, liberal father is supportive of his daughter, however ridiculous her looks. He believes in 'dialogue'—talking things out: 'She discussed it with me first.' And we have the image of rebellious, defiant Heidi, reduced to tears—not so tough really! And we recognise her desperation as she tries a range of separate excuses: the cost, and the indelible nature of the dye. The teachers are well captured, however briefly: 'the teachers twittered.' We get an image of nice old dears, genteel, ladylike disapproval and all the connotations about the type of school that this conjures up.

The success of the portraiture depends to a good degree on Adcock's sharp ear for dialogue. She had a real feel for the style of conversation. She captures the father's defensive terse tones: 'She discussed … we checked …' and the headmistress's long-winded, slightly grand style, conveyed in the complex syntax of the second stanza. We can hear her careful, measured statement: '… not specifically forbidden.' And she captures the casual, pushy, argumentative style of the teenager Heidi: 'And anyway, Dad …'

2 *W. H. Auden* *(1907–1973)*

Wystan Hugh Auden was born at York on 21 February 1907 and educated at Oxford and Berlin. He is considered one of the most important English poets of the nineteen-thirties, writing on political and social themes. A prolific poet, he wrote in a variety of verse forms, composing both humorous and serious poetry. 'Funeral Blues', originally a song in one of his plays, is taken from the volume *Another Time* (1940), which contains many of his best-known poems, such as 'September 1939' and 'Lullaby'. Auden spent much of his life in the United States, becoming an American citizen in 1946. (For fuller information see page 116.)

Funeral Blues

Stop all the clocks, cut off the telephone,
Prevent the dog from barking with a juicy bone,
Silence the pianos and with muffled drum
Bring out the coffin, let the mourners come.

Let aeroplanes circle moaning overhead   5
Scribbling on the sky the message He Is Dead,
Put the crêpe bows round the white necks of the public doves,
Let the traffic policemen wear black cotton gloves.

He was my North, my South, my East and West,
My working week and my Sunday rest,   10
My noon, my midnight, my talk, my song;
I thought that love would last for ever: I was wrong.

The stars are not wanted now: put out every one;
Pack up the moon and dismantle the sun;
Pour away the ocean and sweep up the wood.   15
For nothing now can ever come to any good.

Explorations

First reading

1. What images grab your attention?
2. What do you think is happening in this poem?
3. Do you find it unusual in any way? Explain.

Second reading

4. The first two stanzas create the atmosphere of a funeral. What sights and sounds of a funeral do you notice?
5. It used to be a custom that clocks were stopped in a house where a death had occurred: as well as marking the time of death, this signified that time stood still for the grieving family. But do you think that the signs of mourning have been carried to extremes in the first two stanzas? Examine the actions called for.
6. How do you think the first stanza should be read: in a low, defeated tone, or semi-hysterical, or what? Read it aloud.
7. Read the second stanza aloud.
8. Do you think there might be a change of tone from the third stanza on? Read aloud stanzas 3 and 4.
9. Are you sympathetic to the speaker in this poem?

Third reading

10. What does the third stanza suggest about the relationship between the speaker and the person mourned? Examine each line in detail for the kernel of truth behind the clichés.
11. How do you understand the speaker's state of mind, particularly in the last verse?
12. Do you take this poem to be a serious statement about loss and bereavement, or do you find it exaggerated and 'over the top'? Explain your opinion. Do you think it could be read as a satire, that is, a poem ridiculing, in this case, the public outpouring of emotion at the funerals of famous people? Read the poem again.

Fourth reading

13. What do you think the poem is saying?
14. Look at the imagery again. How does it fit in with what the poem is saying?
15. Read the critical commentary below on 'style'. What elements of a blues song do you find in the poem?
16. What do you like about this poem?

A Critical Commentary

Origins of the poem

It is sometimes difficult to trace the origins of certain Auden poems, because he had the habit of revising his material frequently, incorporating some poems into longer works and generally rewriting. A version of 'Stop All the Clocks' (the first two verses as here, with two others) first appeared in the drama Auden wrote and produced jointly with Christopher Isherwood in 1936, *The Ascent of F6*. In this satirical fable about politics and leadership the song is a 'spoof' of a dirge for a dead political leader. It is a tongue-in-cheek lament, making fun of the gullibility of the public, who insist on making heroes of flawed human beings.

The present version appeared in the collection *Another Time* (1940) and was entitled 'Funeral Blues', one of 'Four Cabaret Songs for Miss Heidi Anderson'. At the time of composition Heidi Anderson was engaged to Auden's friend and collaborator, the Irish poet Louis MacNeice. The music for these was composed by Benjamin Britten.

Readings

This poem can be read either as an elegy or as a satire. If we read it as an elegy we tend to concentrate on the two final stanzas and focus on the depth of feeling, that intense sense of loss that finds expression in the outpouring of unbridled grief:

> He was my North, my South, my East and West
> ...
> The stars are not wanted now: put out every one ...

If we read it as an elegy, these exaggerated sentiments are an attempt to communicate the depth of pain and the fearful grief felt by the speaker. If we read it as a satire, we take our cue from the first two stanzas in particular and view the poem as a satirical treatment of public mourning, as a lament with exaggerated sentiments and imagery that succeeds in ridiculing the practice of the public funeral and is critical of the outpouring of popular grief for a public figure.

Style

On first reading this poem one is struck by the ludicrous imagery and the wildly exaggerated emotions. The reader may not be sure whether this is comic or tragic. But if we consider the poem's origins as a blues song it may help our understanding. The critic John Fuller sees the poem as 'a good pastiche of the stoical lament and flamboyant imagery of the traditional blues lyric.' In other words, the style is a mixture of features from the lament and the blues lyric, and Auden has exaggerated these. So, we find an overstatement of the usual blues sentiment in lamenting a dead lover. This exaggerated feeling is carried in the imagery, which varies from the stately and solemn—

> Silence the pianos and with muffled drum
> Bring out the coffin, let the mourners come

—to the comic 'Put the crêpe bows round the white necks of the public doves.' We find the blues style also in the use of clichés:

> He was my North, my South, my East and West,
> My working week and my Sunday rest.

Banal and much-used metaphors such as these help convey the notion that these feelings are felt by everybody, by ordinary people. They foster the idea that this grief is universal. Blues rhythms too are suggested in the metre. We get these long, rolling sentences, for example in the third stanza; and then the division of some lines into two introduces a counter-rhythm and a regular beat: 'I thought that love would last for ever: I was wrong.'

The satire

The satirical effect is created through exaggeration. The realistic sounds, silences and colours of a funeral are evoked in the first two stanzas: stop all the clocks, silence the pianos, muffled drum, aeroplanes moaning, crêpe bow, black cotton gloves. The long *o* and *u* sounds help create the atmosphere of mourning: phone, bone, drum, come. But it all goes over the top into melodrama, through the use of extremes: 'Prevent the dog from barking' and 'Let aeroplanes circle moaning overhead | Scribbling in the sky the message: He is Dead.' The flamboyant American advertising culture is quite inappropriate for conveying the announcement of a death; this bad taste heightens the sense of satire. The somewhat hysterical tone of the opening ('Stop all the clocks, cut off the telephone') adds to the melodrama, as do the extremes of feeling in

> Pour away the ocean and sweep up the wood.
> For nothing now can ever come to any good.

But do you think there might be a hint of real grief and sorrow behind this melodramatic exaggeration? Consider, for instance, the third stanza. Could line 1 be read as meaning 'He was the whole world to me,' line 2 as 'He was always in my thoughts, both at work and leisure,' and line 3 as 'He was at the centre of all my moods, happy or depressed' (noon or midnight)?

It might be useful to list (in your own words) the speaker's feelings for the dead person; then examine the final stanza in some detail. Why do you think he chooses the references he does? Why the sun, moon, and stars? Why does he feel he will no longer need the ocean or the wood? Could these have been their favourite places?

Do you find that the two final stanzas prompt you to consider that this poem communicates genuine feeling and depth of emotion?

3 *Elizabeth Bishop* (1911–1979)

Elizabeth Bishop with bicycle in Key West

Born in Worcester, Massachusetts, Elizabeth Bishop spent much of her childhood with her maternal grandparents in Nova Scotia, Canada, a situation that provided the material for some of her writing. She travelled widely in Europe and South America, settling in Brazil for many years. This too provided material for her poems. Another of her favourite places was Key West, Florida, where she enjoyed fishing. This is reflected in the poem 'The Fish', taken from her first book of poetry, *North and South* (1946). Other volumes were *A Cold Spring* (1955), *Questions of Travel* (1965), and *Geography III* (1976). Her poems often encourage us to look beneath the surface and discover the uniqueness and strangeness of everyday experience. She frequently explores the unsatisfactory, unhappy aspects of life. (For fuller information see page 117.)

The Fish

I caught a tremendous fish
and held him beside the boat
half out of water, with my hook
fast in a corner of his mouth.
He didn't fight.   5
He hadn't fought at all.
He hung a grunting weight,
battered and venerable
and homely. Here and there
his brown skin hung in strips   10
like ancient wallpaper,
and its pattern of darker brown
was like wallpaper:
shapes like full-blown roses
stained and lost through age.   15

He was speckled with barnacles,
fine rosettes of lime,
and infested
with tiny white sea-lice,
and underneath two or three   20
rags of green weed hung down.
While his gills were breathing in
the terrible oxygen
—the frightening gills,
fresh and crisp with blood,   25
that can cut so badly—
I thought of the coarse white flesh
packed in like feathers,
the big bones and the little bones,
the dramatic reds and blacks   30

of his shiny entrails,
and the pink swim-bladder
like a big peony.
I looked into his eyes
which were far larger than mine   35
but shallower, and yellowed,
the irises backed and packed
with tarnished tinfoil
seen through the lenses
of old scratched isinglass.   40
They shifted a little, but not
to return my stare.
—It was more like the tipping
of an object toward the light.
I admired his sullen face,   45
the mechanism of his jaw,
and then I saw
that from his lower lip
—if you could call it a lip—
grim, wet, and weaponlike,   50
hung five old pieces of fish-line,
or four and a wire leader
with the swivel still attached,

with all their five big hooks
grown firmly in his mouth.   55
A green line, frayed at the end
where he broke it, two heavier lines,
and a fine black thread
still crimped from the strain and snap
when it broke and he got away.   60
Like medals with their ribbons
frayed and wavering,
a five-haired beard of wisdom
trailing from his aching jaw.
I stared and stared   65
and victory filled up
the little rented boat,
from the pool of bilge
where oil had spread a rainbow
around the rusted engine   70
to the bailer rusted orange,
the sun-cracked thwarts,
the oarlocks on their strings,
the gunnels—until everything
was rainbow, rainbow, rainbow!   75
And I let the fish go.

Notes

[40] **isinglass:** a semi-transparent form of gelatine extracted from certain fish and used in making jellies, glue, etc.

Explorations

First reading

1. How do you visualise the fish? Think of it as a painting or a picture. What details strike you on a first reading?
2. What is your first impression of the speaker in this poem?

Second reading

3. Consider in detail the description of the fish. Which elements of the description could be considered objective or factual? Which elements could be seen as purely subjective on the part of the poet? Which are imagined or aesthetic elements in the description?

4. Do you think the poet's re-creation of the fish is a good one? Explain your views.

Third reading

5. Explore the attitude of the speaker towards the fish over the entire length of the poem. What changes do you notice, and where?
6. Why do you think she released the fish? Explore the text for possible reasons.
7. Do you think this is an important moment for the poet? What does she learn or discover? Where, in the text, is this suggested?
8. Is the poet excited by this experience? Where, in the text, is this suggested? Comment on the tone of the poem.

Fourth reading

9. What issues does this poem raise? Consider what the poem has to say about
   - our relationship with the natural world
   - the nature of creativity
   - moments of insight and decision
   - other themes hinted at.
10. Do you think the imagery is effective in getting across a real understanding of the fish and an awareness of the poet's mood? Explore any two relevant images, and explain how they function.
11. This is quite a dramatic poem. Explain how the dramatic effect is created. Consider such elements as the way the narrative builds to a climax; the ending; the effect of the short enjambed lines; and the speaker's interior debate.
12. What did you like about this poem?
13. Read the critical commentary below, discuss it, and make your own notes on Elizabeth Bishop's technique, that is, her method of re-creating a subject in her poetry.

A Critical Commentary

Background

Elizabeth Bishop discovered Florida and a love of fishing in the late nineteen-thirties. Based on real fishing experiences, her notebooks of the time show images and line fragments that were later developed in 'The Fish'. She worked on the poem during the winter of 1939 and sent a finished draft to Marianne Moore in January 1940, and the poem was first published in the *Partisan Review* in March 1940. It is included in her first published collection, *North and South* (1946).

The speaker: the I and eye

The poem is narrated in the first person, so we get to meet the poet—the 'I' in the poem—directly, as we do in quite a few of Bishop's poems. This gives the experience of the poem an immediacy and an intimacy for the reader. But while the reader may feel closely involved in the drama, there is a hint that the speaker herself is something of an outsider, not a native of the place, the inhabitant of a 'rented boat'. Perhaps this lends a certain objectivity to the drama and the description of it.

We are also introduced here to the famous Bishop 'eye', which sees both the beautiful and the grimy, not only describes surface detail but even imagines the interior:

> the dramatic reds and blacks
> of his shiny entrails,
> and the pink swim-bladder
> like a big peony.

Minute descriptions and the calculated use of detail are a feature of Bishop's poetry. This is how she apprehends the world and comes to grips with experience: through aesthetic re-creation. Detail is important as a basis for understanding.

Bishop re-creates the fish in minute detail. This is how she interiorises it, comprehends it. At first she domesticates it in the imagery, making it familiar by linking it to details of faded everyday living (he is 'homely', 'brown skin hung in strips like ancient wallpaper,' 'shapes like full-blown roses,' 'rags of green weed'). Yet something of its essential wildness, the otherness of its creative being, is retained in some of the descriptions:

> the frightening gills,
> fresh and crisp with blood,
> that can cut so badly …

This is also rendered in war imagery:

> from his lower lip …
> grim, wet, and weaponlike,
> hung five old pieces of fish-line …
> Like medals with their ribbons
> frayed and wavering.

But perhaps the most crucial moment in the poet's comprehension of the fish is when she examines the eyes,

> which were far larger than mine
> but shallower, and yellowed,
> the irises backed and packed
> with tarnished tinfoil
> seen through the lenses
> of old scratched isinglass.

The detail is re-created poetically, using all the echoes and sound effects of alliteration and assonance reminiscent of a Hopkins 'inscaping'—re-creating in words the essence of the thing observed ('shallower', 'yellowed', 'backed and packed', 'tarnished tinfoil'). The detailed re-creation leads to the poet's realisation that these eyes are unresponsive, the fish is oblivious to her, there is no real sentient contact between human and animal.

> They shifted a little, but not
> to return my stare.

There is no question here of humankind's heroic struggle against nature, such as we find in Hemingway's *The Old Man and the Sea*. The experience is not glorified or mythologised but rather rendered as she saw it. 'I always tell the truth in my poems,' Bishop is reported as saying to her students. 'With "The Fish", that's exactly how it happened. It was in Key West, and I did catch it, just as the poem says. That was in 1938. Oh, but I did change one thing; the poem says he had five hooks hanging from his mouth, but actually he only had three. Sometimes a poem makes its own demands. But I always try to stick as much as possible to what really happened when I describe something in a poem' (Wesley Wehr in 'Elizabeth Bishop: conversations and class notes', *Antioch Review*, no. 39, summer 1981).

We notice that, even as she is asserting the absolute integrity of her eye and the accuracy of the descriptive process, she is also aware of the creative demands of the poetic process. The poem is an accurate record, but only up to a point.

A dramatic poem

The critic Willard Spiegelman (in *Centennial Review*, no. 22, winter 1978, reprinted in H.

Bloom (ed.), *Elizabeth Bishop: Modern Critical View*, 1985), reflecting on the dramatic quality of Bishop's poetry, said: 'We do not normally think of Bishop as a poet of struggle; the tension in her poems is mostly internalised, and confrontations, when they occur, are between the self, travelling, moving or simply seeing, and the landscape it experiences.'

This is particularly applicable to this poem. The first and last lines ('I caught a tremendous fish' and 'and I let the fish go') frame this drama. There is little external conflict, though there are hints of military antagonism and danger from the fish. The confrontation framed by these lines is mainly internal.

So why does she release the fish? Was it because of the lack of heroic struggle?

> He didn't fight.
> He hadn't fought at all.

Does the lack of contact in the eyes disappoint her? Or does she release him out of respect for his history of previous successful encounters, a record emblazoned on his lip ('a five-haired beard of wisdom | trailing from his aching jaw'). Perhaps these are part of the decision; but the real moment of truth occurs because of the sudden appearance of the accidental industrial rainbow when the bilge oil gleams in the sun ('where oil had spread a rainbow | around the rusted engine'). Fortuitous, a grim parody of natural beauty, an ironic comment on humankind's relationship with nature this may be, but it provides for the poet a moment of aesthetic unity with the grandeur of the world, and everything is transformed ('everything | was rainbow, rainbow, rainbow!'). It is a moment of revelation, in which this new image of the fish colours the environment and alters her relationship with nature. No longer antagonistic, confrontational, she has metaphorically tamed, re-created and understood the fish.

The ending of the poem is very similar to a Wordsworth nature poem such as 'The Daffodils': the hypnotic vision ('I stared and stared'), the wealth accruing to the viewer ('victory filled up the little rented boat'), and feelings of inspiration and joy through creating a connection with the world, a world that has been transformed by the vision, this moment of epiphany:

where oil had spread a rainbow
around the rusted engine
to the bailer rusted orange,
… until everything
was rainbow, rainbow, rainbow!

The Prodigal

The brown enormous odour he lived by
was too close, with its breathing and thick hair,
for him to judge. The floor was rotten; the sty
was plastered halfway up with glass-smooth dung.
Light-lashed, self-righteous, above moving snouts,   5
the pigs' eyes followed him, a cheerful stare—
even to the sow that always ate her young—
till, sickening, he leaned to scratch her head.
But sometimes mornings after drinking bouts
(he hid the pints behind a two-by-four),   10
the sunrise glazed the barnyard mud with red;
the burning puddles seemed to reassure.
And then he thought he almost might endure
his exile yet another year or more.

But evenings the first star came to warn.   15
The farmer whom he worked for came at dark
to shut the cows and horses in the barn
beneath their overhanging clouds of hay,
with pitchforks, faint forked lightnings, catching light,
safe and companionable as in the Ark.   20
The pigs stuck out their little feet and snored.
The lantern—like the sun, going away—
laid on the mud a pacing aureole.
Carrying a bucket along a slimy board,
he felt the bats' uncertain staggering flight,   25
his shuddering insights, beyond his control,
touching him. But it took him a long time
finally to make his mind up to go home.

Notes

[23] **aureole:** a celestial crown represented in pictures as a golden circle above the head of martyrs and saints

Explorations

Pre-reading

1. What does the title of the poem lead you to expect?

First reading

2. Were any of your expectations met on reading the poem?
3. How do you see the character in this poem?
   - What is he doing? How does he live?
   - Why is he there?
   - Does he find any satisfaction in his work?
   - What helps him endure his exile?
4. What details of the scene affected you most?

Second reading

5. Examine the final five lines. What do you think the 'shuddering insights, beyond his control' might be? Re-create his thoughts as you imagine them here.
6. Bishop appeals to a range of senses—smell, sight, sound, touch—in order to re-create the atmosphere of the place. Examine a sample of each type of image and discuss the effect.
7. How would you describe the atmosphere of the place? Is it one of unrelieved misery or is there some contentment in it? Refer to the text.
8. Examine the poet's attitude to the prodigal. Do you think she is condemnatory, sympathetic, or neutral? Discuss, with reference to the text.
9. What is your own attitude to the prodigal?

Third reading

10. What are the main human issues raised by this poem?
11. Briefly, express the theme of the poem.
12. Bishop's poetic technique involved really looking at the detail of her subject matter. Where do you think this works best in this poem?

A Critical Commentary

Genesis of the poem

Elizabeth Bishop said that the poem originated from her thoughts when one of her aunt's stepsons offered her a drink of rum in the pig-sty at about nine o'clock in the morning during her trip to Nova Scotia in 1946. Perhaps that was the final spark that engendered the poem; but the theme could never have been far from her thoughts, as she herself struggled with alcoholism all her life.

About the time of her thirty-eighth birthday, on 8 February 1949, she fell into a deep trough of depression. In an effort to rally herself out of it she went on a holiday to Haïti, from where she wrote to Marianne Moore to say that she had finished some poems, including 'The Prodigal'. Ironically, on her return from Haïti she went into a long and heavy drinking bout. 'The Prodigal' was published in the *New Yorker* on 13 March 1951.

Theme and development

This poem deals with the exile of the alcoholic. Like all good poetry, it functions at the level of the individual in the narrative but also at a universal level, exploring the metaphorical exile of alcoholism: the isolation, the skulking, the deception and hiding, the lack of control, aspirations rather than action. (Where do these feature in this poem?) There is enormous human understanding in the poem. Despite the physical grossness of odour and ordure, the heart can still lift to the religious impulse ('the lantern—like the sun, going away—| laid on the mud a pacing aureole') or thrill to the romantic beauty of nature ('the sunrise glazed the barnyard mud with red; | the burning puddles seemed to reassure'). In fact the prodigal seems to retain a particularly benign relationship with nature, appreciating the delicacy of even these animals ('light-lashed … a cheerful stare') and maintaining a comfortable domesticity between animal and human ('the pigs stuck out their little feet and snored'). Nature here is a bringer of wisdom. The bats' 'uncertain staggering flight' is the spur to his self-awareness, his moment of 'shuddering insights', and so his eventual turning back.

The poem is depressingly realistic in its evocation of filth and human abasement:

> even to the sow that always ate her young—
> till, sickening, he leaned to scratch her head.

But it is noble and uplifting in its awareness of the spark of soul that still flickers even in the most abject circumstances.

Form
The poem is structured as two sonnets of a rather loose nature. Each has the requisite fourteen lines, and the first one maintains the conventional octave-sestet division, but the rhyming schemes are eccentric, if not absent altogether. The rhythm is a mixture of iambic pentameter and four-stress lines.

Filling Station

Oh, but it is dirty!
—this little filling station,
oil-soaked, oil-permeated
to a disturbing, over-all
black translucency.   5
Be careful with that match!

Father wears a dirty,
oil-soaked monkey suit
that cuts him under the arms,
and several quick and saucy   10
and greasy sons assist him
(it's a family filling station),
all quite thoroughly dirty.

Do they live in the station?
It has a cement porch   15
behind the pumps, and on it
a set of crushed and grease-
impregnated wickerwork;
on the wicker sofa
a dirty dog, quite comfy.   20

Some comic books provide
the only note of colour—
of certain colour. They lie
upon a big dim doily
draping a taboret   25
(part of the set), beside
a big hirsute begonia.

Why the extraneous plant?
Why the taboret?
Why, oh why, the doily?   30
(Embroidered in daisy stitch
with marguerites, I think,
and heavy with grey crochet.)

Somebody embroidered the doily.
Somebody waters the plant,   35
or oils it, maybe. Somebody
arranges the rows of cans
so that they softly say:
ESSO-SO-SO-SO
to high-strung automobiles.   40
Somebody loves us all.

Notes
[24] **doily:** a small ornamental table-napkin

[25] **taboret:** a type of stool

[32] **marguerites:** daisies

Explorations

Pre-reading

1. Think about the title. What do you see?

First reading

2. Describe the atmosphere this poem creates for you. What details appear to you to be significant in creating this? Discuss them.

Second reading

3. Plan the shots you would use if you were making a film of this scene. Describe what you see in each shot, and explain your choice of detail.

4. Is there any progression or development of complexity in this film? How do you understand it?

5. What do the doily, the taboret and the begonia add to the atmosphere?

Third reading

6. What is it about this scene that fascinates the poet—the forecourt, the domestic details, or something else? Discuss.

7. How do you understand the 'somebody' in stanza 6?

Fourth reading

8. Do you think the poet is discovering a truth and making a statement about life? If so, what? Discuss this.

9. Read the critical commentary below and discuss this as an interpretation of the poem.

10. Write your own notes on the theme of the poem, the poet's philosophy, her poetic method, and the style and tone of the poem.

11. Do you find any evidence of wit or humour in this poem? Explain.

A Critical Commentary

A celebration of the ordinary

Many of Elizabeth Bishop's poems show a fascination with the exotic, with travel, with the mysterious forces in nature, and with the extremes of human experience, but she is also a poet of the ordinary, the everyday, the mundane and banal. She is interested in both the extraordinary and the ordinary.

And the scene we are introduced to at the beginning of this poem is not just the antithesis of beauty, it is unmitigated ugliness: 'oil-soaked, oil-permeated,' 'crushed and grease-impregnated wickerwork,' 'a dirty dog.' What Bishop does is to focus her well-known curiosity on this everyday dull scene and probe its uniqueness and mystery. She finds its meaning through her usual poetic method: the accumulation of detail and a probing beneath the surface of the seen.

The domestic gives meaning to life

What is revealed as the details pile up is evidence of domesticity, even in this greasy, grimy world of oil and toil: the flower, the 'taboret (part of the set),' the embroidered doily; and even the dirty dog is 'quite comfy.' In a parody of metaphysical questioning,

> Why the extraneous plant?
> Why the taboret?
> Why, oh why, the doily?

the poem searches for answers, for reasons why things are so, for some harmony or coherence at the heart of this grimy scene. The answer appears in the last stanza, where there are indications of an anonymous domestic presence.

> Somebody embroidered the doily.
> Somebody waters the plant.

For Bishop, domesticity is the greatest good, and establishing domestic tranquillity is what gives meaning to life. She has elevated this into

'Interior with Calder Mobile' — painting by Elizabeth Bishop

a philosophy in place of a religious outlook. Indeed this last stanza has been read as a parody of the great theological 'argument from design', used as an indication of the existence of God.

In Bishop's 'theology', is the Great Designer feminine? Certainly we could argue that the world of work described here operates on the male principle. The 'several quick and saucy | and greasy sons' and even the 'big hirsute begonia'—all evoke a male world of inelegant, rude and crude health. In contrast, the domesticity is achieved mainly through the female principle:

> Embroidered in daisy stitch
> With marguerites, I think,

and it is this principle that provides order, coherence and meaning ('arranges the rows of cans') and is a proof of love ('somebody loves us all').

Tone

There are some complicated and subtle shifts of tone throughout this poem. From the somewhat offhand tone of the opening line ('Oh, but it is dirty!') she first takes refuge in descriptive detail. Some critics have read the beginning of the poem as condescending ('little filling station,' 'all quite thoroughly dirty'). The flashes of wit may give some credence to that interpretation ('be careful with that match!' and the comic-book of 'certain colour').

But the poet is gradually drawn into the scene and becomes involved; the stance of detached outside observer no longer provides complete protection for her. She is engaged intellectually at first ('why, oh why, the doily?'), and, as she uncovers what gives coherence and meaning to the scene, an emotional empathy is revealed ('somebody loves us all'). Perhaps this is as much a *cri de cœur* of personal need as it is an observation. But the wit saves the poem from any hint of sentimentality:

> Somebody waters the plant,
> or oils it, maybe.

In general, could we describe the tone of the poem as wryly affectionate? Or do you read the tone of the ending as bemused, as the poet is left contemplating the final irony that love is a row of petrol cans?

4 *William Blake* (1757–1827)

William Blake was one of the foremost English poets of the Romantic period. A visionary, he was particularly interested in the emotional, psychological and spiritual side of the human being. His most well-known writings are the short lyrical poems of the volumes *Songs of Innocence* (1789) and *Songs of Experience* (1794), which Blake himself described as 'showing the two contrary states of the human soul.' 'A Poison Tree' is taken from *Songs of Experience*. (For fuller information see page 119.)

A Poison Tree

I was angry with my friend:
I told my wrath, my wrath did end.
I was angry with my foe:
I told it not, my wrath did grow.

And I water'd it in fears,   5
Night and morning with my tears;
And I sunned it with smiles,
And with soft deceitful wiles.

And it grew both day and night,
Till it bore an apple bright;   10
And my foe beheld it shine,
And he knew that it was mine,

And into my garden stole
When the night had veil'd the pole:
In the morning glad I see   15
My foe outstretch'd beneath the tree.

Notes

a poison tree: the poison tree of Java, so noxious that even a touch is fatal

[10] **an apple bright:** symbol of temptation, from the Garden of Eden story

[14] **night had veil'd the pole:** the North Pole, which Blake sometimes used as an image of evil; here night has covered the northern hemisphere in darkness

Explorations

Pre-reading

1. Are you the kind of person who can tell people straight out if they annoy you, or do you suffer in silence and bear a grudge?

(*a*) Think about a time when you had to tell some 'home truths' to a friend. What happened? (*b*) Think about a time when you really resented someone or something but didn't voice your anger or other feelings. Describe it.

First reading

2. In the first two stanzas, how does Blake deal with his anger?
3. What image of the speaker do you form from this?
4. Stanzas 3 and 4 employ symbolism to continue the story. Explain the significance of the apple, the garden, and the 'foe outstretch'd beneath the tree.'

Second reading

5. What insights into human nature does this poem provide for you? Would you agree that Blake is completely honest in confronting the unpleasant side of life?
6. Do you find this poem depressing, uplifting, instructive, or what? Explain your reaction to it.

Third reading

7. Briefly express what you understand as the theme or moral of the poem.
8. Do you think the poem is effective? Consider, for example, whether you think the imagery appropriate to this kind of poem; whether the rhymes might mislead us and so conceal the dark philosophy of the poem; whether the simplicity of the piece is powerfully effective or off-putting.

A Critical Commentary

Theme or moral

The moral of this poem is that anger that is expressed is easily forgotten ('I told my wrath, my wrath did end'), whereas anger that is stored up, particularly anger towards one who is not a friend, can be destructive.

The poem shows a deep insight into human psychology, particularly into the darker side of human nature. For example, it suggests that our anger is sometimes fuelled by our insecurity, spurred on, perhaps, by unfounded or irrational fears about the other person: 'And I water'd it in fears.' It understands how we sometimes nurture anger or hatred as if it were a tender plant to be 'water'd' and 'sunned'. The deceptiveness and hypocrisy we practise, concealing our real feelings, is captured:

> And I sunned it with smiles,
> And with soft deceitful wiles.

Perhaps the most frightening aspect of the entire episode is the realisation that anger ruins the person himself, making him actually 'glad' to behold suffering and death:

> In the morning glad I see
> My foe outstretch'd beneath the tree.

Blake's advice would contradict the usual Christian doctrine about exercising self-restraint and forbearance. He feels that it is better to 'spit it out' than to keep a gripe hidden and allow it to fester and so destroy or pervert both participants.

Imagery and symbolism

The central image is the poison tree of Java: the fact that anger is a poison tree with fatal effects. The apple of temptation is a much-used Christian symbol. The image of night—the veiled North Pole—has suggestions of sinister darkness, which fits in well with the theme of human darkness. It is interesting and perhaps unexpected to find nature used as a symbol of evil and death. Natural imagery is used also to describe psychological processes. Dealing with feelings is compared to nurturing a plant: 'water'd it in fears … sunned it with smiles.' The metaphorical garden is the garden of the poet's life and experiences.

5 Eavan Boland *(born 1944)*

Prominent among the many concerns of Eavan Boland is the place of the woman writer in Irish literature, mythology, and history. She writes about how women have been exploited, marginalised, and kept from the centre of influence in society; but she also writes about the experience of women as mothers, as in the poem 'This Moment', which is taken from the volume *In a Time of Violence* (1994). Some poems in that collection deal with national and historical violence; an earlier volume, *The War Horse* (1975), also deals with how violence, and particularly the Northern 'troubles', encroaches on our lives. 'Child of Our Time' is taken from this volume. (For fuller information see page 120.)

Child of Our Time
(for Aengus)
Yesterday I knew no lullaby
But you have taught me overnight to order
This song, which takes from your final cry
Its tune, from your unreasoned end its reason;
Its rhythm from the discord of your murder   5
Its motive from the fact you cannot listen.

We who should have known how to instruct
With rhymes for your waking, rhythms for your sleep,
Names for the animals you took to bed,
Tales to distract, legends to protect   10
Later an idiom for you to keep
And living, learn, must learn from you dead,

To make our broken images, rebuild
Themselves around your limbs, your broken
Image, find for your sake whose life our idle   15
Talk has cost, a new language. Child
Of our time, our times have robbed your cradle.
Sleep in a world your final sleep has woken.

Background

The poem was inspired by a press photograph showing a firefighter carrying a dead child out of the carnage of the Dublin bombings in May 1974.

Explorations

First reading

1. If you hadn't read the title or the last three lines, what might suggest to you that it was written to a child? Examine stanzas 1 and 2.

2. The speaker acknowledges that it was the child's death that prompted her to compose this poem: 'You have taught me overnight to order | This song.' How does she feel about the child's death in the first stanza? Examine the words and phrases describing the death: 'your final cry,' 'Your unreasoned end,' and 'the discord of your murder.' What do these phrases tell us about the way the poet views the death?

3. In the second stanza, notice that the main clause consists of the first word and the final five words in the stanza: 'We … must learn from you dead.' The rest of the stanza is a parenthesis and relates to 'we', presumably the adult society. (*a*) In what way has adult society failed, according to the poet? (*b*) What particular aspect of child-rearing and education does she focus on? (*c*) 'Later an idiom for you to keep | And living learn.' In your own words, what do you think is meant by this? ('Idiom' here means 'style of expression'.)

4. In the third stanza the child's body is described poetically as 'your broken image'. What does this picture suggest to you?

5. What do you think she has in mind when she says that we need (*a*) to rebuild 'our broken images … around your limbs' and (*b*) to 'find … a new language'?

6. Does the speaker find any ray of hope for the society in which this calamity occurred? Refer to the text of the third stanza.

Second reading

7. Consider this poem as an elegy, a meditation on death. What ideas on that subject are explored or suggested?

8. Can this be read as a public or political poem? Explain, with reference to the text.

9. Concerning the poet's feelings, do you find here a sense of personal sorrow or community guilt and sorrow? Explain your thinking.

Third reading

10. The poem might be seen as a mixture of dirge and lullaby. What elements of dirge or of lullaby, or both, do you find? Consider the theme, the choice of language, the imagery, the repetitions.

A Critical Commentary

A reading of the poem

First and foremost, this is an elegy for the untimely death of a child. It bemoans the senselessness and irrationality of the child's slaughter in an act of public violence.

> This song, which takes from your final cry
> Its tune, from your unreasoned end its reason
> Its rhythm from the discord of your murder …

In the second stanza the keen sense of loss is encouraged by the mournful litany of the literary rituals of childhood, naming again the associations of intimate moments, the rituals around sleeping and waking:

> rhymes for your waking, rhythms for your sleep
> Names for the animals you took to bed,
> Tales to distract, legends to protect …

This sense of loss is compounded by guilt, in that it is the adults who should have been the guardians and guides of the child.

> We who should have known how to instruct
> With rhymes for your waking …

The elegy finishes in a prayer that adult society will learn from this horror. This is expressed in the paradox 'and living, learn, must learn from you dead.' The hope is that society will construct a better method of social interaction, so that the death will not have been in vain ('find, for your sake whose life our idle | Talk has cost, a new language').

The poem is also a searing condemnation of violence. Society stands accused ('our times have robbed your cradle'), accused also of this barbarous irrationality ('your unreasoned end … the discord of your murder'). The only hope is that society would awaken to the reality of its actions and that the child might 'Sleep in a world your final sleep has woken.'

The poem could also be read as a comment on the failure of communication. The entire poem is couched in language terminology. It is a 'lullaby', a 'song', inspired by a 'final cry', a 'tune' with 'rhythms.' In the second stanza loss is expressed in terms of language deprivation and child-rearing seen in terms of language-fostering: 'rhymes for your waking,' etc. The only way forward from this conflict and violence is described as 'a new language'. So the failure of language is associated with death and destruction. But language is the only bulwark against chaos; and this is the positive message of this bleak poem. Poetry, the most artistic expression of language, can be created out of this pain, this 'tune' from 'your final cry'. It signals a victory of order over chaos, reason 'from your unreasoned end,' rhythm from 'discord'. It offers a chance to rebuild broken images, to visualise a better society.

Feelings

A delicate balance of emotions is achieved in this poem. The brutal reality of the killing is never denied; the fact of death is faced squarely in 'And living, learn, must learn from you dead,' where the placing of the last word in the line gives it finality and emphasis. But the references to death are sometimes veiled in poetic terms: 'your final cry,' 'your final sleep,' etc. Or they are intellectualised, as in 'the discord of your murder.' Here the aspect of death dwelt on is its discordance, its out-of-tuneness, the disharmony of death. The child's broken body is rendered as 'your broken image'. The inversion of the natural order of life and death in the killing of a child is expressed in the paradoxes 'from your final cry | Its tune'; 'from your unreasoned end its reason'; 'Its rhythm from the discord of your murder.' Her consideration of this death is poeticised or intellectualised to some degree.

But this is no anodyne reaction. Feelings of grief, loss and guilt and a resolution to learn a better way are all conveyed. Yet there is a delicacy and gentleness to the mourning, made all the more poignant by the fact that the poem is a sort of final lullaby; so the slightly euphemistic treatment is appropriate. Death is a kind of sleep: 'Sleep in a world your final sleep has woken.' Altogether the poem seems to be an interesting combination of dirge and lullaby.

This Moment

A neighbourhood.
At dusk.

Things are getting ready
to happen
out of sight.   5

Stars and moths.
And rinds slanting around fruit.

But not yet.

One tree is black.
One window is yellow as butter.   10

A woman leans down to catch a child
who runs into her arms
this moment.

Stars rise.
Moths flutter.   15
Apples sweeten in the dark.

Explorations

First reading

1. What do you see in this scene? List the items.
2. What senses, other than sight, are involved, or hinted at?
3. Do you think this scene unusual or very ordinary? Explain. What do you think the poet is celebrating here?
4. Yet there is a hint of the mysterious about the scene. Where is this, and what do you think is suggested?

Second reading

5. What do you think is the most significant image in the poem? How does the poet draw attention to its importance?
6. Do you notice any sense of dramatic build-up in the poem? Examine the sequence of ideas and images.

7. Explore the imagery. What do the images contribute to the atmosphere? What is suggested, for example, by 'one window is yellow as butter' and by 'apples sweeten in the dark'?

Third reading

8. What is the central moment in this poem all about?
9. What do you think the poem is saying about nature?
10. Do you think it is making a statement about the experience of women? Explain your ideas.

Fourth reading

11. Read and discuss the critical commentary below. Does it add anything to your own thoughts on the poem? Explain. Add to your notes.

A Critical Commentary

A reading of the poem

At one level this is a simple nature lyric celebrating the moment of dusk in the suburbs. The scene is filled with the usual furniture of a suburban evening: darkening trees, lighted windows, stars, moths, children, and mothers calling them in. It is a romantic evocation of suburban twilight, creating an atmosphere of calm, of continuing growth, ripeness, and natural abundance: 'One window is yellow as butter … Moths flutter. | Apples sweeten in the dark.' Boland is celebrating the ordinary, having discovered that even banal suburban routines can stimulate the poetic in her.

Yet for all its outward ordinariness there is a hint of the mysterious.

> Things are getting ready
> to happen
> out of sight.

This might refer simply to nature's continuing growth in the secrecy of night ('Apples sweeten in the dark') or to some deeper significance of this scene. Notice that the really significant part of the moment is the reuniting of mother and child. There is a subtle dramatic build-up to this, with intimations that something is being held back slightly: 'Things are getting ready | to happen … But not yet.' The intervening images serve to heighten the wait for the finally revealed moment:

> A woman leans down to catch a child
> who has run into her arms
> this moment.

This stanza is emphasised by having the only significant activity in the poem: 'leans,' 'to catch,' 'has run.' With that activity 'this moment' has arrived. So the moment celebrated is maternal, a physical demonstration of the bond between mother and child, with all its connotation of love, security, and protection.

The fact that this is happening everywhere, in suburbs all over the world, gives it a universal significance, lends a mythic quality to the gesture. The woman in the poem is connected to all women in history who must have performed a similar action.

So the poem is about dusk, a moment of transition in nature, but it is also about a universal moment in woman's experience: the confirmation of maternal love.

Ideas in the poem

- The ordinary beauty and richness of nature at the mysterious hour of dusk.
- That the suburbs can be poetic.
- That significant moments are moments of human encounter.
- A woman sharing in the universal experience of motherhood.

6 *Emily Dickinson* (1830–1886)

Emily Dickinson was born and lived all her life in Amherst, Massachusetts. She seems to have suffered some kind of psychological crisis in her early thirties, which resulted in her withdrawal from society. She became somewhat eccentric, 'the myth' of Amherst, who didn't meet strangers or visitors and who spoke to friends from behind a half-closed door or shrouded in shadow at the head of the stairs. She produced a great number of rather cryptic poems of a most unusual form. When she died she was found to have left almost two thousand poems and fragments, in which she explored themes of love, pain, absence and loss, doubt, despair and mental anguish, and hope, among others. Hardly any were published in her lifetime, and their true worth and originality were not appreciated for many years. (For fuller information see page 120.)

'Hope' is the thing with feathers

'Hope' is the thing with feathers—
That perches in the soul—
And sings the tune without the words—
And never stops—at all—

And sweetest—in the Gale—is heard—   5
And sore must be the storm—
That could abash the little Bird
That kept so many warm—

I've heard it in the chillest land—
And on the strangest Sea—   10
Yet, never, in Extremity,
It asked a crumb—of Me.

Explorations

Pre-reading

1. Consider briefly what part 'hope' plays in your own day-to-day life.
2. If you had to represent it figuratively in a painting or an image, how would you describe it?

First reading

3. How does the poet visualise hope?
4. Examine the analogy in detail. List the qualities or characteristics of hope suggested by each of the images in the first stanza. Pry beneath the obvious. For example, what does 'sings the tune without the words' suggest? What is the effect of that description of hope as 'the thing' with feathers?
5. What aspects of hope are suggested in the second stanza? What does the sound-effect of the word 'abash' contribute to this picture? What is the effect of the adjective 'little'?
6. In the third stanza, which qualities are a repetition of suggestions already encountered and which are new?
7. How do you interpret the last two lines? Do they indicate the strength or a weakness

in the virtue of hope? It depends on whether you read the third line as part of the meaning of the previous two or read it with the last line. Experiment with both readings. Is there some ambiguity, and does this show a weakness in the virtue of hope?

Second reading

8. Do you think the bird analogy is successful? Explain your views. What other metaphors for hope could you advance?
9. What insights into the nature of hope did you get from reading this poem?
10. How would you describe the mood of the poem? Suggest one way in which you think this is created in the text.

Third reading

11. What do you notice about the technical features of the poem: punctuation, sentences, the use of capital letters, etc. Explore the effect of any one of these.
12. Would you agree that the extraordinary imagery is one of the best features of this poem? Develop your answer with specific references to the text.

A Critical Commentary

A reading of the poem

This is one of Emily Dickinson's 'definition' poems. She is exploring a psychological condition, using a concrete analogy or metaphor. She has explored hope in other poems, variously describing it as a 'strange invention', a 'subtle glutton', and now 'the thing with feathers'. Through this bird metaphor she examines the various qualities and characteristics of hope, in so far as they can be described at all.

The association of hope with a bird is common enough in religious symbolism: the spirit or divine inspiration is often represented

as a dove. Dickinson maintains this spiritual aspect of hope ('perches in the soul'); but she is also at pains to establish its difference, its strangeness, its absolute otherness, in case we accept the bird analogy too literally. It is 'the thing' with feathers, a not quite definable quality of spirit. It is undemonstrative, unshowy, a silent presence ('sings the tune without the words'). It is permanent, perpetual, always there—a quality emphasised by Dickinson's unusual punctuation ('never stops—at all—'). That final dash might be taken to suggest that the process is continuing.

Characteristics of sweetness and warmth,

very tangible qualities, are emphasised in the second stanza. Hope's indomitable nature and particular value in time of crisis are also stressed ('and sweetest—in the Gale—is heard').

The third stanza introduces something of a more personal experience of hope with the introduction of the first person by the poet ('I've heard'). Again the value of hope in extreme circumstances is featured ('in the chillest land,' 'on the strangest Sea'). Its absolute strength, its independence and the lack of demands it makes on its host body are emphasised.

> Yet, never, in Extremity,
> It asked a crumb—of Me.

For Dickinson, hope is an independent gift, a spiritual gift perhaps. It is delicate and fragile, yet strong and indomitable, and this paradoxical quality is reflected in the image

> And sore must be the storm—
> That could abash the little Bird.

The tiny creature is not disconcerted or abashed by anything but the most dreadful of storms.

There is also the suggestion that hope is a presence not easily defined ('the thing with feathers').

Mood

Emily Dickinson's poems are sometimes bleak affairs, examining such painful conditions as despair, alienation, mental anguish, and unhappy love. But this is an exceptionally optimistic poem, which radiates a mood of buoyant self-confidence: 'I've heard it in the chillest land.' The optimistic tone is reflected too in the references to music ('And sings the tune … Sweetest—in the Gale—is heard—') and warmth ('That kept so many warm'). The forward motion of the lines, with Dickinson's strange punctuation, also helps to suggest that this is a continuing state of mind, not just a temporary high point.

> 'And never stops—at all—'

Imagery

The poem is structured around the central metaphor of the bird as hope, and this is extended in references to feathers, singing, etc.

Many of Dickinson's most startling metaphors and images consist of abstract and concrete elements yoked together, and we see this here in 'Hope is the thing …' It is as if by putting the two unlikely opposites together she is suggesting how really extraordinary is the virtue of hope.

A narrow Fellow in the Grass

A narrow Fellow in the Grass
Occasionally rides—
You may have met Him—did you not
His notice sudden is—

The Grass divides as with a Comb—   5
A spotted shaft is seen—
And then it closes at your feet
And opens further on—

He likes a Boggy Acre
A Floor too cool for Corn—   10
Yet when a Boy, and Barefoot—
I more than once at Noon
Have passed, I thought, a Whip lash
Unbraiding in the Sun
When stooping to secure it   15
It wrinkled, and was gone—

Several of Nature's People
I know, and they know me—
I feel for them a transport
Of cordiality—   20

But never met this Fellow
Attended, or alone
Without a tighter breathing
And Zero at the Bone—

Background

Across the Main Street in Amherst was the 'Dickinson Meadow', where Emily might have encountered the 'narrow Fellow' in a 'Boggy Acre'. Always averse to publication, the poet objected that 'it was robbed of me' when her sister-in-law Susan and Samuel Bowles arranged to publish the snake poem. It was printed in the *Republican* on 14 February 1866.

Explorations

First reading

You might approach this poem as a sort of literary riddle and explore the clues carried by the connotations and sounds of words and images.

1. Consider the 'narrow Fellow'. What is actually seen of him? Is this enough to identify the creature with any certainty? What does the title lead you to expect?
2. There are incidental indications of his presence. Where are they, and what do they add to our understanding of the 'narrow Fellow'?
3. How do you imagine the speaker? What 'persona' or character does the speaker adopt for this narrative? (See the third stanza.) Do you think this is in any way significant?

Second reading

4. Consider the metaphorical descriptions of the creature. Perhaps the most exciting is 'Whip lash'. What are the connotations of the words? What does the term suggest about the creature? Do these connotations clash with the image of it 'unbraiding in the sun'?
5. How did it move when the speaker bent to pick it up?
6. In general, what is your impression of the qualities and nature of this creature?
7. Are there any attempts to make the creature seem less threatening? Refer to the text.
8. What does 'Barefoot' add to the atmosphere of the scene? Who is barefoot? When did this happen?
9. Was the speaker less troubled by this when in her youth? What is the speaker's present or adult reaction to an encounter with the 'narrow Fellow'? Refer to the text. What does 'Zero at the Bone' suggest about her feelings?

Third reading

10. What does the poem convey to us about the writer's attitudes to nature? Support your ideas with references to the text.
11. Do you think this is an effective evocation of a snake? Support your answer with references to the text.
12. Would you agree that there is real fear beneath the apparent casualness of this poem?

Fourth reading

13. 'When she opened her eyes to the real hidden beneath the daily, it was to the peculiarity, awesomeness, and mystery of it' (John Robinson). Would you agree with this interpretation of the poem?

A Critical Commentary

Dickinson and nature

Essentially, this poem is concerned with Emily Dickinson's attitude to nature, in particular her sense that the natural world was distinctly different. In this she differed from Emerson, who thought the entire world, human and non-human, was in harmony and could be known and understood by humankind.

Dickinson is much more wary. She professes to have an amicable relationship with nature:

> Several of Nature's People
> I know, and they know me—
> I feel for them a transport
> Of cordiality—

This is suggestive of a polite acquaintance more than any emotional attachment or real closeness. It displays a somewhat reserved sense of neighbourly tolerance for Earth's creatures. But even that does not hold for this particular creature, the 'narrow Fellow'. Though there is some effort to personalise him—perhaps as a gentleman rider ('occasionally rides—you may have met Him')—and to refer to his likings ('a Boggy Acre'), the poet's essential reaction is one of great unease. This shock on meeting is registered in the disjointed, awkward syntax, the faltering words of 'His notice sudden is.' We notice her feeling of threat coming through in the descriptions. Consider, for example, 'Whip lash': it captures the speed, agility and wild unpredictability of the creature but it also has connotations of sudden threat, injury, pain, a lethal strike. And at the end of the poem she explicitly records her fear; she feels threatened to the marrow of her bones:

> Without a tighter breathing
> And Zero at the Bone—

For Dickinson, nature is to be treated warily; there are times when it is prudent to keep out of the way.

The method of her portrayal of the snake conveys how peculiar, mysterious and elusive nature is. In format, this is a sort of riddle poem. The snake is not named, indeed is never fully seen, apart from the glimpse of 'a spotted shaft'. We just get clues to its passing: 'the Grass divides as with a Comb … and opens further on.' Its purpose or place in the scheme of things is beyond the speaker's comprehension: it just moves through the poem as a series of images. We never learn enough to understand its nature or even to identify it. It makes occasional appearances, which surprise or frighten. It is altogether outside everyday experience—totally 'other'. Dickinson's poetic method here reveals her attitude to nature: as Jerusha McCormack put it (in *ATE Journal*, no. 7), 'her method then, is not deliberately elusive, but an imitation of the bafflement she herself finds in the obscurity of natural things and their refusal to confess to significance. They might be mastered but they cannot be understood.'

Imagery

There is an element of creative unexpectedness in Emily Dickinson's imagery, for example in the depiction of the snake as an occasional rider or the bog as 'a Floor too cool for Corn.' This is a feature of her poetry in general. The purpose of some of the imagery here seems to be an attempt to humanise nature (the narrow fellow 'occasionally rides'; 'Nature's People'), or it is an attempt to domesticate it ('the Grass divides as with a Comb'). The domestic and the strange are brought together. Again the natural is viewed in domestic terms, where the bog is seen as 'a Floor'. Ultimately, this attempt to domesticate nature through the imagery fails, and the essential wildness of the snake reasserts itself in the image of 'Whip lash', conveying, as we saw, grace and agility, but also threat.

Dickinson's imagery is pared down to its simple essence in an image such as 'Zero at the Bone'. In a strange configuration of the abstract and the concrete she succeeds in finding expression for a primal inner terror.

Some general points on Emily Dickinson's poetry

Searching for meaning

Many of Dickinson's poems are struggling to find meaning in the experience being investigated, experiences such as the nature of hope, the feeling of despair, the experience of breakdown, what it might be like to die, the essential nature of bird or reptile.

Even the structure of some of the poems makes it clear that what is happening is an investigation, a struggle to name or master the experience. She uses analogies and similes in an attempt to understand. She attempts to define abstracts in terms of concrete things ('"Hope" is the thing with feathers'). Here she is struggling to understand, using analogical terms. Some of the poems are structured as riddles, for example 'A narrow Fellow'. This is a circuitous exploration of a phenomenon that is gradually made clearer but is never fully named. Indeed it resists being named.

Some critics refer to the rhetorical quality of her poems. Not only is she debating with herself but she is using devices to argue and convince us of her position. Notice the appeal to the reader in 'A narrow Fellow': 'You may have met Him—did you not.'

Telling dramatic stories

For all the elusiveness of her subject matter and the roundabout nature of her poetic method, there is a strong narrative structure in many of Dickinson's poems. Many are told in the first person and constructed as reminiscent narratives, for example 'A narrow Fellow'. She takes us through a sequence of images, inside or outside the head, exposing us to a series of problems or confused feelings, which mostly lead on to a dramatic if sometimes inconclusive ending. This is the essential structure of story. And they are dramatic: they deal with dramatic moments of discovery and insight, such as in 'Hope ...' and 'A narrow Fellow'.

Sparseness

Sparseness and economy of word and image are essential features of Dickinson's poetry. Consider:

The Grass divides as with a Comb
A spotted shaft is seen—

Punctuation

The most idiosyncratic feature of Dickinson's punctuation is her use of the dash. At first this was viewed as sloppy punctuation, indiscriminate, just another example of her unpreparedness for publication. Then it was argued that the dashes had a rhetorical rather than a grammatical function. Because some of them in the original manuscripts were sloping it was even felt that they might be hints for the pitch of a reading voice.

Nowadays readers accept them as a conscious feature of her punctuation, and they are seen as fulfilling a function somewhere between a full stop and a comma. It can be argued that a dash represents a long pause, linking what has gone before and what is to follow. It facilitates continuity and gives the impression of immediacy, that is, that these ideas, fears, terrors and images are only just being processed by the mind. Reader and speaker are just now making these explorations and discoveries.

The dash fulfils a number of functions. The dash at the end of a poem might suggest continuity, that the debate is not finished or the feeling continues (see 'A narrow Fellow'). The dash affects the pace and rhythm of the line. It is used for dramatic pausing, deliberately slowing the pace. And so we hear the sound of Hope in the midst of that long period of turmoil: 'And sweetest—in the Gale—is heard—' It prolongs the moment.

Capitalisation

Dickinson's method of capitalisation has been a source of much discussion and questioning. The eighteenth-century style of using a capital letter for the initial letter of all nouns had died out. Besides, she did not use a capital for every noun. So was her practice just a personal style or had it a purpose? Present-day scholars feel that she used capitals for emphasis, drawing attention to words that carry the weight of the central imagery and meaning and so provide a line of emphasis through the poem. So we can view the capitalised words as stepping-stones through the meaning.

We can see this at work in the third stanza of 'A narrow Fellow'. Boggy Acre, Floor and Corn create the essential pastoral scene. Boy and Barefoot introduce that element of drama, the exposed danger yet an everyday risk that a country boy might take. Noon is one of those personal words she uses in many different contexts and with different meanings; here it may just refer to time of day or to the period of peak activity in her life. 'Whip lash' is the central image in the entire stanza, reflecting the essential energy, wildness and lethal beauty of the snake. Its other side, its more lethargic nature, is captured in that sun-basking image 'Unbraiding in the Sun.' So the capital letters take us through the most important ideas and images of the stanza.

Imagery

Emily Dickinson's poetry is primarily visual. Image follows image in a technique that might be seen nowadays as cinematic. Consider the sequence of images in 'A narrow Fellow': 'a narrow Fellow in the Grass … The Grass divides as with a Comb—| A spotted shaft is seen—| And then it closes at your feet | And opens further on—' And this is followed by the sequence of images from the Boggy Acre stanza, as sequenced above. So we have this sequence of detailed miniature images taking us through the field and the poem. Dickinson thinks in images. They are not ornamental: their function is to carry the thought of the poem.

Many of her really exciting images consist of abstract and concrete elements yoked together, as with hope or the thing with feathers.

She uses similes and metaphors in an attempt to understand by analogy, as she does in 'Hope'. The metaphor poem 'Hope' resembles a particular kind of didactic metaphor, central to the tradition of Protestant preaching, indeed to all religious preaching. This was known as an 'emblem' and might be a picture or other religious object, from which meaning and a moral were elaborately constructed. Perhaps this is one of the bases of Dickinson's metaphorical style.

Many of her images are pared down to a mere phrase, to their barest essentials. This economy leads to a certain cryptic quality in the imagery and often lends itself to ambiguity. But ambiguity was a conscious feature of her

style. The reader is expected to work at these cryptic images, such as 'Zero at the Bone'.

We find a great variety and range of imagery in Dickinson's poetry generally: the natural world, legal matters, military affairs, everyday banal bits and pieces, even the ghoulish or macabre features. But in these two poems the imagery comes chiefly from the natural world.

Form and metre

The majority of Dickinson's verses are based on the hymn format and the ballad quatrain. They consist of quatrains with alternate lines of eight and six syllables. This was known in the hymn books as 'common metre'. For a good example of this examine 'Hope'. But notice that the metre is not always completely regular.

The ballad or hymn format suited her, as it satisfied her instinct for economy and facilitated the tight constructions to which she was led by her liking for definition, antithesis, and paradox.

'Hope' is the thing with feathers—
That perches in the soul—
And sings the tune without the words—
And never stops—at all.

There is a slight reminiscence of the hymn in her work, particularly in the tendency towards epigram and aphorism ('and sweetest—in the Gale—is heard'). The strong narrative line in her poems shows a similarity with the ballad; but she does not feel bound by a regular metre and displays the confidence and originality to vary it.

Neither is she totally bound by the quatrain format. We find an eight-line stanza in 'Narrow Fellow'. Altogether we find a flexible approach to metre and stanza, with a strong inclination to the ballad or hymn format that suited her.

Rhyme

Again we find much flexibility and, some would say, originality. Though there is a deliberate intention to rhyme, quite a deal of it comes out as off-rhyme or half rhyme, such as soul—all, storm—warm in 'Hope'.

7 *Paul Durcan* *(born 1944)*

Among the more notable of Paul Durcan's many collections are *The Berlin Wall Café* (1985), *Daddy Daddy* (1990), *A Snail in My Prime* (1993), *Christmas Day* (1996) and *Greetings to Our Friends in Brazil* (1999). He focuses on contemporary Ireland, particularly the west, and also on themes of political violence, love and marriage, and religion. He is well known for his satires directed at church and state and for his zany wit. But much of his most moving poetry springs from his own life experience, for example the breaking up of his marriage in *The Berlin Wall Café* and the love-hate relationship with his father in *Daddy, Daddy*. 'Going Home to Mayo, Winter 1949' is taken from the collection *Sam's Cross* (1978). (For fuller information see page 123.)

Going Home to Mayo, Winter 1949

Leaving behind us the alien, foreign city of Dublin
My father drove through the night in an old Ford Anglia,
His five-year-old son in the seat beside him,
The rexine seat of red leatherette,
And a yellow moon peered in through the windscreen.   5
'Daddy, Daddy,' I cried, 'Pass out the moon,'
But no matter how hard he drove he could not pass out the moon.
Each town we passed through was another milestone
And their names were magic passwords into eternity:
Kilcock, Kinnegad, Strokestown, Elphin,   10
Tarmonbarry, Tulsk, Ballaghaderreen, Ballavarry;
Now we were in Mayo and the next stop was Turlough,
The village of Turlough in the heartland of Mayo,
And my father's mother's house, all oil-lamps and women,
And my bedroom over the public bar below,   15
And in the morning cattle-cries and cock-crows:
Life's seemingly seamless garment gorgeously rent

By their screeches and bellowings. And in the evenings
I walked with my father in the high grass down by the river
Talking with him—an unheard-of thing in the city.   20

But home was not home and the moon could be no more outflanked
Than the daylight nightmare of Dublin city:
Back down along the canal we chugged into the city
And each lock-gate tolled our mutual doom;
And railings and palings and asphalt and traffic-lights,   25
And blocks after blocks of so-called 'new' tenements—
Thousands of crosses of loneliness planted
In the narrowing grave of the life of the father;
In the wide, wide cemetery of the boy's childhood.

Notes

[4] **Rexine:** the brand name of a type of artificial leather used in upholstery

Explorations

First reading

1. In the first part of the poem, what does the child notice about the journey? What aspects give it a magical quality for him?
2. What does the young boy like, in particular, about the family home in Turlough? What do you notice about the atmosphere of the place and how is it created? Look at the sights and sounds.
3. In the first part of the poem, what evidence is there that the child is unhappy in Dublin?

Second reading

4. What do you think he means by the phrases 'But home was not home' and 'the moon could be no more outflanked'?
5. What images are used to signify the city, and what atmosphere is created? Describe the city as you think the speaker sees it.
6. In the poem, how does life in the city contrast with life in the country?
7. How do you think the poet feels about both the country and the city? What exactly leads you to say this?

Third reading

8. What do you discover about the relationship between father and son in this poem?
9. Do you think Durcan captures well the child's view of the world? Refer to specific images or phrases of dialogue to support your views.
10. How do you understand the final three lines of the poem?

Fourth reading

11. Briefly explain the main themes you find in the poem. What has it to say about the country versus the city; one's place of origin; holidays; dreams and reality; a child's view of the world?
12. On the evidence of this poem, would you consider Durcan to be an idealist, a nostalgic person, or what?
13. Do you find this to be a sad or a happy poem? Comment.

A Critical Commentary

A reading of the poem: two cultures

The poem deals directly with the contrast between urban life and rural culture, between present and past. The village is a romantic, welcoming place, with an old-fashioned, magical charm about it—'all oil-lamps and women.' It has a gentle, feminine identity, in contrast to the hard, powerful, masculine city: 'blocks after blocks of so-called "new" tenements.' The country is a known place, a place of heritage, where they belonged: 'my father's mother's house.' This is in marked contrast to the impersonal 'alien, foreign city of Dublin.'

The village is an exotic place, particularly to a child. There is the novelty of the unusual: 'my bedroom over the public bar below.' It is all beautifully chaotic, with an animal wildness, a naturalness, that is quaintly appealing.

> And in the morning cattle-cries and cock-crows:
> Life's seemingly seamless garment gorgeously rent
> By their screeches and bellowings.

Contrast this with the rigid divisions and barren orderliness of the city, with its 'railings and palings and asphalt and traffic-lights.'

The village is a place that fostered intimacy between father and son:

> I walked with my father in the high grass down
> by the river
> Talking with him—an unheard-of thing in the
> city.

The city is associated with loneliness, isolation, and death. The tenements are seen as graveyards, with 'thousands of crosses of loneliness' that somehow become a reminder of actual death for the father. For him, death is more real, perhaps because it is more immediate—and so the shape of the grave is more clearly defined as 'the narrowing grave.' But the city carries an aura of death even for the child, for whom death is less immediate and obvious: 'In the wide, wide cemetery of the boy's childhood.' Perhaps there is a hint too that the city proved the cemetery of the boy's dreams.

The poet displays a yearning for the village of Turlough that is almost religious in its intensity. Like a religious exile, he is 'going home,' with all the excitement and anticipation that entails. Consequently he is deeply disappointed when he realises that it is a temporary stay, that 'home was not home.' Turlough means life and excitement for him; the city means exile and death.

A child's view of the world

Part I communicates a child's view of life, a magical world full of possibilities:

> 'Daddy, Daddy,' I cried, 'Pass out the moon.'

The journey becomes a symbolic quest for the promised land: names of towns are reeled off as in a religious litany. And in this magic place, all is transformed, and children are no longer treated as inferior.

> I walked with my father in the high grass down
> by the river
> Talking with him …

Father and son

The relationship with his father provided a good deal of grief for Paul Durcan, but we see little of that here. The portrait of the father is typically masculine, associated with driving, energy, and direction, with going places. There is a hint of aloofness, in that the intimacy of conversation is unusual, 'unheard-of thing in the city.' Yet on this occasion father and son collaborate on the quest ('no matter how hard he drove he could not pass out the moon'). An interlude of closeness and co-operation is provided by the return to the village; it is as if the ideal relationship is attainable only in this hallowed place.

Imagery

The image of a journey, which is central to the poem, achieves a certain symbolic significance here. It is both a real journey and a magical quest for origins, for the perfect place, for happiness. The drive through the night has its counter-image in the 'daylight nightmare of Dublin city' and so helps to link both halves of the poem, the perfect dream and the hard-working reality. The images evoking rural life have a biblical quality to them: 'oil-lamps and women,' 'cattle-cries and cock-crows'; and the metaphor of most obvious biblical significance, 'Life's seemingly seamless garment gorgeously rent.' The effect is to suggest that this is a good and holy place, as well as a place obviously teeming with life.

In contrast, pictures of the city are cold, non-human, and divisive rather than fostering life: railings and palings, blocks of flats; and in some surreal way they become associated with crosses and death.

8 Robert Graves (1895–1985)

The descendant of a distinguished Anglo-Irish family but born and educated in England, Robert Graves is probably better known for his autobiography, *Goodbye to All That* (1929), and for his historical novels *I, Claudius* and *Claudius the God* than for his poetry, of which he produced a great many volumes. 'Hedges Freaked with Snow' is a section of 'Three Songs for the Lute' in *New Poems, 1962*. The volume features some very bleak love poems. (For fuller information see page 123.)

Hedges Freaked with Snow

No argument, no anger, no remorse,
No dividing of blame.
There was poison in the cup—why should we ask
From whose hand it came?

No grief for our dead love, no howling gales   5
That through darkness blow,
But the smile of sorrow, a wan winter landscape,
Hedges freaked with snow.

Notes

freaked: 'freak' can mean (a) to fleck or streak with colour or (b) a sudden causeless change of mind, a capricious humour

[7] **wan:** pale, of sickly complexion

Explorations

Pre-reading
1. Have you ever broken off with a friend (or boy-friend or girl-friend)? Were you full of hurt or anger, or could you be detached about it? Think about it.

First reading
2. What is your first impression of the poet's attitude here?

3. 'There was poison in the cup.' What does this suggest to you about how the relationship ended? What might have happened? Imagine a scenario.
4. 'Why should we ask | From whose hand it came?' Why do you think he doesn't want to talk about it? Is he callous, or afraid, or

what?

5. 'No grief for our dead love ...' How do you think the speaker feels here? Does this fit in easily with a reading of the speaker as callous and unconcerned? How do you understand the speaker's feelings?

Second reading

6. 'The smile of sorrow': imagine where you yourself might need to put on a smile of sorrow. Describe what it feels like to put on such a front. What does this image suggest about the speaker's feelings here?
7. Think about the images of nature in this poem. What atmosphere do they create?

What do they suggest about the relationship?

Third reading

8. What does this poem reveal to you about love?
9. What does it say about human beings? Does it leave you with a bleak or a dignified view of humanity? Explain briefly.
10. How do you imagine his former lover might have reacted when she read this poem? Compose a letter she might have written to the poet, setting out her feelings.
11. Outline your feelings for the speaker of this poem. Do you feel sorry for him, angry with him, or what? Explain.

A Critical Commentary

Theme

This is a poem about breaking up a relationship gracefully: parting with dignity, without blame or recriminations; refusing to squabble, but with resignation, keeping up a dignified front, 'the smile of sorrow.'

Tone

The note of calm dignity, the determined civility of the speaker is one of the most impressive things about this poem. The repetition of the word 'no' shows his absolute resolve to be civilised: 'No argument, no anger ...' He admits that their relationship was poisoned and stoically accepts it, refusing to search for blame.

But this is not a callous, 'couldn't care less' attitude: there is evidence of real sadness in the plaintive 'No grief for our dead love.' Though it is couched in the negative, there is a sense of tender mourning here. We are also conscious of the emotions that are barely held in check: 'no howling gales | That through darkness blow.' The emotional bleakness is evoked in the 'smile of sorrow' and through the winter landscape. The tone is one of resigned despondency, bleak acceptance that it is all over. The speaker shows

'stiff upper lip' human dignity at its best.

Imagery

Graves uses natural imagery to communicate feelings and emotions. The more obvious ones include the 'howling gales' and 'the wan winter landscape.' 'Hedges freaked with snow' is quite subtle and ambiguous, as it could refer to both the flecks of colour and the changes of mind in the relationship. Either way the natural imagery reflects the human dynamics in the poem. The contradictory image 'smile of sorrow' embodies the mixed feelings of the speaker—sorrow and resignation. The startling image of the poisoned cup carries the real unvarnished pain of the break-up.

Style

This is a stylish, polished lyric. We notice the variation of line lengths and the regularity of the three-stress second and fourth lines of each stanza. The 'no' repetitions reinforce the negative atmosphere. There is a conventional rhyme between lines 2 and 4 and some alliteration for emphasis: 'smile of sorrow'; 'wan winter.' It is a crafted, controlled piece that carries well the controlled emotion.

9 *Michael Hartnett (born 1941)*

Born in Croom, County Limerick, Michael Hartnett has lived in London, Madrid, Dublin, and Newcastle, County Limerick. A bilingual poet, among his collections are *Anatomy of a Cliché* (1968), *A Farewell to English* (1975), from which 'Death of an Irishwoman' is taken, *Do Nuala: Foidhne Chrainn* (1984), *Inchicore Haiku* (1985), and *Poems to Younger Women* (1989). He finds the inspiration for many of his poems in the local community and environment but is also very conscious of the broader European tradition of literature. (For fuller information see page 124.)

Death of an Irishwoman

Ignorant, in the sense
she ate monotonous food
and thought the world was flat,
and pagan, in the sense
she knew the things that moved   5
at night were neither dogs nor cats
but púcas and darkfaced men
she nevertheless had fierce pride.
But sentenced in the end
to eat thin diminishing porridge   10
in a stone-cold kitchen
she clenched her brittle hands
around a world
she could not understand.
I loved her from the day she died.   15
She was a summer dance at the crossroads.
She was a cardgame where a nose was broken.
She was a song that nobody sings.
She was a house ransacked by soldiers.
She was a language seldom spoken.   20
She was a child's purse, full of useless things.

Explorations

First reading

1. 'She ate monotonous food.' What sort of food do you imagine she ate?
2. Though she may not have believed literally that the world was flat, what does this statement suggest about her knowledge of the modern world?
3. What do her views on nocturnal happenings reveal about her?
4. What is your general impression of the character and views of the woman? How do you visualise her—age, dress, appearance, speech, etc.? Base your impressions on suggestions in the text.

Second reading

5. 'But sentenced in the end ...' What does this phrase suggest? Comment on the woman's situation in old age. Is it dignified, comfortable, or what?
6. What images best convey her plight in old age? Explain what they suggest to you.

7. What do we learn of her past life from the poem?
8. 'I loved her from the day she died.' What do you think he means by this statement?
9. Comment on the relationship between the speaker and the woman. What is his attitude to her? Explain his feelings for her: what exactly did he like about her?

Third reading

10. Why do you think the poem is entitled 'Death of an Irishwoman' rather than 'Death of an Old Woman'? What evidence in the poem supports the title?
11. Is the mood of this poem one of unrelieved sombreness and loss, or is there some balancing happiness? Explain your opinion.
12. What issues or themes do you think are dealt with in this poem?
13. What affected you most in this poem?
14. Do you think the poet is nostalgic for the past? What might lead you to this conclusion?

A Critical Commentary

A reading of the poem

This is a portrait of an old rural woman, grown unadventurous with age, for whom food (the 'thin diminishing porridge') has become as monotonous and unsustaining as her life. She lives an insular existence, uneducated about the wider world. This is communicated in the exaggerated claim that she thought the world was flat. Her lack of comprehension of the modern world is registered with great feeling in that image:

> she clenched her brittle hands
> around a world
> she could not understand.

Her primitive philosophy is dominated by superstitions, by the non-rational forces in life, púcas, leprechauns, and magic—a view of life that isolates her further from the modern world. The grave-cold of extreme old age is reflected in the words and images: thin; stone-cold kitchen; brittle hands. Altogether it is a portrait of a woman who has sadly outlived her time, out of place in the world, retaining little but her 'fierce pride'.

But she once had a life of vivacity, fun, danger, adventure, and even historical significance: 'a summer dance at the crossroads'; 'a cardgame where a nose was broken'; 'a house ransacked by soldiers' (presumably in the 1919–1923 period). And so she represents the history and culture of an earlier generation. Perhaps the poem could be read as a celebration of a fading culture and way of life: 'a song that nobody sings'; 'a language seldom spoken'.

It is also very much a child's view of the world: the love of the old woman, curiosity about the past, a child's fascination with the obsolete ('a child's purse, full of useless things').

So it is both a personal poem, commemorating a loved one, and a cultural commemoration.

10 Séamus Heaney *(born 1939)*

Born into a farming background at Bellaghy, County Derry, in 1939, Séamus Heaney was educated at St Columb's College, Derry, and Queen's University, Belfast. He now lives in Dublin. His first volumes of poetry, *Death of a Naturalist* (1966) and *Door into the Dark* (1969) are filled with the characters, scenes, customs, flora and fauna of his country background. He also began to explore geography and archaeology as symbols of Ireland's spirit and troubled history. The bog becomes central to his imaging and thinking of Ireland, and in the 'bog poems' he finds an oblique way of examining the sacrificial killings, the power of religion, and the deadly demands of myth. Here he is exploring primarily the consciousness of his own nationalist community, the Irish experience of invasions, most particularly in the volume *North* (1975); but he also writes a great deal about domestic values, family love, and rural traditions. Among his volumes of poetry are *Field Work* (1979), *Station Island* (1984), *The Haw Lantern* (1987), *Seeing Things* (1991), and *The Spirit Level* (1996). In 1995 he was awarded the Nobel Prize for Literature. (For fuller information see page 124.)

The Forge

All I know is a door into the dark.
Outside, old axles and iron hoops rusting;
Inside, the hammered anvil's short-pitched ring,
The unpredictable fantail of sparks
Or hiss when a new shoe toughens in water.   5
The anvil must be somewhere in the centre,
Horned as a unicorn, at one end square,
Set there immovable: an altar
Where he expends himself in shape and music.
Sometimes, leather-aproned, hairs in his nose,   10
He leans out on the jamb, recalls a clatter
Of hoofs where traffic is flashing in rows;
Then grunts and goes in, with a slam and flick
To beat real iron out, to work the bellows.

Explorations

Pre-reading

1. Read the title only. Jot down all the images that come into your head—what you might expect to see in the forge.

First reading

2. What do you actually see in this picture of the forge?

3. Where is the speaker standing in this poem? Do you think this might be significant? Why? What can he see? What can he not see?

Second reading

4. What can we say about the blacksmith from his appearance and manner? Refer to the text.

5. How do you think the smith views his work? Read again lines 13 and 14.

6. How does the poet view the smith's work? Read again lines 6–9. Do you think he has respect, or even reverence, for the blacksmith's art? Explain.

Third reading

7. What do you think is the poet's theme here?

8. Could the poem be read in a symbolic way—that is, as dealing with a subject other than the surface one of the work of a blacksmith? If so, how?

9. Read the section 'Theme' in the critical commentary below. Do you agree, or do you think this is too far-fetched? Comment, with reference to the text.

10. Which images do you think work best at evoking the atmosphere of a forge? What do they suggest to you?

11. It has been said that one of Heaney's particular gifts is that of vivid portraiture. Do you think this poem could be used as evidence of that talent? Explain, with reference to the text.

or

12. Would you agree with the following criticism by James Simmons?

'The Forge', from which the title of the book is taken, is shapely and vivid at first but fails to stand as a metaphor for the creative act. It becomes a cliché portrait of the village smithy. The smith has hairs in his nose and remembers better times. He retreats from the sight of modern traffic 'to beat real iron out, to work the bellows.'

Give your opinion on both the metaphor and the portrait of the village smithy.

Fourth reading

13. What do you notice about the style of language used? Is it poetic, prosaic, conversational, or what?

14. What elements of the poem do not work very well for you? Explain, with reference to the text.

15. Read the critical commentary below and decide which points are relevant to your own notes on this poem.

A Critical Commentary

Theme

At one level, this might be read as another descriptive poem celebrating local craftsmanship and exploring cultural roots—a nostalgic poem of social history. Such a reading leaves one unsatisfied, an outsider rebuffed by an inarticulate and rude, if talented, smith.

The real subject of this poem is the mystery of the creative process. The work of the forge serves as an extended metaphor for the beating out of a work of art, the crafting of poetry. The reader, like the speaker in this case, is outside, peering in at the mystery. One can catch glimpses of beauty in the making ('the unpredictable fantail of sparks'), or hear snatches of its elegant sound (the 'short-pitched ring' or the 'hiss'), but the secret of its construction remains a mystery, inaccessible to the non-artist. Just as in 'The Diviner', the onlookers can see the event but cannot themselves perform it or even understand it.

Creativity is a fabulous process, the stuff of legend, of mediaeval romance: the anvil is a horned 'unicorn'. But it is also a sacred process, and the smith is its high priest:

> at one square,
> Set there immovable: an altar
> Where he expends himself in shape and music.

The making of art is not the exclusive preserve of intellectuals and the 'chattering classes' but can be born of even the uncouth and uncommunicative ('hairs in his nose, he leans out ... grunts and goes in').

Art is not necessarily anchored to the here and now. The artist withdraws from the modern world to create ('He ... recalls a clatter | of hoof where traffic is flashing in rows ... grunts and goes in, with a slam and flick | To beat real iron out ...').

So the poem deals with the mystery and the sacredness of art and at the same time puts before us the ordinariness of the artist.

Origins of the image

This is probably based on Heaney's experience of a real forge: Devlin's forge at Hillhead, not far from Mossbawn, where the Heaneys first lived during the poet's youth. From this forge he borrowed the anvil to lend realism to his part as a blacksmith in a Bellaghy Dramatic Society production about the 1798 rebellion.

So the ordinary bric-à-brac of life is endowed with metaphysical meaning and poetic significance by the writer. But the image has literary echoes also. Smiths featured in the work of Gerard Manley Hopkins, a poet much admired by Heaney. Hopkins uses the smith as a symbol of human strength, beauty and Christian courage in 'Felix Randal' and as a metaphor for God in 'The Wreck of the Deutschland', where he sees the God-smith

forging humankind to what shape he wills:

> With an anvil-ding
> And with fire in him forge thy will
> Or rather, rather then, stealing as Spring
> Through him, melt him but master him still.

Joyce too, through Stephen Dedalus, utters that famous arrogant statement of artistic *raison d'être* in *Portrait of the Artist as a Young Man*, where he resolves to 'forge in the smithy of my soul the uncreated conscience of my race.' So for Heaney, the forge had both a strong physical and a literary presence.

Imagery and sound

All the imagery in this poem is generated by the forge and its surroundings. The discarded bric-à-brac ('old axles and iron hoops rusting') recalls the real disorder out of which true beauty is created. The unexpected glory of sparks ('the unpredictable fantail of sparks') provides the only flash of colour in the otherwise Stygian gloom. Darkness is the predominant backdrop colour here. In fact a number of poems in the same volume—'The Outlaw', 'Gallarus Oratory', and 'The Forge'—feature dark places, enclosed spaces, which, paradoxically, are places of great energy and creativity, whether biological, spiritual, or artistic. So here too the dark is seductive and creative, enticing and explosive. Would you agree with the critic who said that Heaney here presents 'an image of the poet as master of the powers of darkness'?

The central image is the anvil, which Heaney allows to have a couple of different implications, associating its horn with the mythical beast of mediaeval romance and its square end with a religious altar. So both the romantic and the sacred aspects of creativity are fostered.

Sound is an essential feature of pictorial composition for Heaney. At a conscious level we are aware of the musical quality of the verse, the onomatopoeic 'ring', 'hiss', 'slam' and 'flick' and the alliteration of 'grunts and goes.' But there are also subterranean musical echoes within words, which provide a background resonance. For example the flat *e* and *a* sounds in 'somewhere', 'square' and 'altar' focus on the weight of the anvil and its central importance.

Form

The poem is structured as a Petrarchan sonnet, with the octave devoted to the forge and the sestet providing a shift in focus to the smith. This division allows the anvil as 'an altar' to be emphasised at the pivotal point of the poem.

Other than that it is not technically effective as a sonnet: the pentameter rhythm is uneven, the rhyming scheme is irregular (*abba cddc, efgfeg*), with the sestet most uneven. Some of the rhymes are off-rhymes rather than true. One could see this as a failure of technique, a lack of verbal sophistication; or could one see it as a naturalness that fits the often conversational rhythms of language ('he leans out on the jamb, recalls a clatter | Of hoofs ...') and the rough subject?

Sunlight
(from 'Mossbawn: Two Poems in Dedication')

There was a sunlit absence.
The helmeted pump in the yard
heated its iron,
water honeyed

in the slung bucket   5
and the sun stood
like a griddle cooling
against the wall

of each long afternoon.
So, her hands scuffled   10
over the bakeboard,
the reddening stove

sent its plaque of heat
against her where she stood
in a floury apron   15
by the window.

Now she dusts the board
with a goose's wing,
now sits, broad-lapped,
with whitened nails   20

and measling shins:
here is a space
again, the scone rising
to the tick of two clocks.

And here is love   25
like a tinsmith's scoop
sunk past its gleam
in the meal-bin.

Background

'Mossbawn' refers to the townland and the family home where Heaney grew up, a place that was for him, as home is for all children, the centre of the world and the source of all life and energy.

In a radio broadcast (BBC Radio 4, 1978, printed in *Preoccupations*, 1980), Heaney said:

> I would begin with the Greek word, *omphalos*, meaning the navel, and hence the stone that marked the centre of the world, and repeat it, *omphalos, omphalos, omphalos* until its blunt and falling music becomes the music of somebody pumping water at the pump outside our back door. It is Co. Derry in the early 1940s. The American bombers groan towards the aerodrome at Toomebridge, the American troops manoeuvre in the fields along the road, but all of that great historical action does not disturb the rhythms of the yard. There the pump stands, a slender, iron idol, snouted, helmeted, dressed down with a sweeping handle, painted a dark green and set on a concrete plinth, marking the centre of another world. Five households drew water from it. Women came and went, came rattling between empty enamel buckets, went evenly away, weighed down by silent water. The horses came home to it in those first lengthening evenings of spring, and in a single draught emptied one bucket and then another as the man pumped and pumped, the plunger slugging up and down, *omphalos, omphalos, omphalos*.

Mary Heaney was his aunt, a kind of second mother to him, for whom he had a special affection. She features in a number of his poems: as one of the family women in 'Churning Day', both as a young girl and as a woman taking the young Séamus on a trip to the seaside in 'In Memoriam Francis Ledwidge', and as the planter of a memorial tree in 'Clearances'. She represents the old secure, stable way of life, a sense of community and traditional rural values.

Explorations

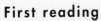

First reading

1. What is described here?
2. What details stand out on a first reading?

Second reading

3. Think of the poem as a picture in two panels: the yard and the kitchen. (*a*) Study the detail of each scene and discuss the significance of each piece of detail. What era is evoked by the detail? (*b*) Examine the portrait of Mary Heaney. What kind of person is she? (*c*) Describe the atmosphere created in each scene and explain how it is created.

Third reading

4. This is the opening poem in a volume that deals with violence, conflict, and conquest, for the most part. Does this surprise you? Explain.

5. In that context, what do you think is the significance of the poem? What does this poem suggest about the poet's values and attitudes to living?
6. Do you think there is any significance in the change from past tense to present tense that occurs from stanza 5 onwards?
7. Explain your own reaction to this poem.

Fourth reading

8. Do you think the poet is yearning for the security of childhood in this poem? Explain, with reference to the text.
9. It has been said that Heaney is often preoccupied with his own roots, celebrating the customs, rituals, atmosphere and skills of the farming community that nurtured him. Do you think that applies to this poem? Explain, with reference to the text.

A Critical Commentary

Significance of the poem

Given the context of this poem in a volume dealing primarily with violence, past and present, are we justified in viewing the piece as somewhat escapist? The poet has created a timeless zone of slow days, domestic ritual, natural and human warmth, and companionable silence—a safe haven amid the surrounding violence. We are taken back in time to childhood, pictured here as the golden age of innocence and security. (In general, childhood is not sentimentalised by Heaney: see 'Death of a Naturalist', 'Mid-Term Break', and 'The Early Purges'.) Is this nostalgic escapism or a search for alternative human values, values no longer found in present-day society?

Values

The values featured here are domestic: the value of unspectacular routine work ('now she dusts the board | with a goose's wing'); the practice of simple culinary skills ('her hands scuffled | over the bakeboard')—the routine of a life pared down to its absolute essentials of bread, water, and love. Far from suggesting deprivation, these bare essentials are imbued with a sense of mystery, a sense of the sacramental, suggesting a religious simplicity of life: the water is 'honeyed', 'the scone rising,' and 'here is love.'

Family feeling is important here. Love grows out of simple, shared domestic tasks; love flourishes in a very ordinary unspectacular setting, among ordinary unglamorous people ('broad-lapped, | with whitened nails | and measling shins'), flowering in the silent spaces between people.

> And here is love
> like a tinsmith's scoop
> sunk past its gleam
> in the meal-bin.

Love is associated with the simplest of staple food, lurking in the life-giving meal, unspectacular ('a tinsmith's scoop') yet vital.

The values of silence and peace are also stressed ('sunlit absence,' 'each long afternoon,' 'here is a space again,' 'the tick of two clocks'). All these values are found by reaching back to a pre-modern time. All the props of the scene suggest an earlier age: the pump in the yard, a griddle cooling, the reddening stove, a goose's wing, the meal bin. They are rural values, born of a simple life, emanating from a bygone age. Yet they are made to appear poignantly appealing, offering an ideal way of living.

Atmosphere

The atmosphere created is one of warmth, serenity, and quiet vitality. This is achieved primarily through the imagery and symbolism. Images of sunlight and heat predominate ('a sunlit absence,' 'water honeyed,' 'the sun stood | like a griddle cooling | against the wall,' 'the reddening stove'). The 'helmeted' pump is both actual and symbolic, a soldier on sentry duty protecting the household; but, more importantly, the pump is in immediate contact with the hidden springs of the earth, the source of life. Its water is somehow mysteriously transformed ('honey'). As the critic Michael Parker says, it 'serves as an icon or symbol for the subterranean energies of the place and people.' The sun too is captured by the scene, reduced to domestic proportions '(like a griddle cooling').' The bread and water are also life symbols. The alliterative language ('helmeted', 'heated', 'honeyed') creates a melodic flow, which also helps to build this atmosphere of 'mellow fruitfulness'. Heaney himself is reported as saying that it was intended to be a description of the experience of a foetus in the womb.

But the atmosphere is not lazy. There is a quiet energy in this poem, achieved partly through the style of verse. A great deal is packed into these very short lines. The resulting *enjambment* or continuation of ideas—not just from one line to the next but also from one verse to the next—creates a sense of contained energy. The erratic activities and pauses in the aunt's baking ritual contribute also to this

sense of restlessness ('now she dusts the board,' 'now sits,' 'here is a space | again').

A Constable Calls
(From 'Singing School')

His bicycle stood at the window-sill,
The rubber cowl of a mud-splasher
Skirting the front mudguard,
Its fat black handlegrips

Heating in sunlight, the 'spud'   5
Of the dynamo gleaming and cocked back,
The pedal treads hanging relieved
Of the boot of the law.

His cap was upside down
On the floor, next his chair.   10
The line of its pressure ran like a bevel
In his slightly sweating hair.

He had unstrapped
The heavy ledger, and my father
Was making tillage returns   15
In acres, roods, and perches.

Arithmetic and fear.
I sat staring at the polished holster
With its buttoned flap, the braid cord
Looped into the revolver butt.   20

'Any other root crops?
Mangolds? Marrowstems? Anything like that?'
'No.' But was there not a line
Of turnips where the seed ran out

In the potato field? I assumed   25
Small guilts and sat
Imagining the black hole in the barracks.
He stood up, shifted the baton-case

Further round on his belt,
Closed the doomsday book,   30
Fitted his cap back with two hands,
And looked at me as he said goodbye.

A shadow bobbed in the window.
He was snapping the carrier spring
Over the ledger. His boot pushed off   35
And the bicycle ticked, ticked, ticked.

Explorations

First reading

1. What descriptive details of the bicycle did you notice as you read this poem? Did they seem to you in any way significant?
2. What details of the description of the policeman did you think significant? What type of character is suggested by these details?

Second reading

3. What do you think is the boy's attitude to the bicycle, as described in the poem? Where and how is this attitude communicated to the reader?
4. What is the relationship between the participants in this encounter: the policeman, the boy, and his father? Examine the imagery, the dialogue, and the actions of those involved.

Third reading

5. Can you understand how the boy feels? Explain.
6. Do you think the poem faithfully represents how a young person might feel in this situation? Examine your own experiences to test the truth of the poem.
7. Outline the main themes of this poem, as you understand them.
8. From your reading of this poem, would you agree that one of Heaney's strengths as a poet is his ability to create realistic descriptions in minute detail?

Fourth reading

9. Do you think the poet here shows a natural sympathy for victims, for the underdog in society?
10. Do you think this poem might be read as a metaphor for the feelings of the nationalist community in Northern Ireland? Explain, with reference to the text.
11. Read the critical commentary below and add to your own notes on the significance of this poem.
12. What is your evaluation of this poem's truth and significance?

A Critical Commentary

This is one of a set of six autobiographical poems entitled 'Singing School', which deal with the development of Heaney's sense of identity as a poet and as a member of the Northern nationalist community. It records the poet's sense of fear and guilt experienced as a child when he encountered a figure of the law. Perhaps it is meant to be symptomatic of the uneasy nationalist relationship with the forces of law and order; but in truth it could be describing 'any child's encounter with a threatening figure of remote authority' (James Simmons).

The bicycle is described in images and sounds that suggest ugliness and crude strength. The *ow* sound in 'cowl' has a crude primitiveness, and the assonance of 'fat black' emphasises the suggestions of ungainly strength in the adjectives. The 'spud' of the dynamo continues to build, both in image and sound, the pervasive atmosphere of crude, even brutal, strength. Perhaps there is also a hint of aggression, possibly life-threatening, in that dynamo metaphor, 'gleaming and cocked back' (as in a gun?). The feeling of oppression is created quite overtly, indeed without a great deal of subtlety, in the image at the end of the second stanza:

> The pedal treads hanging relieved
> Of the boot of the law.

And all of this is created before we meet the policeman.

The policeman never comes across as a person but is defined in terms of his uniform and accoutrements. A series of disjointed references to the 'heavy ledger', the 'polished holster', 'the braid cord looped into the revolver butt' and 'the baton-case' establish the figure of military authority, while the only human reference, to the upside-down cap ('The line of its pressure ran like a bevel | In his slightly sweating hair'), does not serve to humanise this figure but rather repels us further. Under this stern figure of authority the

agricultural survey returns have assumed the status of a day of reckoning, and the 'heavy ledger' becomes the 'doomsday book'. The brisk official tone of the questioning enhances the impersonal nature of this encounter.

> 'Any other root crops?
> Mangolds? Marrowstems? Anything like that?'
> 'No.'

There are quite divergent critical views on the truth of this poem. Some read the poem as a very specific political statement, with the policeman as the embodiment of the Protestant state and the young boy experiencing the fear, guilt and alienation of the dispossessed Catholics. Others, such as James Simmons ('The trouble with Séamus' in *Séamus Heaney*, edited by Elmer Andrews), are of the opinion that this is a false reading. He feels that this is quite a weak poem, describing ordinary exaggerated childish fears, and that it doesn't add very much to our understanding of the nationalist identity.

> The father may have been making a few false returns, but the child has heard of 'the black hole in the barracks' and fears that his father may be carried off for his crimes. This is a pleasant little story, vividly told, but there is little about it to justify its place in a short sequence. A Protestant poet might write an exactly similar piece. False returns and a fear of the law are probably universal, but in the context of Heaney's poem, the very vagueness of the story must be generally thought to be one more example of the horrors of being a Catholic in Northern Ireland.

How do you read this poem?

The critic Edna Longley, writing about the falseness of the ending ('His boot pushed off | And the bicycle ticked, ticked, ticked'), speaks of 'the caller's bike becoming, even from the child's eye view, an implausibly melodramatic time-bomb.' Do you find this poem real or melodramatic?

11 *John Hewitt* *(1907–1987)*

John Hewitt was born in Belfast and educated at Methodist College and Queen's University. He considered himself to be of a liberal Protestant mind in religion but radical in social policy. He worked in the Belfast Museum and Art Gallery from 1930 until 1957. Above all else he was devoted to Ulster, and his poems deal with the culture and heritage of the province and its political and religious divisions. He also wrote about childhood memories and personal themes; but he is most famous for his nature poems capturing the life of the Glens of Antrim. (For fuller information see page 128.)

The Green Shoot

In my harsh city, when a Catholic priest,
known by his collar, padded down our street,
I'd trot beside him, pull my schoolcap off
and fling it on the ground and stamp on it.

I'd catch my enemy, that errand-boy,   5
grip his torn jersey and admonish him
first to admit his faith, and when he did,
repeatedly to curse the Pope of Rome;

schooled in such duties by my bolder friends;
yet not so many hurried years before,   10
when I slipped in from play one Christmas Eve
my mother bathed me at the kitchen fire,

and wrapped me in a blanket for the climb
up the long stairs; and suddenly we heard
the carol-singers somewhere in the dark,   15
their voices sharper, for the frost was hard.

My mother carried me through the dim hall
into the parlour, where the only light
upon the patterned wall and furniture
came from the iron lamp across the street;   20

and there looped round the lamp the singers stood,
but not on snow in grocers' calendars,
singing a song I liked until I saw
my mother's lashes were all bright with tears.

Out of this mulch of ready sentiment,   25
gritty with threads of flinty violence,
I am the green shoot asking for the flower,
soft as the feathers of the snow's cold swans.

Explorations

Pre-reading

1. How would you describe the culture of your own locality and environment? What do you notice about the dominant attitudes in your school, housing estate, class, or family? It might help to
   - list three things your community values
   - list three things your community is strongly against
   - describe how important or regular customs are practised
   - say whether any group of people is badly treated.

Discuss these questions.

First reading: lines 1–9

2. Visualise the incident in the first stanza. Notice the different styles of walking: 'padded', 'trot'. What is suggested here about the different attitudes of each of the participants? What do you think might be the significance of the gesture with the school cap?

3. What does the gesture reveal about the attitude to the priest? What does it reveal of the mentality of those who thought it a proper thing to do?

4. What was your own reaction to it?

5. Imagine the feelings of the priest. Write a diary entry for the incident as he might have written it.

6. Do you think that class as well as religious difference plays a part in the conflict in the second stanza? Where is this indicated?

7. What might be the thoughts of the errand-boy?

Second reading: stanzas 3–6

8. Describe the atmosphere in the house on Christmas Eve. How is this created?

9. What does this episode reveal about the relationship between the boy and his mother? What do we learn about the character of the boy? Does it accord at all with the youth of the first two stanzas?

10. In what way is the incident significant? How does the poet read it, and why does he think it significant? Read the last stanza.

Third reading

11. What do you think Hewitt means by the last two lines? Put the idea in your own words.

12. Do you think the poet has a good eye for detail? Explain.

13. In general, what is the poet saying about

his cultural background?

14. Do you think people can overcome and outgrow their upbringing and the culture of

their particular environment? Discuss this.

15. What insights did the poem give you into the culture of Northern Ireland?

A Critical Commentary

A reading of the poem

This poem explores the poet's roots. It is a journey into his past, recalling significant events of his Belfast boyhood and analysing the Protestant street culture and ethos that shaped him. As he himself says, he is exploring the mulch that fed this green shoot.

He focuses on some contradictory aspects of his upbringing. On the one hand there is the religious bigotry that encouraged the public humiliation of Catholic clergy and the bullying of Catholic messenger-boys. These are the crude expressions of religious supremacy and arrogance that were the daily features of life in his 'harsh city', where he was 'schooled in such duties by my 'bolder friends.' He recalls in specific detail these 'threads of flinty violence,' as he terms them. But he also remembers vividly a moment of 'ready sentiment', when, with seasonal appropriateness, mother and child inside the window savoured the music of the Christmas carols. Here we see the loved and cherished boy who is fiercely protective of his mother (too young to understand that she is crying from sentiment, not hurt). This is the same boy who in later years behaved cruelly to Catholic priests and errand-boys. Hewitt is caught by these contradictions in his upbringing: fierce, protective love existing side by side with religious hatred, sentimentality and violent bigotry together. And he ends the poem with an entreaty or a wish that he might flower or develop into something pure, gentle, and aesthetically pleasing, despite the mixed cultural mulch that fostered him in youth.

> I am the green shoot asking for the flower,
> soft as the feathers of the snow's cold swans.

This is a narrative poem, structured in three sections. The first nine lines focus on his youthful acts of bigotry. Stanzas 3–6 recall that sentimental Christmas Eve. And the final stanza moves back from the personal narrative, analyses the episodes, and concludes with the hope that one can overcome or transcend one's background.

Hewitt's method is to recall symbolic gestures and significant moments that are symptomatic of his culture and upbringing. He defines them as moments of sentimentality and violence but leaves the reader to draw out the detailed significance from these accurately drawn images. The central metaphor of the poem is a horticultural one. He thinks of his roots literally as if he were a plant, the 'green shoot'. His aspirations too, his hopes of growth and development, are communicated in this metaphor—'asking for a flower.'

12 *John Keats (1795–1821)*

One of the most important poets of the English Romantic period, John Keats was born in London on 31 October 1795. The eldest of four surviving children, he had lost both parents by the time he was fifteen, and his subsequent life was dogged by financial hardship and illness. Though he qualified as a surgeon and apothecary, he discarded that career for poetry. Among the best known of his long narrative epic poems are 'Endymion', 'Hyperion', and 'Lamia'. Among the shorter verse we find 'La Belle Dame sans Merci', the five Great Odes, and the ode 'To Autumn', all composed in that extraordinarily productive year of 1819. Keats had nursed his brother Tom, who died of tuberculosis in December 1818, and he himself died of the disease on 23 February 1821 in Rome, where he is buried. (For fuller information see page 129.)

La Belle Dame sans Merci

O what can ail thee knight at arms
Alone and palely loitering?
The sedge has withered from the Lake
And no birds sing!

O what can ail thee knight at arms   5
So haggard and so woe begone?
The squirrel's granary is full
And the harvest's done.

I see a lilly on thy brow
With anguish moist and fever dew,   10
And on thy cheeks a fading rose
Fast withereth too—

I met a Lady in the Meads
Full beautiful, a faery's child

Her hair was long, her foot was light   15
And her eyes were wild—

I made a Garland for her head,
And bracelets too, and fragrant Zone:
She look'd at me as she did love
And made sweet moan—   20

I set her on my pacing steed
And nothing else saw all day long
For sidelong would she bend and sing
A faery's song—

She found me roots of relish sweet   25
And honey wild and manna dew
And sure in language strange she said
'I love thee true'—

She took me to her elfin grot
And there she wept and sigh'd full sore   30
And there I shut her wild wild eyes
With kisses four.

And there she lulled me asleep
And there I dream'd—Ah Woe betide!
The latest dream I ever dreamt   35
On the cold hill side.

I saw pale kings and Princes too
Pale warriors, death pale were they all;
They cried 'La belle dame sans merci
Thee hath in thrall.'   40

I saw their starv'd lips in the gloom
With horrid warning gaped wide
And I awoke and found me here
On the cold hill's side

And this is why I sojourn here   45
Alone and palely loitering;
Though the sedge is wither'd from the Lake
And no birds sing—

'La Belle Dame Sans Merci': painting by
Sir Frank Dicksee (1853–1928)

Notes

La belle dame sans merci: this was the title of a mediaeval ballad composed by Alain Chartier in 1424. The name comes from the terminology of courtly love in mediaeval literature and means 'the beautiful lady without mercy'. This 'mercy' has been described (by Brian Stone in *The Poetry of Keats*, 1992) as 'the sort of gracious kindness which prompts a woman to accept a lover's pleas'

[3] **sedge:** a kind of coarse grass

[9] **lilly:** lily, meaning white or pale in colour

[13] **meads:** meadows

[18] **zone:** girdle or ornate belt

[29] **elfin:** fairy (the word originally referred to a diminutive supernatural being in Arthurian legend)

[29] **grot:** grotto, i.e. cave

[40] **in thrall:** enslaved, in her power

Background

The poem was composed on 21 April 1819 in Keats's journal letter to George and Georgina and was published in Hunt's new journal, the *Indicator*, on 10 May 1820. The text used here is the draft in that letter rather than the slightly altered published version.

Explorations

First reading

1. What is your first impression of the atmosphere in this poem? What do you see, hear, and feel? Reread and jot down significant phrases and images.

Second reading

2. Is there a change of speaker in the fourth stanza? Who is speaking from then onwards? Who asked the questions in the first three stanzas?

3. (*a*) Describe the knight's present condition. (*b*) What happened to him?

4. What are the indications, as the tale progresses, that the woman is an enchanter?

5. How is the otherworldly atmosphere created in this tale of enchantment? Consider
- the woman
- the landscape details and imagery
- the dream
- the archaic language

- the metre (see the section 'A ballad' in the critical commentary below).

Third reading

6. What view of love is behind this poem? Read the critical commentary below and discuss it.

7. (*a*) How do you understand the theme of this poem? (*b*) Do you think the ballad is an appropriate form of poem for this theme? (See the critical commentary below.)

8. Do you think this poem is meant to instruct us? If so, comment on the moral.

9. 'The poem has a very simple view of good and evil.' Would you agree with this statement? Explain your views.

10. What elements of the poem did you find most effective?

A Critical Commentary

Love, corruption, and death

This is one of three poems by Keats dealing with love between a man and a superhuman woman (see also 'Endymion' and 'Lamia'), and only in Endymion is there a happy outcome. Here, as in 'Lamia', we are dealing with an enchanter, this time a murderous one. La Belle Dame is the fatal woman-figure often found in romantic literature who seduces the knight and thereby fatally weakens him. She is viewed as a 'demon muse' by the critic Katherine Wilson (in *The Nightingale and the Hawk: A Psychological Study of Keats's Ode*); but whether or not she is inspirational, she is certainly fatal. Love is here associated with death. Some commentators have wondered whether this is an expression of Keats's own feelings of guilt about love. Robert Graves (in

The White Goddess) took a more complex view and felt that 'the Belle Dame represented love, death by consumption ... and poetry all at once.'

But the knight here did not succeed in resisting, has been fatally corrupted, and is languishing ('palely loitering'). So we presume that he was in some degree responsible, to some extent a compliant partner in the seduction. Corruption follows seduction in the world of this poem.

This is another of Keats's poems to feature the human being in a strange transitional state. It is as if the knight has been transported beyond the reality of this life and visited the underworld, where he encountered others seduced like himself. He managed to return, but fatally weakened.

Background

Establishing a biographical rationale for a poem is risky at the best of times. Here it is doubly so, because the evidence is definitely circumstantial. But Aileen Ward (in *John Keats: The Making of a Poet*) makes a number of fascinating points about the background circumstances. Earlier in that month of April 1819, Keats had come across a bundle of love letters to his late brother Tom from Amena, a mysterious French acquaintance of Tom's school friend Charles Wells. There had been a long sentimental correspondence between the two, with Wells as intermediary. Tom had even gone to France in a vain effort to meet her. Now Keats discovered that it had all been a cruel hoax by Wells, and he was furious at the strain that had been inflicted on his already dying brother. This may not have been the conscious inspiration for the poem, but it lends a certain poignancy to the figure of the pale knight and the theme of love, delusion, and betrayal.

Ward also draws attention to the fact that Keats himself exhibited a fear of involvement in his own love affair with Fanny Brawne about this time, writing: 'Ask yourself my love whether you are not very cruel to have so entrammelled me, so destroyed my freedom.' Though he was enormously drawn to her, the writing of poetry had a superior claim on him, and he seemed to see the two in opposition. Though the experience of love was the life blood of his poetry, yet he seemed to shy away from the actual. 'If I were to see you today it would destroy the half comfortable sullenness I enjoy at present into downright perplexities,' he wrote to her in September of that year. 'I love you too much to venture to Hampstead, I feel it is not paying a visit, but venturing into a fire ... knowing well that my life must be passed in fatigue and trouble, I have been endeavouring to wean myself from you.' Whether the last sentence refers to his personal and financial circumstances or to his notion of the life of a poet is not clear; but his ambiguity about love and his fear of involvement at that time may well be reflected in 'La Belle Dame sans Merci'.

Mediaeval resonances in the poem

Keats had a particular fascination with the mediaeval, and this is one of the last of the poems in which he used the literature and folklore of the Middle Ages.

- Consider the title (see the note on page 52 above).
- The name 'la belle dame sans merci' comes from the terminology of courtly love and refers to the withholding of the lady's favours.
- A characteristic of the mediaeval supernatural ballad was the seduction of a human being by one of the faeries, who took power from men by luring them into making love.
- Spenser's 'Faerie Queene', which was a model for some of Keats's work, also features an enchanter from the mediaeval world.
- The mediaeval ballad sometimes featured a wasteland that could be made green again through the intervention of a virtuous knight.

A ballad

The poem exhibits many of the classic characteristics of the ballad form:

- the themes of love, war, or death, often exhibited as a supernatural encounter
- narration through dialogue
- archaic language and phrasing
- simplicity of vocabulary
- the repetition of phrases
- dramatic qualities of action and conflict
- ballad metre, usually four-line stanzas of four, three, four and three stresses. This moved the story along at a fairly swift pace. Keats has altered this to produce a slower and more haunting rhythm: he lengthened the second line by a foot and shortened the last line by two feet, using a spondee as a weighty last foot :

∪ — ∪ — ∪ — ∪ —
O what | can ail | thee knight | at arms

∪ — ∪ — ∪ — ∪
Alone | and palelly loitlering?

∪ — ∪ — ∪ ∪ ∪ —
The sedge | has withlered from | the Lake

∪ — — —
And no | birds sing!

To Autumn

Season of mists and mellow fruitfulness,
Close bosom-friend of the maturing sun;
Conspiring with him how to load and bless
With fruit the vines that round the thatch-eves run;
To bend with apples the moss'd cottage-trees,   5
And fill all fruit with ripeness to the core;
To swell the gourd, and plump the hazel shells
With a sweet kernel; to set budding more,
And still more, later flowers for the bees,
Until they think warm days will never cease,   10
For Summer has o'er-brimm'd their clammy cells.

Who hath not seen thee oft amid thy store?
Sometimes whoever seeks abroad may find
Thee sitting careless on a granary floor,
Thy hair soft-lifted by the winnowing wind;   15
Or on a half-reap'd furrow sound asleep,
Drows'd with the fume of poppies while thy hook
Spares the next swath and all its twined flowers:
And sometimes like a gleaner thou dost keep
Steady thy laden head across a brook;   20
Or by a cyder-press, with patient look,
Thou watchest the last oozings hours by hours.

Where are the songs of Spring? Ay, where are they?
Think not of them, thou hast thy music too,—
While barred clouds bloom the soft-dying day,   25
And touch the stubble-plains with rosy hue;
Then in a wailful choir the small gnats mourn
Among the river sallows, borne aloft
Or sinking as the light wind lives or dies;
And full-grown lambs loud bleat from hilly bourn;   30
Hedge-crickets sing; and now with treble soft
The red-breast whistles from a garden-croft;
And gathering swallows twitter in the skies.

Notes

[7] **gourd:** a large fleshy fruit

[15] **winnowing:** the process of separating grain from chaff (the covering of the grain) at harvest time: the beaten corn is thrown in the air, and the wind blows off the lighter chaff

[18] **swath:** a row of corn as it falls when reaped

[19] **gleaner:** a person gathering ears of corn left by the reapers

[25] **barred clouds:** clouds patterned in bars

[25] **bloom:** used as a transitive verb and meaning to give a glow to

[28] **sallows:** low-growing willow trees

[30] **bourn:** a small stream

[32] **croft:** a small agricultural holding

Explorations

First reading

1. Decide to concentrate either on what you see or on what you hear as you listen to this poem or read it aloud to yourself. What elements of either sights or sounds make an impression on you?
2. On a first reading, what particular qualities of the season are being celebrated?

Second reading

3. What do you think is a central statement in the first stanza? Why?
4. What particular aspect of autumn is depicted in the first stanza?
5. Which of our senses is engaged primarily when we read this first stanza?

Third reading

6. Comment on the mood of the second stanza.
7. What are your impressions of the personifications of autumn in the second stanza? What is suggested about the season, and about humankind's relationship with nature?

8. Why do you think the poet enquires about the songs of spring in the third stanza?
9. Would you describe the mood of this final stanza as nostalgic, depressed, perfect contentment, or what? Examine the mood in detail.

Fourth reading

10. In general, what aspects of the season appeal to the poet?
11. Choose two examples of Keats's use of sensuous language that strike you as particularly effective, and say why you think so.
12. Keats's poetry is preoccupied with the quest for beauty. Explain how this poem can be seen as part of that search. Refer to specific examples.
13. Keats's other great poetic battle was with change and decay. Is there any evidence of that here?
14. Would you consider this a successful nature poem? Give two reasons, referring to the text.

A Critical Commentary

Background

This ode was written on 19 September 1819. The circumstances of its composition were alluded to briefly in a letter Keats wrote to his friend John Reynolds on Tuesday 21 September:

> How beautiful the season is now—How fine the air. A temperate sharpness about it. Really, without joking, chaste weather—Dian skies—I never lik'd stubble fields so much as now—Aye better than the chilly green of the spring. Somehow a stubble plain looks warm—in the same way that some pictures look warm—this struck me so much in my Sunday's walk that I composed verses upon it ...

'The Cornfield 1826': painting by John Constable (1776–1837)

Theme

The poem celebrates the natural abundance of autumn. Certain aspects of the season are celebrated in each stanza: the rich fruiting of the vegetable world (stanza 1); the varied and thrilling musical sounds of the animals, birds, and insects (stanza 3); and the calm, lethargic mood of the season, with which human activities and moods are completely in tune (stanza 2).

Furthermore, Keats celebrates the beauty of the season in the full knowledge that it is transient, part of the changing cycle of life.

> Where are the songs of Spring?
>   Ay, where are they?
> Think not of them, thou hast thy music too,—
> While barred clouds bloom the soft-dying day.

Structure

Outwardly at least, the poem has a very clear, even symmetrical structure. Each stanza examines an element of the season: stanza 1, the vegetable world; stanza 2, human activities; stanza 3, animals, birds, and insects. The critic Walter Jackson Bate (in *Keats: Twentieth-Century Views*) has explored the complexity and tension beneath the surface. Each stanza concentrates on a dominant aspect of autumn but at the same time preserves an element of its opposite. For example, the theme of the first stanza is ripeness, the maturity of autumn fruit, yet growth is still going on ('to set budding more, and still more'). 'So process is continuing within a context of attained fulfilment.' We find a similar but opposite pattern in the second stanza: the activities of harvesting are mainly represented through images of stillness and inactivity. In the third stanza the birds, animals and insects are portrayed in active, concrete imagery full of energy and life, yet there are hints of transience and death also ('the small gnats mourn' and 'gathering swallows twitter in the skies'). So beneath the simple structure we find something of Keats's paradoxical complexity.

Other critics have noted the logical progress of the poem as it moves slowly through the season: pre-harvest ripeness in the first stanza, followed by the harvesting of stanza 2 and the post-harvest 'stubble-plains' of the third stanza.

The day provides a further symmetry for the structure of the ode: morning ('the maturing sun') in the first stanza, through the activities of the day in the second, to evening ('the soft-dying day') of the third stanza.

Personification of autumn

Personified autumn is addressed throughout all three stanzas ('close bosom-friend of the maturing sun' in stanza 1; 'thou hast thy music too' in stanza 3). The autumn of stanzas 1 and 3 is very real, the images concrete, depicting the actual sights of the season ('the moss'd cottage-trees'; 'the stubble-plains with rosy hue'; 'the red-breast whistles from a garden-croft').

But the second stanza features an elaborate and varied personification of the season as a person engaged in the various activities of harvesting—or not engaged, because three of the four poses depict postures of casual inactivity ('a kind of beautiful lethargy,' as Brian Stone describes it): 'sitting careless on a granary floor,' sound asleep or drugged on a furrow, or just calmly watching the oozings of the cider press. The only activity is performed in the third picture, that of the gleaner balancing a load on her head as she crosses a brook. Even that activity is stately and unhurried, the balancing tension conveyed by the line bisection of the phrase 'keep | steady.' Most critics are agreed that these figures show the human at one with the natural world, interacting with calm empathy.

Less readily agreed is whether this is a masculine or a feminine personification. Stone feels that the first figure is feminine, influenced perhaps by the languid delicacy of the 'hair soft-lifted by the winnowing wind.' The third figure, of the gleaner, he also takes as feminine, as this work was traditionally performed by women and children. The sleeping reaper he takes to be male, and the watcher of the cider press could be of either sex, though he sees it as male. His conception is coloured by social history. Cedric Watts sees the entire personification as of indeterminate sex, though traditionally it has been regarded as masculine. Helen Vendler views the stanza as a totally feminine personification of autumn: 'Keats's goddess of autumn, nearer to us than pagan goddesses because, unlike them, she labours in the fields and is herself thrashed by the winnowing wind, varies in her manifestation from careless girl to burdened gleaner to patient watcher, erotic in her abandon to the fume of poppies, intimate of light in her bosom friendship with the maturing sun, worn by her vigil over the last oozings.' Leon Waldoff agrees, seeing Autumn as a goddess of fruition and plenty, taking her place with the imaginative figures of the other odes: a feminine soul (Psyche), a bird whose mournful song was heard by Ruth, a mysterious urn, and a goddess of melancholy. How do you see it?

A poem of Keats's mature outlook on life

Though the great odes have many elements in common, strictly speaking they are not a sequence. Yet we are justified in finding in this ode a development of thought and tone that indicates a more mature, integrated outlook on life. In this respect 'To Autumn' is a fitting culmination to the odes. Gone is the restless searching after beauty in 'Ode to a Nightingale' and 'Ode on a Grecian Urn'; gone the quest for permanence; no more headlong flight and attempts to escape the horrors and suffering of life ('Ode to a Nightingale'). Past too is the conflict between beauty and transience, joy and sorrow, which was partially resolved in 'Ode on Melancholy', with the realisation that melancholy is in everything, an intrinsic part of the search for beauty and joy. Here the restlessness has eased, replaced by the fulfilled and lethargic spirit of autumn.

The human spirit is at ease with the world rather than in flight from it. There is a hint that the eternal search for better might still haunt the poet's soul ('Where are the songs of Spring? Ay, where are they?'), but it no longer presents itself with the same desperate need as in 'Ode on a Grecian Urn' ('Ah, happy, happy, boughs! that cannot shed your leaves'). Here thoughts of spring are pushed aside ('Think not of them, thou hast thy music too'). And it is this acceptance of life as it is, in all its transient beauty, that we find in the third stanza, which exemplifies Keats's mature philosophy. He is accepting here that maturity, death and regeneration are interconnected. The faint hints of death in the 'soft-dying day', 'the small gnats mourn' and the 'light wind' that 'dies' are an integral part of the season that includes 'the stubble-plains with rosy hue,' the 'full-grown lambs,' and the 'gathering swallows.' He is accepting the transient nature of existence, but this no longer takes from his enjoyment. As Leon Waldoff says, 'Keats gives expression to a keen sense of transience and loss, but it is integrated into an acceptance of a natural process that includes growth as well as decay.'

This is not to suggest that Keats has suddenly become harshly realistic. This ode paints an idealised picture of the English countryside, a green land of plenty, with the pace of life unhurried and humankind in tranquil empathy with nature. The poem exhibits a mixture of realism and what Cedric Watts calls 'consolatory fantasy'. It is as if all this richness just appeared spontaneously. He has chosen to hide the toil, the sweaty labour, the peasant squalor. Would a Marxist critic say this was a dishonest poem? At any rate, in choosing the representative features of autumn Keats has exercised an 'optimistic selectivity' (Watts).

Tone

Readers are generally agreed on the calm tone of this poem. There are no descriptive passages, hardly any qualifications and no dramatic debate such as we find in the other odes. Instead we find a calm assurance, both in the fruitfulness of the season (stanza 1) and in its value (stanza 3) ('thou hast thy music too'). The tranquillity and serenity of stanza 2 are obvious.

But it is a valediction, a farewell to the season; and the awareness of coming winter is felt particularly in the third stanza, as we have seen. Yet it is not sentimental, being saved perhaps by the wealth of apt detail and precise description, which give a balanced context for the hints of mourning and the sense of impending loss ('in a wailful choir the small gnats mourn | Among the river sallows').

Imagery

As usual, the images assail the whole range of our senses, often simultaneously in the synaesthetic imagery characteristic of Keats. (*Synaesthesia* is the fusion of two or more senses in the one image, as in the tactile-visual 'touch the stubble-plains with rosy hue.') This allows us to experience what is being described in a real, three-dimensional way. Keats also makes a dominant appeal to one particular sense in each of the three stanzas: tactile in stanza 1, visual in stanza 2, and auditory in stanza 3. For example, in stanza 1 the abundance, the sumptuousness, the ripe plenty of autumn are communicated in tactile imagery, in particular through the full, weighty verbs ('load,' 'bend,' 'fill,' 'swell the ground,' 'plump the hazel shells,' 'set budding').

The images of the second stanza are visual in the main, personifying autumn in human poses that are relaxed yet alert (in three of the four), communicating, according to Bate, 'energy caught in repose' ('sitting careless on a granary floor, | Thy hair soft-lifted by the winnowing wind,' 'by a cyder-press, with patient look'). The critic Ian Jack suggested that the pictorial details are probably inspired by paintings; but Keats concentrates on realistic detail of harvest operations (the granary, winnowing, a gleaner, a cider press). This weight of concrete, detailed imagery, combined with apt observation, gives this poem a sense of actuality, which saves it from becoming mere bucolic fancy, even though the details are selective and avoid unpleasant reality, as we saw earlier. The densely packed nature of the imagery also fosters the sense of actuality. This density often results from the poet's habit of packing a number of elements, often hyphenated, into a single image ('close bosom-friend', 'moss'd cottage-trees', 'a half-reap'd furrow', the 'soft-dying day').

The music of the language

Qualities of the season are carried not just by the imagery but also by the very sounds of the words, in dense patterns of alliteration, assonance, onomatopoeia and musical echoes that reverberate throughout the poem. For example, in the first stanza the sensuousness of the season is conveyed through the soft alliterative *m* sounds of 'mists', 'mellow' and 'maturing' and the tacky 'clammy cells'. The sense of calm fullness comes through the long vowels of 'trees', 'bees', and 'cease'. And 'swell', 'hazel', 'shells' and 'kernel' might suggest bells echoing across the autumn stillness. The onomatopoeic 'winnowing wind' gives a lift to the otherwise lethargic second stanza, a calmness perfectly rendered by the sibilant *s* sounds and the lazy long vowels of 'watchest the last oozings hours by hours.' The third stanza plays the music of autumn in its auditory imagery but also through the actual sounds of the words. For example, the inherent tinge of sadness is carried in the long vowels of 'mourn', 'borne', and 'bourn'.

The ode form

The ode is a formal, dignified and heavyweight form of lyric poetry, usually of some length. It is derived from an ancient Greek form that was often sung or accompanied by music. Odes were relatively new on the scene in English poetry, Wordsworth's ode 'Intimations of Immortality', written in 1815, being one of the more well-known contemporary ones. In earlier odes, such as 'Ode to a Nightingale', Keats used a ten-line stanza composed of a Shakespearean quatrain, *abab*, followed by a Petrarchan sextet, *cde cde*. In 'To Autumn' he increased the weighty stanza even further by inserting an extra line, to make a couplet of lines 9 and 10. So we get a long eleven-line stanza of iambic pentameters, rhyming *ababcdedcce*. When taken together with the simplicity of diction, these full, heavy stanzas are perfect for conveying the richness, melody and serenity of the season.

13 *Philip Larkin* *(1922–1985)*

Born in Coventry and educated at Oxford, Philip Larkin worked as a librarian all his life, notably at Queen's University, Belfast, from 1950 to 1955 and at the University of Hull from then onwards. 'At Grass' is from an early collection, *XX Poems*, published in 1951. Other volumes include *The Less Deceived* (1955), *The Whitsun Weddings* (1964), and *High Windows* (1974). (For fuller information see page 132.)

At Grass

The eye can hardly pick them out
From the cold shade they shelter in,
Till wind distresses tail and mane;
Then one crops grass, and moves about
—The other seeming to look on—   5
And stands anonymous again.

Yet fifteen years ago, perhaps
Two dozen distances sufficed
To fable them: faint afternoons
Of Cups and Stakes and Handicaps,   10
Whereby their names were artificed
To inlay faded, classic Junes—

Silks at the start: against the sky
Numbers and parasols: outside,
Squadrons of empty cars, and heat,   15
And littered grass: then the long cry
Hanging unhushed till it subside
To stop-press columns on the street.

Do memories plague their ears like flies?
They shake their heads. Dusk brims the shadows.   20
Summer by summer all stole away,
The starting-gates, the crowds and cries—
All but the unmolesting meadows.
Almanacked, their names live; they

Have slipped their names, and stand at ease,   25
Or gallop for what must be joy,
And not a fieldglass sees them home,
Or curious stop-watch prophesies:
Only the groom, and the groom's boy,
With bridles in the evening come.   30

Notes

[24] **Almanacked:** listed in a racing almanac, a register of racehorses

Background

'At Grass', dated 3 January 1950, was printed in *XX Poems* (1951) and also included in *The Less Deceived* (1955).

Andrew Morton (in *Philip Larkin: A Writer's Life*) traces the biographical background of the poem. The poet's father had died in 1948 and Larkin moved with his mother to Leicester. He found living with his mother very difficult, and though he and Ruth Bowman had become engaged in 1948, the relationship was going stale. In contrast, his friends, such as the Amises, seemed to be happy and prospering. The poem was written during the Christmas holiday after a visit to a cinema where he saw a film about the retired years of a racehorse called Brown Jack.

From the evidence of Larkin's working notebook it seems that the idea of personal failure preoccupied him at this time. Perhaps the poem too can be seen to embody a statement about success and failure, albeit about outliving one's successes. Fame and glory are seen here from a different viewpoint.

Stud farm in England, c.1950

Explorations

First reading

1. On a first reading, what do you notice about (a) the setting or scene, (b) the horses, (c) the time of day, and (d) the general mood of the poem?

Second reading

2. In the first stanza, did you notice the quiet, undramatic opening? How is this achieved? What words or phrases contribute to it? Explain.

3. Do you find that this poem offers a realistic description of grazing racehorses? Explain, with reference to particular words and phrases.

4. Are there any details that slightly spoil the romantic scene of gently grazing retired horses? Explore this possibility.

5. What elements of a typical race meeting do you think are well caught in stanzas 2 and 3?

Third reading

6. It is as if this scene was viewed from a distance by the poet. Explore how the sense of distance is created in the first three stanzas. What effect has this on the tone of the poem?

7. Explore the poetic use of language in the fourth stanza. (a) What atmosphere do you think is evoked by line 2? (b) Technically, how is the sense of easeful and untraumatic departure communicated in the third line? Examine the sounds of the words. (c) What is suggested to you by 'the unmolesting meadows'? Do you find this phrase in any way startling or slightly disturbing? (d) What part does rhyme play in the creation of atmosphere? (e) Consider the phrase 'their names live; they'. What do you think is the effect of the punctuation of that phrase and of its particular place in the stanza?

8. How would you describe the atmosphere in stanza 5? Consider the phrases 'have slipped their names' and 'not a fieldglass sees them home' in this context. What is the effect of the poet's presumption that they gallop 'for what must be joy'?

9. Examine the natural, homely, undistressing evocation of death in the last two lines. It comes not as the Grim Reaper but as the unthreatening and totally familiar 'groom' and 'groom's boy'. The long vowels of these words are soothing, and semantically they suggest care, comfort, and feeding; yet the finality of it is not disguised. The inverted word order of the final line emphasises that all activity ends in that final verb. Do you think this portrayal of death is effective and suitable in the context of the poem?

Fourth reading

10. Would you agree that the tone of this poem is unemotional and detached? How is this achieved? Consider the speaking voice (first person, third person, or what?), the sense of distance or perspective, and the effect of the style of description (a succession of brief pictures, often unconnected, like a series of untitled photographs).

11. Comment on the sources and effectiveness of the imagery.

12. Read the critical commentary below, discuss it, and decide on your own reading of this poem. Make headings to summarise your views.

13. What do you particularly like about this poem? Or what do you find less than satisfactory?

A Critical Commentary

Levels of meaning

At one level this is a naturalistic description of retired racehorses in a field at evening. The movements of these highly strung animals are realistically described, caught by the tense, uneasy rhythm of the language: 'one crops grass … moves about … the other … to look on … stands … again.' They are endowed with a certain pathos because the poet wonders if, like humans, they remember their days of glory, the thrill of winning ('the long cry hanging unhushed'; 'do memories plague their ears like flies?'). And he goes on, with a sense of humour: 'they shake their heads.' But of course this is also a naturalistic horse gesture from these beautifully evoked animals that 'stand at ease' or 'gallop for what must be joy' as they wait until 'the groom, and the groom's boy, | With bridles in the evening come.'

But this is not just a romantic chocolate-box scene. There are some ominous details that trouble this notion of bucolic bliss, even in the first stanza. Why are they sheltering in the 'cold shade'? And does that phrase carry its associations of death, as it does in classical mythology? The s sounds of 'shade', 'shelter' and 'distresses' create an uneasy effect. That the wind 'distresses' tail and mane further reinforces the notion that this is not an idyllically happy scene. The coldness and the dusk and these other details suggest the coming of death. And this becomes a poem about the end of life.

It is a retrospective look at life. Fame, competition, success and the moments of drama and glory are viewed in perspective from the point of view of the end. These successes are not downgraded because of approaching death: they are valued and celebrated ('their names live'; 'two dozen distances sufficed | To fable them'). But, as one critic assessed it, 'these worldly successes are put in the context of a full life and viewed somewhat hazily and dispassionately from the standpoint of the end.' So the poem portrays a controlled celebration of life. Achievements are celebrated but realistically seen in context. Note the irony of 'not a fieldglass sees them home.'

There is a sense too that the poet is trying, but not fully succeeding, to understand the meaning of it all—the meaning of life. The speaker seems to be always at a distance, either attempting to make out the scene or else attempting to attribute motive. There is the physical distance ('the eye can hardly pick them out,' 'the cold shade'); the metaphysical or mental distance, where the poet does not quite understand but attempts to attribute motive ('the other seeming to look on,' 'gallop for what must be joy'); and, finally, there is a time distance ('fifteen years ago, perhaps,' 'faint afternoons'). The effect of this is generally to blur the focus a little, to introduce a note of hazy uncertainty, a slight bewilderment about the meaning of it all.

So the philosophy that underpins the poem is that life is to be enjoyed, success celebrated, but the ultimate meaning or purpose is none too clear. Andrew Motion feels that this poem 'manages to suggest deep admiration for human lives well-lived and safely over.' He thinks that Larkin's feelings of regret and disappointment, which produced the poem, are transformed into appreciation: 'It is an envious poem which shows no trace of envy's corrosions.' Do you understand what he means by this statement, and would you agree with it?

Themes

- The celebration of life from the standpoint of the end
- The struggle to find significance and meaning in life
- The gentleness and naturalness of death

Readings of the poem

It is a measure of the depth and richness of this

poem that critics have interpreted it in widely divergent ways. Here are some of them. Examine each in the light of your own reading of the poem.

- A. Alvarez (in *The New Poetry*, 1962) says that this is a traditional pastoral poem, nostalgic in tone, 'elegant and unpretentious and rather beautiful in its gentle way.' (We have touched on this reading in 'Levels of meaning' above.)
- Andrew Motion says it is a philosophical poem about life.
- Blake Morrison (in *The Movement: English Poetry and Fiction of the 1950s*, 1986) calls it 'a post-imperial poem'. He says the poem expresses feelings of loss and regret, such as might have been felt by the British people around 1950, when the poem was written. But can the horses be seen as symbols of empire?
- Tom Paulin says the poem shows Larkin's conservative approach to literature and his class prejudice; that Larkin affects or attempts to take on a classical style—for instance in the use of 'cold shade', with its classical connotations, and also that the horses are like retired generals, 'emblems of the heroic'; and that the reference to grooms shows Larkin's support of the British class system. What is your reaction to this reading?
- James Booth (in *Philip Larkin: Writer*, 1992) says that 'if an ideological subtext could be detected in "At Grass" it would not be one of imperial nostalgia, but of animal welfare,' relating it to other poems in which Larkin shows an intense identification with the plight of animals, such as 'Myxomatosis' and 'Take One Home for the Kiddies'. Booth also points out that Larkin left a legacy to the Royal Society for the Prevention of Cruelty to Animals.

Do these readings provide some insight for your own interpretation of the poem?

The Explosion

On the day of the explosion
Shadows pointed towards the pithead:
In the sun the slagheap slept.

Down the lane came men in pitboots
Coughing oath-edged talk and pipe-smoke,   5
Shouldering off the freshened silence.

One chased after rabbits; lost them;
Came back with a nest of lark's eggs;
Showed them; lodged them in the grasses.

So they passed in beards and moleskins,   10
Fathers, brothers, nicknames, laughter,
Through the tall gates standing open.

At noon, there came a tremor; cows
Stopped chewing for a second; sun,
Scarfed as in a heat-haze, dimmed.   15

> *The dead go on before us, they*
> *Are sitting in God's house in comfort,*
> *We shall see them face to face—*
>
> Plain as lettering in the chapels
> It was said, and for a second   20
> Wives saw men of the explosion
>
> Larger than in life they managed—
> Gold as on a coin, or walking
> Somehow from the sun towards them,
>
> One showing the eggs unbroken.   25

Background

This poem, dated 5 January 1970, was probably inspired by a television documentary on the mining industry that Larkin watched with his mother during the Christmas holidays of 1969. The literary influence on it is most likely D. H. Lawrence, with his descriptions of mining villages. Larkin had read Lawrence avidly in earlier years. The poem is included in the collection *High Windows* (1974).

Explorations

First reading

1. On a first reading, what details made most impression on you?
2. What happens in the poem?

Second reading

3. What do you notice about the village? Examine all details carefully.
4. What information are we given about the miners? Explore details of dress, habit, manner, mood, philosophy.
5. Are there any hints, either in the imagery or the method of narration, that a disaster was about to happen? Examine stanzas 1 to 4 for any signs of the ominous.
6. Do you think the poet's description of the explosion is effective? Explain your thinking on this.
7. The fifth stanza marks a division between two quite different halves in this poem. How do the last ten lines differ from the first four stanzas? How would you describe the atmosphere in the last ten lines? What words or phrases contribute to this?
8. What is suggested in stanza 8? What is the effect of the imagery in this stanza?
9. What do you think is the effect of the last line?

Third reading

10. What does the poet want us to feel in this poem, and how does he achieve this?
11. What statement about life, society and people do you think the poet is making here? Refer to details in the poem.
12. Is this a poem you might remember five years from now? Why?

A Critical Commentary

Themes explored

This is a narrative poem about an industrial catastrophe in a mining village, a pithead explosion resulting in the deaths of many men of all ages from that community. The catastrophe is dealt with obliquely: no details of the carnage, horror or pain are recorded; rather is it almost euphemistically described:

> At noon, there came a tremor; cows
> Stopped chewing for a second; sun,
> Scarfed as in a heat-haze, dimmed.

Indeed it is all the more powerful for that. Death is seen here as unexpected, coming out of the sun. Death is unfair, indiscriminate ('fathers, brothers').

Larkin is recording how fragile humankind is in the face of blind fate. There is a heavy sense of foreboding about this poem ('shadows pointed towards the pithead'). They seem impelled 'through the tall gates standing open.' Are humans a mere pawn of fate, innocently, happily trooping towards their destruction?

Larkin is also impressed by how fragile communities are. There is a graphic evocation of village community here—'slagheap slept,' 'lane,' 'men in pitboots,' 'beards and

moleskins'—which may owe a great deal to D. H. Lawrence. But is this not a somewhat idealised community, full of masculine camaraderie ('coughing oath-edged talk and pipe-smoke') and good humour ('nicknames, laughter'), a somewhat simplistic picture of a simple people innocently exploring the grandeur of nature ('one chased after rabbits; lost them') and comforted in adversity by their religious beliefs ('the dead ... face to face')? Perhaps Larkin's point is that even ideal communities are powerless when confronted with wanton fate.

If not totally indifferent, nature seems at best to register the human disaster only for a moment ('cows | Stopped chewing for a second; sun, | Scarfed as in a heat-haze, dimmed'). Yet it is also nature that produces the hope in this poem, with that poignant image of the unbroken eggs. The human nest or community might be devastated, but the natural one survives. The wives too provide a continuity. Is woman a symbol of survival for Larkin? Certainly life goes on in this poem, and there is a powerful sense of continuity, as in 'The Trees'.

Imagery

There is a graphic evocation of the mining village, achieved through a wealth of realistic detail: pit-boots, pipe smoke, beards, and moleskins—all details of human accoutrements. Through this imagery the living, breathing reality is conjured up.

Romanticised images of nature (rabbits, larks' eggs, etc.) suggest the innocent preoccupations of children. But nature's other face is also hinted at ('in the sun the slagheap slept'). The alliteration emphasises the ugly amorphous mass, and there is a hint of possible threatening activity from the sleeping giant. But the image we are left with is that of the unbroken eggs, which become a symbol for survival and continuity at the end of the poem.

Religious imagery and scriptural allusions

('the dead … sitting in God's house,' 'plain as lettering in the chapels') give the poem a broader scope and a cosmic significance. We are made to see humankind against the broad tapestry of Heaven and Earth, and humans become heavenly beings ('Gold as on a coin, or walking | Somehow from the sun').

Tone

On the surface this appears to be a neutrally descriptive poem, merely logging details. Indeed the pace of the rhythm rolling along somewhat monotonously would reinforce this impression. The speaker is at pains to keep his distance and remain uninvolved: 'it was said' and 'wives saw.' He avoids personal comment. Yet that discipline seems to break down in the last line, where the pathos of that final image of the unbroken eggs and the ironic contrast with the shattered community releases all that held-back emotion. It is easy then to feel Larkin's empathy for the village. The emotion is all the more powerful for having been bottled up.

Metre

The metre is mainly non-rhyming trochaic tetrameter:

$$- \; \smile \quad - \; \smile \quad - \quad \smile \quad - \; \smile$$

Shadows | pointed | towards the | pithead

$$- \quad \smile \quad - \; \smile \quad - \; \smile \quad - \quad \smile$$

One chased | after | rabbits; | lost them

$$- \; \smile \quad - \quad \smile \quad - \quad \smile \quad - \; \smile$$

Fathers, | brothers, | nicknames, | laughter.

Trochaic metre has been used to give an easy sing-song lilt to children's narrative poetry, for example by Longfellow in 'Hiawatha' (Larkin claimed he was not aware he was using a metre similar to Longfellow's). In 'The Explosion' the gently lulling monotony of this metre hides the awful reality of the subject. This is a further bleak irony in the poem, that it is the story of a disaster told in childish rhythms. Yet it is very effective and is maintained until the final line, which serves to further emphasise that line and so add to the emotion.

Cut Grass

Cut grass lies frail:
Brief is the breath
Mown stalks exhale.
Long, long the death.

It dies in the white hours   5
Of young-leafed June
With chestnut flowers,
With hedges snowlike strewn,

White lilac bowed,
Lost lanes of Queen Anne's lace,   10
And that high-builded cloud
Moving at summer's pace.

Notes

[10] **Queen Anne's lace:** a parsley-like plant, sometimes used in herbal medicine

Explorations

Pre-reading

1. From your own experiences, list what you have noticed about a June day in the countryside.

First reading

2. What elements of nature's activity does the poet focus on?

3. Do you find the poet's attitude to the cut grass particularly sensitive? Explain.
4. What is suggested by the image of 'the white hours' of 'young-leafed June'?
5. 'Lost lanes of Queen Anne's lace': what do you see when you read this line? What atmosphere does it conjure up?

Second reading
6. What exactly is Larkin's main idea about the season, as communicated in this poem? State it briefly in your own words.
7. What part do the sounds of words play in the creation of atmosphere in the poem?
8. 'While the main focus may be on the exuberance of nature in June, we are also aware of the transience of life, the swift passage of time and the changing seasons in this poem.' Comment.

Third reading
9. Do you think this poem is effective? Explain your own reaction to it.
10. Examine Larkin's assessment of the poem in the section 'Imagery' in the critical commentary below. Do you agree with his views?

A Critical Commentary

Theme
This graceful lyric deals with a common enough theme: the cycle of life in nature. But it approaches this topic with great immediacy and not a little drama. The poet marks how death can coexist with beauty in the freshness of a June day. Grass is cut to make hay, and 'long the death. | It dies in the white hours | Of young-leafed June.' The poem emphasises the frailty of life, but this is more than balanced by the rich, abundant beauty of nature ('hedges snowlike strewn'), with its medicinal properties ('Queen Anne's lace') and elegant energy ('high-builded cloud | Moving at summer's pace').

Imagery
The fairly obvious natural imagery of flowers, hedges and clouds had been freshened in a personal way by Larkin ('lost lanes of Queen Anne's lace'). It is reinvigorated by a dramatic personification:

> Brief is the breath
> Mown stalks exhale.

Larkin himself felt that the imagery might be overdone. In a letter to Monica Jones (1 August 1971), after the poem was completed, he said:

> Its trouble is that it's 'music', that is, pointless crap ... About line 6 I hear a kind of wonderful Elgar rhythm music take over, for which the words are just an excuse ... Do you see what I mean? There is a point at which the logical sense of the poem ceases to be added to, and it continues only as a succession of images. I like it all right but for once I'm not a good judge.

Do you agree with his reservations about the imagery? Comment. Do you see what he means about the 'wonderful rhythm'? Explain.

Rhythm and rhyme
Despite the short lines of irregular metre, a slow, elegant pace is achieved, mainly though the use of long vowels. For example:

$$-\quad-\quad-$$

Mown stalks exhale

$$-\quad-$$

Long, long ...

He uses alliteration for musical effect: 'brief is the breath,' 'snowlike strewn,' 'lost lanes of ... lace.' This augments the music of the regular rhyme *abab* of each stanza.

Tone
Is there a certain wistfulness about the poet's contemplation of short-lived beauty? The grass is 'frail', the breath 'brief'. The inappropriateness of any notion of death in the 'white hours | Of young-leafed June' indicates some sadness. This wistfulness is carried on the sounds of the words, as we saw.

14 *Michael Longley (born 1939)*

Born in Belfast of English parents, Michael Longley was educated at the Royal Belfast Academical Institution and Trinity College, Dublin. His early education and local socialisation made him aware of conflicting classes and religious identities. He worked for the Arts Council of Northern Ireland between 1970 and 1991, when he nurtured local talent, attempted to bring the arts at an affordable price to working-class people, and fostered the artistic expression of both sides of the political divide. Among his volumes of poetry are *No Continuing City* (1969), *An Exploded View* (1973), *The Echo Gate* (1979), *Gorse Fires* (1991), and *The Ghost Orchid* (1995). 'Badger' and 'Wounds' are from *An Exploded View*. Some poems in this collection respond to the contemporary upsurge of violence in Northern Ireland; other poems, such as 'Carrigskeewaun', focus on an alternative life-style in the west of Ireland. (For fuller information see page 133.)

Badger

for Raymond Piper

I

Pushing the wedge of his body
Between cromlech and stone circle,
He excavates down mine shafts
And back into the depths of the hill.

His path straight and narrow   5
And not like the fox's zig-zags,
The arc of the hare who leaves
A silhouette on the sky line.

Night's silence around his shoulders,
His face lit by the moon, he   10
Manages the earth with his paws,
Returns underground to die.

II

An intestine taking in
patches of dog's-mercury,
brambles, the bluebell wood;   15
a heel revolving acorns;
a head with a price on it
brushing cuckoo-spit, goose-grass;
a name that parishes borrow.

III

For the digger, the earth-dog   20
It is a difficult delivery
Once the tongs take hold,

Vulnerable his pig's snout
That lifted cow-pats for beetles,
Hedgehogs for the soft meat,   25

His limbs dragging after them
So many stones turned over,
The trees they tilted.

Notes

[2] **cromlech:** a name once given to what are now
called portal tombs—prehistoric stone monuments
consisting of a large flat stone resting horizontally on
two or more upright stones

[14] **dog's-mercury:** the common name of *Mercurialis
perennis*, a herbaceous woodland plant, usually
regarded as toxic

[19] **a name that parishes borrow:** the poet refers
to *broc*, the Irish for 'badger' (in fact the element Broc
found in place-names—for example *Domhnach Broc*,
anglicised Donnybrook—is the man's name Broc)

Explorations

First reading: section I

1. Think of section I as a picture or painting.
   What do you see? Consider the setting
   described, the background, the lighting,
   and the main subject.
2. What do you notice about the badger?
   How do you visualise the animal? Examine
   the connotations of descriptive words and
   phrases, such as 'the wedge of his body';
   'Night's silence around his shoulders'; 'he
   manages the earth.' How do badgers' paths
   differ from those of other animals, and
   what might this suggest about the nature
   of the badger?
3. What is suggested here about the animal's
   relationship with the earth? Consider his
   association with cromlech and stone circle;
   how he 'manages' the earth; how he
   'Returns underground to die.'
4. Do you think the badger has particular

significance for the poet? Explain.
5. How would you describe the atmosphere
   of section I? What words or phrases help
   to create it?

Second reading: section II

6. What do you notice about the badger's diet?
7. What other aspects of the badger's
   environmental function are mentioned in
   section II?
8. 'A head with a price on it': what does this
   line suggest about human attitudes to the
   badger?

Third reading: section III

9. What do you think is happening in section
   III?
10. Contrast the human's treatment of the
    environment in section III with the badger's
    management of the earth in sections I and II.

11. Do you think the poet has some sympathy for the animal in this section? Which phrases or images might suggest this?
12. Explore the ironies in the first stanza of this section.

Fourth reading
13. What point is the poet making about humankind's interaction with the environment?
14. What other themes do you notice in the poem?
15. Would you agree that 'Longley displays the scientific assurance of a naturalist'?
16. 'Longley's view of the west of Ireland is a realistic rather than a romantic one.' On the evidence of the poem 'Badger', would you agree with this statement? Refer to the text to support your argument.
17. Summarise your thoughts and feelings on this poem.

A Critical Commentary

A reading of the poem

This nature poem celebrates that nocturnal woodland creature, the badger, but it also questions humankind's interference in nature. The badger's legendary strength is evoked both in the descriptions ('the wedge of his body') and by his activities ('He excavates ... into the depths of the hill'), which personify him as a muscular miner. There is a sense of uncompromising directness and dependability about his 'path straight and narrow' that contrasts with the deceptiveness of the fox and the giddiness of the hare. That ruggedness is also evident from his indiscriminate diet: he can cope with the poisonous dog's-mercury and the tough briars as well as the gentler bluebells.

But it is his relationship with the earth that is most interestingly portrayed. Longley sees the badger as a sort of horticulturalist: he 'manages the earth with his paws'; he facilitates the growth of great oak trees ('a heel revolving acorns'). The picture comes across of an animal at one with the earth, the caretaker of the hill, which in turn takes care of him in death. The animal's close association with prehistoric tombs lends him an even greater aura of significance. Somehow he becomes a symbol of the earth's ancientness, its longevity and mythological power. Longley himself has said that he thinks of animals as spirits. He tries to have an animal in each of his books.

The poem also deals with humankind's destructiveness and cruelty, its interference in the natural world. The poet's criticism of this is communicated through the bleak ironies of section III: digging out the digger, the bitter euphemism of this process being described as a forceps birth, the irony of being 'delivered' to his death.

> It is a difficult delivery
> once the tongs take hold.

There is sympathy for the 'vulnerable ... pig's snout' and implicit condemnation of the brutal treatment ('his limbs dragging after them') and also of the environmental disturbance:

> So many stones turned over,
> The trees they tilted.

This treatment is in marked contrast to the badger's careful management of the earth, unaided by machines or 'tongs' of any kind. A clear environmental statement is made here, but it is subtly put across through the contrast rather than by any kind of didactic statement.

Tone

This is a tough, unsentimental poem recording the perennial secret workings of nature. True, it does romanticise the badger somewhat—

> Night's silence around his shoulders,
> His face lit by the moon

—but it also records the violence, the suffering

and the destruction of nature and creatures. Behind that wealth of observed details and naturalist's knowledge we can detect a tone of admiration for the animal's strength and its management of the woodland ('His path straight … not like the fox's zig-zags …'), and we can certainly feel his sympathy for the vulnerable animal in section III.

Wounds

Here are two pictures from my father's head—
I have kept them like secrets until now:
First, the Ulster Division at the Somme
Going over the top with 'Fuck the Pope!'
'No Surrender!': a boy about to die,   5
Screaming 'Give 'em one for the Shankill!'
'Wilder than Gurkhas' were my father's words
Of admiration and bewilderment.
Next comes the London-Scottish padre
Resettling kilts with his swagger-stick,   10
With a stylish backhand and a prayer.
Over a landscape of dead buttocks
My father followed him for fifty years.
At last, a belated casualty,
He said—lead traces flaring till they hurt—   15
'I am dying for King and Country, slowly.'
I touched his hand, his thin head I touched.

Now, with military honours of a kind,
With his badges, his medals like rainbows,
His spinning compass, I bury beside him   20
Three teenage soldiers, bellies full of
Bullets and Irish beer, their flies undone.
A packet of Woodbines I throw in,
A lucifer, the Sacred Heart of Jesus
Paralysed as heavy guns put out   25
The night-light in a nursery for ever;
Also a bus-conductor's uniform—
He collapsed beside his carpet-slippers
Without a murmur, shot through the head
By a shivering boy who wandered in   30
Before they could turn the television down
Or tidy away the supper dishes.
To the children, to a bewildered wife,
I think 'Sorry Missus' was what he said.

Notes

[3] **Ulster Division:** a division of the British army in the First World War

[3] **Somme:** a river in north-eastern France, the scene of continuous heavy fighting during the First World War, particularly from July to November 1916

[4] **going over the top:** soldiers climbing out of the trenches and attacking across 'no man's land'

[6] **the Shankill:** the area of Belfast around the Shankill Road, inhabited mainly by Protestants

[9] **London-Scottish padre:** the chaplain of the London-Scottish Regiment of the British army, of which Longley's father was a member

[10] **resettling kilts:** the chaplain flicks down the dead soldiers' kilts to allow them some dignity in death

[24] **lucifer:** an old name for a match

Background

In his autobiographical chapters *Tuppenny Stung*, Michael Longley elaborates on his father's wartime experiences.

Having lived through so much by the time he was thirty, perhaps my father deserved his early partial retirement. At the age of seventeen he had enlisted in 1914, one of thousands queuing up outside Buckingham Palace. He joined the London-Scottish by mistake and went into battle wearing an unwarranted kilt. A Lady from Hell. Like so many survivors he seldom talked about his experiences, reluctant to relive the nightmare. But not long before he died, we sat up late one night and he reminisced. He had won the Military Cross for knocking out single-handed a German machine-gun post and, later, the Royal Humane Society's medal for gallantry: he had saved two nurses from drowning. By the time he was twenty he had risen to the rank of Captain, in charge of a company known as 'Longley's Babies' because many of them were not yet regular shavers. He recalled the lice, the rats, the mud, the tedium, the terror. Yes, he had bayoneted men and still dreamed about a tubby little German who 'couldn't run fast enough. He turned around to face me and burst into tears.' My father was nicknamed Squib in the trenches. For the rest of his life no-one ever called him Richard.

Soldiers from the Royal Irish Rifles during a break from fighting at the Battle of the Somme in 1916

Explorations

First reading
(focus on the first half of the poem).

1. The first part of the poem is taken up with the 'two pictures from my father's head.' Explore the first picture (lines 3–8). What are your thoughts about this?

2. Interpret the father's reaction (lines 7 and 8). *or*

3. Compose a brief diary extract that the father might have written on the evening following the attack.

4. Explore the second picture (lines 9–11).

What are your thoughts on this?

5. Reflect on the two images. What do they suggest to you about people at war? Jot down all the ideas suggested by these pictures.

6. Read lines 12–15. What do you discover about the effects of war on the father?

7. From a reading of the first part of this poem, what do you discover about Longley's father?

8. Comment on the relationship between father and son. Refer to specific words and phrases.

Second reading
(focus on the second half of the poem)

9. What is happening in the second part of this poem? Read it a number of times. If you are still confused, examine the first three lines very carefully.

10. At this surreal burial ceremony the poet inters an odd collection of objects and images. (*a*) Comment on the significance of the objects directly connected to the father. What is revealed about the father and the relationship between father and son? (*b*) Explore the images of violence. What do you see? What do they suggest to you about the society?

11. 'A shivering boy who wandered in': compose an interior monologue of the imagined thoughts of this boy.

Third reading

12. Examine the structure or division of this poem into two parts. How do the two parts relate? What point is the poet making here?

13. Comment on the themes explored in this poem. What view of life is presented?

14. Do you think the poet is angry, saddened or depressed by these happenings? Refer to specific phrases and lines.

15. Would you agree that this poem shows the ordinary human being as insignificant and powerless in the face of violence? Refer to specific incidents in the text.

16. Comment on any feature of the poet's style you consider significant. You might consider the impact of the imagery; the humour; the tone of the piece; the surreal nightmarish effects; the realism; or any other.

A Critical Commentary

A reading of the poem

The figure of his father features prominently in Michael Longley's poetry. The dead father is graphically and sympathetically realised and the father-son bond asserted in such poems as 'In Memoriam', 'Wounds', 'Last Requests', and 'Laertes'. The poet's relationship with his father in 'Wounds' is characterised by intimacy and tenderness. There is an intimacy about their style of communication: 'two pictures from my father's head' suggests a perfect non-verbal understanding, which the poet has kept 'like secrets.' The caress is tender, repetitive, and comforting: 'I touched his hand, his thin head I touched.' The father's sense of humour, even if a little grim, indicates the easiness of the relationship: 'I am dying for King and Country, slowly.' (This refers to the link between his final illness and the old war wounds; see 'In Memoriam': 'In my twentieth year your old wounds woke | As cancer.') In these repeated father-son exchanges Longley is probing his own identity and defining his background.

Much has been written about the supposed identity crisis of the Ulster Protestant writer, shakily situated between the conflicting claims of the English and Irish literary traditions and outlooks. As Terence Brown points out in another context (in *Northern Voices*, 1975), Longley is a lyric poet nurtured in the English and classical traditions, 'attempting to come to terms with the fact that he was born in Ireland of an English father and that he now lives in a Belfast shaken almost nightly by the national question, violently actualised.' This family experience of immigration might be seen to mirror the experience of the Ulster Protestant as immigrant. We catch some of this confusion, this incomprehension of the local view, in the father's bemused reaction to the Ulster soldiers' sectarian slogans and battle cries of 'No surrender.'

> 'Wilder than Gurkhas' were my father's words
> of admiration and bewilderment.

He expresses admiration presumably for their courage but bewilderment at the sectarian sentiment.

Something of the same bewilderment is evident in the poet's own reaction to present-day violence, when he describes the murder of the bus conductor:

> Shot through the head
> By a shivering boy who wandered in
> Before they could turn the television down.

The air of incomprehension, this slight sense of distance from local realities, which may be the inheritance of the immigrant, is shared by father and son.

In summary, the poet is establishing his identity as the son of a courageous English soldier. There is no direct discussion of an identity crisis, either literary or political; but we do register a sense of bewilderment, something of the outsiders' air of detachment in the attitudes of both father and son towards Ulstermen at war. Longley is using his father's First World War experiences as a perspective on present-day atrocities. Patricia Craig (in *Contemporary Irish Poetry*, edited by Elmer Andrews) says that the violence of the trenches is 'brought up smack against the dingier violences of present-day Belfast.' Whether it is more or less dingy in the poet's eyes is debatable. The grotesqueness of the slaughter and the indignities of violent death are emphasised in both the world war and the present-day killings. The 'landscape of dead buttocks' that haunted his father for fifty years is hardly less bizarre than the recent image of

> Three teenage soldiers, bellies full of
> Bullets and Irish beer, their flies undone.

What is different and shocking about the portrayal of modern violence in the poem is its invasion of the domestic scene:

> Before they could turn the television down
> Or tidy away the supper dishes.

It is almost casual, perpetrated by a boy who 'wandered in.' The shocking ordinariness of the violence is underlined by the ridiculous apology 'Sorry, missus': it is as if he had just bumped into her accidentally in the street. Death is delivered to your sitting-room with a casual, polite apology.

Issues raised in the poem: Longley's sense of identity

- The poet is defining himself by describing his family background.
- The English military background is an important and accepted facet of the poet's identity.
- The sensitive and humorous portrait of his father communicates an easy and tender father-son relationship.
- The father figure is important generally in the poet's life: that long-dead man is still a powerful reality.
- The violent city is part of his identity also.

Violence

The 'wounds' of the title refers to old war wounds, lingering psychological wounds (haunting images), and new wounds.

The world of the poem is a world of violence, whether legitimised as war or condemned as illegal acts. Does the poem differentiate between war-violence and present-day atrocities?

Other points:

- the less than glorious reality of war
- the indignity of violent death
- the increasing ordinariness of violence—terror at the heart of the domestic
- the casual, wanton nature of present-day violence.

Tone

The opening is conversational, personal. The speaker is sharing a confidence, inviting us in: 'Here are two pictures … I have kept them like secrets …' There is evidence of a certain wry humour, which successfully deflates any possible attempt at glorifying either his father or the war ('I am dying for King and Country, slowly'; 'A packet of woodbines I throw in, | A lucifer'). Is a note of critical irony detectable in the chaplain's fussiness about dress in the face of death, and a hint of religious cynicism in the apparent indifference of God to human suffering and evil ('the Sacred Heart of Jesus | Paralysed')? The emotional impact is frequently disguised behind the relentless listing of details, but it is there, for example in 'heavy guns put out | The night-light in a nursery for ever.' And the understatement of the last line packs quite an emotional punch.

Visual impact

This particularly visual style relies heavily on Longley's eye for incongruous details, such as the sectarian battle cries as they go over the top; the chaplain with the stylish backhand; the domestic details of the three teenage soldiers, lured to their deaths by the promise of sex; the bus conductor who 'collapsed beside his garden slippers.' And they all make the point about how brutally unglorious death is.

15 *John Montague* *(born 1929)*

Born in New York of Irish parents, John Montague returned as a boy to what remained of the family farm at Garvaghy, County Tyrone. He was educated at St Patrick's College, Armagh, and University College, Dublin, and has been a university lecturer in America, France, and Ireland. A prolific poet, he is probably most famous for his volume *The Rough Field* (1972), in which he investigates his personal and historical experience of Northern Ireland. (For fuller information see page 136.)

The Cage

My father, the least happy
man I have known. His face
retained the pallor
of those who work underground:
the lost years in Brooklyn   5
listening to a subway
shudder the earth.

But a traditional Irishman
who (released from his grille
in the Clark St I.R.T.)   10
drank neat whiskey until
he reached the only element
he felt at home in any longer: brute oblivion.

And yet picked himself
up, most mornings,   15
to march down the street
extending his smile
to all sides of the good,
all-white neighbourhood
belled by St Teresa's church.   20

When he came back
we walked together
across fields of Garvaghy
to see hawthorn on the summer
hedges, as though   25
he had never left;
a bend of the road

which still sheltered
primroses. But we
did not smile in   30
the shared complicity
of a dream, for when
weary Odysseus returns
Telemachus should leave.

Often as I descend   35
into subway or underground
I see his bald head behind
the bars of the small booth;
the mark of an old car
accident beating on his   40
ghostly forehead.

Notes

[1] **My father:** James Montague sold his farm to raise money for a business venture that proved unsuccessful; he failed to find work and, after involvement in republican activities in County Tyrone, emigrated to the United States in 1925; so perhaps he had reason to be unhappy

[33] **Odysseus:** king of Ithaca and legendary Greek hero of Homer's epic poem *The Odyssey*; he survived the Trojan War, but for ten years the sea god Poseidon prevented him from returning home; Montague sees his father's long exile in terms of the trials of Odysseus

[34] **Telemachus:** in *The Odyssey*, the son of Odysseus and his wife, Penelope

Background

In 1952 John Montague accepted a scholarship to study in the United States and intended to visit his father in New York. But, coincidentally, the father returned home and they were able to spend some time together before John went to postgraduate school at Yale University in 1953; hence the reference to Telemachus leaving after Odysseus' return.

Explorations

First reading

1. On a first reading of the poem, did you notice any reasons that might account for the father being 'the least happy man'?

2. Consult the notes above on the father and on Odysseus and Telemachus. What do they add to your understanding of the father's situation?

3. How many different locations or scenes do you notice in this poem?

Second reading: stanzas 1–3

4. Consider the atmosphere of New York as portrayed in the poem. What sounds do you hear? What do we discover of the people, the environment, etc.? Do you think the poet manages to make it real for the reader? What image made you think?

5. Examine the portrayal of the father. What physical descriptions are given, and what might they suggest about the man? What do you notice about his working conditions? Do you think he is happy in

his job? Why, according to the poet, does he drink so much? Has he any redeeming qualities? Refer to phrases or lines to support your answers.

6. The poem is entitled 'The Cage'. Where does this image occur, and what does it refer to? What does it suggest about the father's attitude?

7. Do you think the portrait of the father is a totally depressing one? Explain your views with reference to the poem.

Third reading

8. What is the poet's attitude to his father? Does he resent his father's drinking, admire him, feel sorry for him, remember him with affection, or what? Refer to lines or images in your answer.

9. Briefly, what do you consider to be the theme of the poem?

10. Would you consider this to be a powerful portrayal of the Irish emigrant? Explain your view with reference to the text.

11. What features of the poem do you find to be most successful? Consider effective characterisation; clear, concrete imagery; simple narrative structure; the ability to evoke sympathy without overdoing it; painful honesty; or any other feature.

A Critical Commentary

A reading of the poem

At a basic level, this poem can be seen as a comment on Irish social history, or at least on one aspect of it: emigration. It deals with the phenomenon of the dissatisfied, embittered exile, emphasising the feelings of unfulfilment ('the lost years'), the captivity of work ('The Cage', 'released from his grille'), and the yearnings to return to the native place ('weary Odysseus returns').

At a personal level this is a family poem, a fairly complex portrait of the poet's father, whom he paints warts and all but not without some sympathy. There is no attempt to romanticise the man. He is 'the least happy | man I have known,' unfulfilled and embittered, feeling he has wasted his life, spending

> the lost years in Brooklyn
> listening to a subway
> shudder the earth.

There are historical echoes of the Irish navvy in this image, the emigrant toiling in the bowels of a foreign earth. Caged to his work, his father drinks himself stupid in an effort to escape the reality, until

> he reached the only element
> he felt at home in

any longer: brute oblivion.

Yet the man's tenacity, his efforts at keeping up an outward show and his good manners are recognised in the third stanza: 'picked himself | up, most mornings … extended his smile …' The contradictory aspects of his life in exile, the inner pain and the outward show of normality, are registered and admired. Weary of it all, he returns, to limited satisfaction.

Montague compares his father to the wandering warrior Odysseus. While that allusion carries suggestions of heroism, it does not predict a happy ending. Odysseus' wealth had been squandered; he returned unrecognised at first, a stranger in his own house. Here too there are all the strains of the returned exile. The physical place may remain unchanged, but it is impossible to pick up the pieces where one left off: people change, go their separate ways, develop different dreams and goals ('But we | did not smile in | the shared complicity | of a dream'). It is ironic here that as the father returns, the son is preparing to leave (see the notes on the father above). Altogether, this is a picture of a life lacking fulfilment, a lonely exile and a lonely end.

Yet there is no bitterness in the father-son

relationship. The poet states bald facts as he sees them, and he is not unsympathetic to his father's plight. But there is little real closeness beyond that temporary companionship as they 'walked together | across fields of Garvaghy.' However, the poet does retain pervasive memories of that injured man.

Imagery

The facial images are those of a less than healthy man: 'pallor'; 'the mark of an old car | accident beating on his | ghostly forehead.' They suggest a man worn down by life. There are a number of references to descending underground, creating the impression of a human being driven underground. This impression is fostered by the prevailing metaphor of the cage: entrapment, life's possibilities closed off, freedom restricted. The romantic images of nature, on the other hand, glamorise the native Garvaghy. The images seem to fall along the old rural-urban divide, denigrating the city and exile but romanticising the countryside and Ireland. So the imagery powerfully reinforces the theme of the problems of exile.

16 Eiléan Ní Chuilleanáin (born 1942)

Eiléan Ní Chuilleanáin's first volume of poetry, *Acts and Monuments* (1972), from which 'Swineherd' is taken, won the Patrick Kavanagh Award. Many of the poems focus on the relationship between human beings and the natural world. In later volumes she focuses more sharply on questions of female identity. Among her collections are *Site of Ambush* (1975), *The Rose Geranium* (1982), and *The Magdalene Sermon* (1989). (For fuller information see page 136.)

Swineherd

'When all this is over', said the swineherd,
'I mean to retire, where
Nobody will have heard about my special skills
And conversation is mainly about the weather.

I intend to learn how to make coffee, at least as well   5
As the Portuguese lay-sister in the kitchen
And polish the brass fenders every day.
I want to lie awake at night
Listening to cream crawling to the top of the jug
And the water lying soft in the cistern.   10

I want to see an orchard where the trees grow in straight lines
And the yellow fox finds shelter between the navy-blue trunks,
Where it gets dark early in summer
And the apple-blossom is allowed to wither on the bough.'

Explorations

First reading: first stanza

1. What do you imagine are the 'special skills' of the swineherd?
2. Do you think the swineherd is proud of these 'special skills' or somewhat ashamed? Where is this suggested?

3. In what situations, usually, do people talk about the weather? Why do you think the swineherd might look forward to this?
4. In what tone of voice do you think the first stanza should be spoken – excited, tired, determined, or what? What phrases would

you emphasise in a reading? Why?

5. Where do you think the swineherd works? Look to the second stanza also for clues.

Second reading

6. Lines 5–7: What do you think of the swineherd's ambitions in these lines? Do you find them unusual? Explain. (A lay-sister was a nun who didn't take full religious vows and was given the more menial tasks in the convent, work such as cooking, cleaning, laundry, etc).

7. Eiléan Ní Chuilleanáin has said that she based the poem on her experience of a convent in Belgium where her aunt was Reverend Mother and where there actually was a Portuguese lay-sister in the kitchen. She has also said that she envisaged the swineherd as female.
   (a) Do you think it a little ironic that the swineherd might envy the lowly lay-sister?
   (b) What aspects of the theme of women and work does the poem focus on? What is the poem saying to you about this?

8. Lines 8–10: What does the speaker think she would enjoy? What does she want out of life?

Third reading

9. Lines 11–14: What do you notice about the speaker's ideal place? In what part of the world do you think she might find this? Is it real or completely imaginary?

10. What does the poem suggest to you about people's dreams?

11. Do you think the imagery is effective at communicating hopes and dreams, both the ordinary and the more exotic? Comment on any two images from this point of view.

Fourth reading

12. Compose a conversation the swineherd might have had, during her working day, with the Portuguese lay-sister in the kitchen.

13. Do you see the swineherd as a strong or a weak personality? Consider the way she phrases her wishes.

14. 'The poet has a particular love of nature.' Would you agree?

A Critical Commentary

A reading of the poem

The swineherd in the convent is dreaming about what she will do when she retires. She has spent her life in a menial job, doing what is traditionally considered masculine work and which she euphemistically refers to as 'special skills'. There is a suggestion that she wishes to put this past life firmly behind her and engage in everyday chores. It is ironic that these are equally menial even if they are considered feminine tasks! Perhaps she considers them a step up the social ladder, a fact which further emphasises her lowly situation. More liberating is her wish to have the leisure and the time to appreciate the beauty of ordinary natural processes, such as:

> Listening to the cream to the top of the jug
> And the water lying soft in the cistern.

The sensuous luxury of these images suggests a complete contrast to her former existence. Also in sharp contrast is the ordered beauty of the ideal landscape she pictures in the last four lines, suggestive of a romantic scene further south in Europe where it gets dark early and the days are so calm as not to disturb the apple blossom.

So the poem deals with dreams and aspirations: the yearning for the simplicity of formulaic conversation (such as about the weather); the need to perform simple domestic tasks; the luxury of time to appreciate the things all around; but above all, the ability to reinvent oneself and find another life. The desire for natural beauty is also a powerful need, as in the last four lines.

Ní Chuilleanáin focuses on the lives of marginalised female figures in this poem, women in religious communities, women who do unglamorous tasks and she points to their need for fulfilment and for beauty in their lives.

The poem is structured as a dramatic monologue and this gives it an intimacy and a directness that makes it easy for us to appreciate the speaker's feelings.

17 *Siegfried Sassoon* (1886–1967)

Siegfried Sassoon in military uniform, 1915

Sassoon enlisted in the British army on the first day of the First World War and was one of the few poets to survive the fighting. He is best known for his satirical poems of disillusionment with the war, such as 'The Hero', 'Base Details', and 'The General'. 'Everyone Sang' celebrates the sense of freedom and escape felt at the end of the war. In 1919 Sassoon became literary editor of the *Daily Herald* and achieved notice for his semi-autobiographical writings, beginning with *Memoirs of a Fox-Hunting Man* (1928) and *Memoirs of an Infantry Officer* (1930). (For fuller information see page 137.)

Everyone Sang

Everyone suddenly burst out singing;
And I was filled with such delight
As prisoned birds must find in freedom
Winging wildly across the white
Orchards and dark green fields; on; on; and out of sight.   5

Everyone's voice was suddenly lifted,
And beauty came like the setting sun.
My heart was shaken with tears and horror
Drifted away ... O but every one
Was a bird; and the song was wordless; the singing will never be done.   10

Explorations

First reading

1. 'Everyone suddenly burst out singing.' What circumstances, do you imagine, might give rise to such a spontaneous outburst of joy? You do not need to confine yourself to the circumstances of this particular poem.
2. In this poem, how do you think the poet feels? Indicate three phrases or images that lead you to this conclusion.
3. On a first reading, what do you see? Indicate two images that come to your attention most strongly.
4. Which similes or metaphors do you think convey the sense of freedom most effectively? Give a reason for each choice.

Second reading

5. Do you think this is an emotional moment for the poet? Describe the emotions he is conveying here. Support your answer with references to the text.
6. How does the poet convey the sense of excitement? Think of the choice of language, the imagery, and the structure of the lines.
7. Consider the critical commentary below and list any questions you may have.

Third reading

8. Do you think this poem makes a valuable contribution to the body of war poetry? Comment.

A Critical Commentary

A reading of the poem

This lyric expresses joy and exuberance and communicates a tremendous sense of release and escape now that the war has ended. The mood of excitement and exultation is conveyed through the imagery, particularly that of birds and singing:

> It was filled with such delight
> As prisoned birds must find in freedom
> Winging wildly ...

The alliteration draws attention to the unaccustomed freedom and movement. Sassoon was later to use images of song and the songbird as metaphors for the human soul. Here they certainly convey the delight of the spirit effectively. The music of life is now to be enjoyed. Other images of nature, orchards, green fields and the beauty of the setting sun carry this feeling of goodness and of wholeness. There is almost a mystical quality to the experience; we see this natural empathy between speaker and nature. There is almost a fusion of the poet's spirit with the natural world, a shared understanding that does not require words:

> Beauty came like the setting sun ...
> O but every one
> Was a bird; and the song was wordless ...

The excitement is also carried in the form of the lines. The *enjambment* (running on of lines) gives a breathless quality to the piece, as if the emotion is out of control. The repetition helps in this respect also: 'on; on; and out of sight ... the song ... the singing ...'

It is an emotional piece ('My heart was shaken with tears and horror | Drifting away ...'), celebrating survival. It makes a fitting, optimistic epilogue to a great deal of bleak war poetry. In 'Everyone Sang' the human spirit survives the horrors and can soar again.

18 *William Shakespeare (1564–1661)*

William Shakespeare was born in April 1564 in Stratford-upon-Avon, Warwickshire, the son of Mary Arden, the daughter of a gentleman-farmer, and John Shakespeare, a glover. He was educated locally but left Stratford to follow a career in acting and the theatre. In 1595 he became a shareholder in the acting company known as the Chamberlain's Men, which suggests that he had achieved some wealth. He wrote at least thirty-seven plays in about twenty years, among them such famous titles as *Julius Caesar, Romeo and Juliet*, and *The Merchant of Venice*, as well as the tragedies *Hamlet, Othello, King Lear*, and *Macbeth*. He retired to Stratford in 1613 and died in April 1616. (For fuller information see page 138.)

The sonnet form

At its most basic, a sonnet can be described as a fourteen-line poem with a formal rhyming scheme and a fixed structure for its ideas. There are two principal forms of sonnet, the Petrarchan and the Shakespearean. The Petrarchan sonnet (after Francesco Petrarca, 1304–1375) is structured in two parts. The first eight lines (*octave*) make the chief statement, describe the situation, and pose the question or problem. There follows a turn (or *volta*), featuring a new statement, a refinement of the first statement or a solution to the problem, expressed in the final six lines (*sestet*). Each section may embody a different thought: often the octave is merely descriptive, plainly reporting an event, with the speculation on that event following in the sestet. There may also be a change of mood or tone in the sestet. There is a strict rhyming scheme: *abba abba cdcdcd* (or *cdecde*).

The Petrarchan sonnet has been an influential and popular poetic form. The sonnet was introduced into English poetry in the sixteenth century, reaching its full flowering by the turn of the century. The first English sonneteers, such as Thomas Wyatt and Philip Sidney, followed the Petrarchan model. Shakespeare, a near-contemporary of Sidney's, developed a form of his own, consisting of three groups of four lines each (*quatrains*) and a rhyming couplet to conclude. The couplet was meant to be epigrammatical, a pithy conclusion, rounding off the poem with a moral or a truth. Shakespeare used it in a variety of ways. The quatrains are distinct, separate but linked in theme to the main idea of the sonnet. He favoured the rhyming scheme *abab cdcd efef gg*.

Perhaps because of these numerous divisions in structure, the Shakespearean sonnet tends to read as a reasoned argument. The brevity of the sonnet form demands great discipline from the writer, as well as technical skill with rhyming. It is particularly suitable for the development of a single idea and has been popular as a vehicle for love poetry down through the ages.

Shakespeare's sonnets

Shakespeare's sonnets were first published as a collection in 1609, though they were written some years earlier, the bulk of them probably between 1590 and 1600. Scholars disagree about the exact dating. J. B. Leishman places most of them in the second half of that decade, with one after 1603, while A. L. Rowse feels that the majority of them were probably written before 1595.

There are 154 sonnets in the collection, and they fall into two groups: 1–126, written to an unnamed Friend, and 127–154, to a Dark Lady. Much critical scholarship and energy has been expended over the years in attempts to unmask the identities of both people addressed in the poems. Leishman, for instance, feels that the

Elizabethan lady

The Earl of Southampton, Shakespeare's patron

'Mr. W.H.' to whom the sonnets are dedicated was William Herbert, Earl of Pembroke. Rowse has made a convincing case that the Friend addressed is Henry Wriothesley (pronounced Rithesley), Earl of Southampton and Shakespeare's patron. All we know from the evidence of the sonnets is that the Friend was far above Shakespeare in social position and that he was much younger, being described as 'sweet boy' and 'lovely boy'. Rowse has named the Dark Lady as Emilia Lanier (née Bassano), an Italian courtesan and former mistress of Shakespeare's other patron, Hunsden, the Lord Chamberlain.

Whether these poems are faithful autobiography or a blend of experience and creativity is not really vital to a reading of them. Yet taken together they do tell a story of patronage, friendship, passion, guilt, and disappointment, with all the fervour and uncertainty of any great love affair.

18

Shall I compare thee to a summer's day?
Thou art more lovely and more temperate:
Rough winds do shake the darling buds of May,
And summer's lease hath all too short a date;
Some time too hot the eye of heaven shines,   5
And often is his gold complexion dimmed;
And every fair from fair some time declines,
By chance, or nature's changing course untrimmed:
But thy eternal summer shall not fade,
Nor lose possession of that fair thou ow'st,   10
Nor shall Death brag thou wand'rest in his shade,
When in eternal lines to time thou grow'st.
   So long as men can breathe or eyes can see,
   So long lives this, and this gives life to thee.

Notes

[4] **lease:** a legal agreement allowing the use of land or property for a specified time

[7] **fair from fair:** a beautiful thing from beauty

[8] **untrimmed:** stripped

[10] **thou ow'st:** you own or possess

Explorations

First reading

1. In describing the Friend, Shakespeare first suggests an analogy with a summer's day but then dismisses it. Why does he find the analogy inadequate?
2. What qualities of the Friend are praised, both in direct statement and by implication?
3. What is the poet's underlying worry here, and what is his solution?

Second reading

4. The notion of the transience of youth and the swift fading of summer energy is introduced in line 4. Trace its development through the second quatrain.
5. What view of human life is communicated by the octave of this sonnet?
6. 'But thy eternal summer shall not fade.'

How does the poet go on to justify this paradoxical statement?

Third reading

7. Can you now state the main themes in a few succinct phrases or sentences?
8. How would you describe the tone of the poem: worried, intimate, supremely confident, arrogant, or what? Justify your comments by reference to the text.
9. What does the poem reveal about the writer?

Fourth reading

10. Read the critical commentary below and discuss it.
11. What unanswered questions have you about this poem?

A Critical Commentary

Theme
This poem, praising the looks and temperament of the Friend, asserts the power of verse to give immortality.

Development
At first the poet thinks that a summer's day—with all its connotations of youth, beauty, passion, and energy—might prove a suitable metaphor for his loved one. But on reflection it proves too tempestuous ('rough winds') and erratic ('some time too hot ... often ... dimmed'). Even more worrying is its transience. This awareness of time is highly developed in the first eight lines ('all too short a date'). We are made aware of the brevity and insecurity of summertime—it is merely leased, not owned—and of its erratic nature ('some time', 'often', 'some time'). This is real time described here, impinging on us irregularly, as it does.

But in the third quatrain we come to the paradoxical statement 'thy eternal summer shall not fade.' We are now dealing with metaphorical time, where 'in eternal lines to time thou grow'st.' Death and decay are found in real time, growth and eternity in metaphorical time, in the eternity of poetry. And so 'time' in the first eight lines gives way to the eternity of poetry in the final six.

Imagery
The changing faces of summer are caught in the imagery: the erratic energy ('rough winds') that threatens new growth ('do shake the darling buds of May'); the torrid heat ('too hot the eye of heaven') alternates with cloud ('gold complexion dimmed'). The metaphor here is of face: 'eye', 'complexion', 'fair' (beauty)—the romantic face of summer, which loses its beauty.

The poet uses the contrast of light and shade to suggest life and death: 'the eye of heaven shines' but 'his gold complexion' is often 'dimmed'; 'nor shall Death brag thou wand'rest in his shade.' But the most unexpected metaphor suggesting transience is the legal one of summer's lease, with all the implications of temporary use. Death is personified as a loud braggart and described in classical mythological terms as a sort of wandering in the twilight zone.

Tone
The poet seems to speak with a musing, romantic tone in the octave. Indeed he could very well be talking to himself. But there develops a note of confident defiance in the sestet when he insists that his verse will survive and so give life to the Friend. The frequent use of 'shall' and the repetition of 'so long' in the couplet confirm this tone of defiance. Do you think there is a self-confidence bordering on arrogance in the couplet?

116

Let me not to the marriage of true minds
Admit impediments; love is not love
Which alters when it alteration finds,
Or bends with the remover to remove.

O no, it is an ever-fixèd mark   5
That looks on tempests and is never shaken;
It is the star to every wand'ring bark,
Whose worth's unknown, although his height be taken.
Love's not Time's fool, though rosy lips and cheeks
Within his bending sickle's compass come;   10
Love alters not with his brief hours and weeks,
But bears it out even to the edge of doom.
   If this be error and upon me proved,
   I never writ, nor no man ever loved.

Notes

[2] **impediments:** legal obstacles (a reference to the marriage service in the Book of Common Prayer)

[5] **mark:** a sea marker

[7] **the star:** the North Star

[8] **whose worth's unknown:**

whose astrological influence is uncertain

[8] **his height be taken:** his altitude has been calculated (for navigation purposes)

[9] **Time's fool:** Time's sport or

plaything

[10] **compass:** range

[11] **his:** Time's

[12] **bears it out:** lasts, survives

[12] **edge of doom:** Judgment Day

[13] **upon:** against

Explorations

Pre-reading

1. Read the first one-and-a-half lines. What do you think the poem is going to be about?

First reading

2. What do you notice about this sonnet? List your thoughts, in any order.

3. Shakespeare describes love by comparing it to some things and contrasting it with others. First examine the comparisons in the second quatrain. What do they suggest about the quality of love?

4. Examine the contrasts: lines 2–4 and 9–12. What is suggested about the quality of love here?

Second reading

5. How would you describe the type of love dealt with in this sonnet: erotic love, friendship, soul-mate love, or what? Substantiate your views by reference to the text.

6. Would you consider Shakespeare's idea of love to be unreal and too idealistic? Comment.

7. Examine the couplet. What does it mean? Do you think it makes a good conclusion or not? Explain your view.

Third reading

8. Briefly outline the theme of this poem.

9. Do you think the images used adequately convey the permanence of true love and also the dreadful ravages of time? Examine the effectiveness of one image of each type.

10. How would you describe the tone of this poem: serious, defeatist, confident, arrogant, or what? What words or phrases lead you to this conclusion?

11. 'In this sonnet we find an interesting treatment of love: tender, yet not sentimental.' Discuss this statement, supporting your views by reference to the text.

A Critical Commentary

Theme
This is a poem about ideal love, which the poet feels is a spiritual love or ideal friendship, a 'marriage of true minds' that would survive all vicissitudes and outlast the decline of physical beauty and even the ravages of time.

The notion of ideal love
The poem opens with an allusion to the Book of Common Prayer: 'If any of you know cause, or just impediment, why these two persons should not be joined together in holy matrimony, ye are to declare it ...' So we get the impression right away that the poet is celebrating something special, holy, indeed spiritual (a 'marriage of true minds'). The love in question is platonic: the love of true friendship, a meeting of minds, rather than a sexual encounter. That this is an ideal is quickly borne in on us by lines 2, 3 and 4:

> love is not love
> Which alters when it alteration finds,
> Or bends with the remover to remove.

True love persists, even when it encounters a change of heart or inconsistency on the part of the other person—an ideal rarely attained.

The nautical metaphors of the second quatrain—the sea mark and the North Star—graphically suggest the constancy of love in the midst of turmoil and chaos. It is a guiding light in this dangerous world of ours yet a somewhat mysterious force, though its existence has been well charted ('whose worth's unknown, although his height be taken').

True love survives even when beauty fades. It is not dependent on physical attraction ('Love's not Time's fool, though rosy lips and cheeks | Within his bending sickle's compass come'), and so it lasts 'to the edge of doom.'

This poem is about love in the abstract, the ideal of love, yet it can also be read as a personal statement about Shakespeare's own relationship with the Friend. Indeed at times the rhythms of the language sound like a conversation with the Friend. The speaking voice, 'let me not ... O, no ...' comes through and gives it a very real energy—the honesty and immediacy of conversation rather than the formality of an official address. In this context the couplet attests both to the poet's absolute belief in the existence of an ideal love and to his commitment to the present friendship. Does it not even sound like a challenge to the Friend to try the poet's love, to test its strength, its ideal nature?

The poet is very confident about love. There are feelings of great strength here, yet a sense of tenderness too. It is an interesting treatment of love—not sentimental, yet tender.

Technique
The true value of love is emphasised by contrasts. The poet builds a series of antitheses:
> 'marriage of true minds'—'impediments'
> 'love'—'the remover to remove'
> 'not Time's fool'—'though rosy lips.'

In this way the superiority of love is established. Very often the antithesis is achieved through the repetition of words for effect ('love is not love ... alters when it alteration finds').

The antithesis is also conveyed in the contrasting strands of imagery. The symbols of constancy are the 'ever-fixèd mark' and the North Star. This contrasts sharply with the images of transience (time personified as the king, with love as his jester; the brief hours and weeks; the terminal cruelty of the bending sickle). They contrast too with the images of natural turmoil ('tempests', 'wand'ring bark').

Absolute confidence comes across in the humour and the wit, the ability to engage in word play. For example, the end of the final line, 'I never writ, nor no man ever loved,' could be read as 'no man ever loved (anyone),' or 'I never loved any man.' The humour lifts it above the sentimental.

Shakespeare employs a wide range of

techniques to create effects where needed: alliteration for emphasis, as in 'marriage of true minds' and 'compass come'; metonymy to emphasise the full horror of how time spoils beauty. 'Rosy lips and cheeks' stand for all aspects of physical beauty and good looks.

Fear no more the heat o' the sun

Guiderius:
 Fear no more the heat o' the sun,
 Nor the furious winter's rages;
 Thou thy worldly task hast done,
 Home art gone and ta'en thy wages:
 Golden lads and girls all must,   5
 As chimney-sweepers, come to dust.
Arviragus:
 Fear no more the frown o' the great;
 Thou art past the tyrant's stroke;
 Care no more to clothe and eat;
 To thee the reed is as the oak: 10
 The sceptre, learning, physic must
 All follow this and come to dust.
Guiderius:
 Fear no more the lightning-flash,
Arviragus:
 Nor the all-dreaded thunder-stone;
Guiderius:
 Fear no slander, censure rash;   15
Arviragus:
 Thou hast finish'd joy and moan:
Both:
 All lovers young, all lovers must
 Consign to thee and come to dust.
Guiderius:
 No exorciser harm thee!
Arviragus:
 Nor no witchcraft charm thee!   20
Guiderius:
 Ghost unlaid forbear thee!
Arviragus:
 Nothing ill come near thee!
Both:
 Quiet consummation have;
 And renownèd be thy grave!

Notes

[11] **sceptre:** a royal staff, symbol of rule [11] **physic:** medicine, i.e. doctors [14] **thunder-stone:** a meteorite

Background

This elegy is taken from *Cymbeline* (act IV, scene ii), one of Shakespeare's later comedies (*c.* 1609–10). Set in Roman Britain, it is a play of uneven quality, full of sinister scheming, gratuitous horror, and a great deal of confusion. One of Shakespeare's biographers, Garry O'Connor, likens it to a forerunner of nineteenth-century music-hall entertainment, 'designed to appeal to bored middle-class sophisticates and philistine royal families with a short attention span.' Innogen (the daughter of Cymbeline, king of Britain), while travelling in disguise through the forest has fainted and is presumed dead by her companions (really her disguised half-brothers, Guiderius and Arviragus), who are moved to sing this dirge.

Explorations

First reading

1. Can you imagine the setting, the positions of the speakers, and the position of the person addressed? Describe what you see.
2. In what tone of voice should this be spoken or sung? Why?

Second reading

3. What categories of things are no longer to be feared by the dead person?
4. What view of death is conveyed in this song?
5. Compare this view with references to death found in sonnet 18 ('Shall I compare thee to a summer's day?').

Third reading

6. What picture of society comes across in this song?

Fourth reading

7. How would you describe the mood of this poem? What words or images help create it? What effect has the metre on the mood of the poem?
8. Briefly, set down the main idea of this song.

A Critical Commentary

This is a very moving dirge that nevertheless manages to convey a measured statement about death. Death is a refuge from the extremes of weather, from political tyranny and social injustice, and from the day-to-day struggles of life. Death is comfortable and familiar, a well-earned rest after work.

> Thou thy worldly task hast done,
> Home art gone and ta'en thy wages.

Death is seen as the consummation of life.

There is also the reminder that death is inevitable for all ages and all ranks in society: golden lads and girls; all young lovers; chimney-sweepers; kings, scholars, and doctors. Beauty and youth, the powerful and the learned, as well as the socially insignificant—all must succumb.

It ends with a moving prayer that the dead be protected from all evil of witchcraft or spirits and be allowed a quiet return to the earth, and that the grave be honoured and respected.

19 *Percy Bysshe Shelley* (1792–1822)

The son of an English country gentleman, Shelley was educated at Eton and Oxford, where he spent a rebellious and unhappy youth. Revolutionary in thought, he was anti-religious and anti-monarchy and wrote and spoke publicly on the need for radical social and political reforms. He felt it was the role of the poet to be prophetic and visionary. He lived a fairly unconventional family life, much of it in Italy, where the Shelleys seemed dogged by illness and death. It was here that he wrote some of his best-known poems, such as 'Stanzas Written in Dejection Near Naples', 'Ode to the West Wind', 'Ode to a Skylark', and 'Prometheus Unbound'. (For fuller information see page 139.)

Ozymandias

I met a traveller from an antique land
Who said: Two vast and trunkless legs of stone
Stand in the desert ... Near them, on the sand,
Half sunk, a shattered visage lies, whose frown,
And wrinkled lip, and sneer of cold command,   5
Tell that its sculptor well those passions read
Which yet survive, stamped on these lifeless things,
The hand that mocked them, and the heart that fed:
And on the pedestal these words appear:
'My name is Ozymandias, king of kings: 10
Look on my works, ye Mighty, and despair!'
Nothing beside remains. Round the decay
Of that colossal wreck, boundless and bare
The lone and level sands stretch far away.

Notes

Ozymandias: another name for the Pharaoh Rameses II of Egypt (thirteenth century BC), whose great tomb at Thebes was shaped like a sphinx; it was the Greek historian Diodorus the Sicilian who first referred to it as the tomb of Ozymandias

[1] **antique:** ancient

[4] **visage:** face

[8] **The hand that mocked:** the hand that imitated, referring to the hand of the sculptor

[8] **the heart that fed:** the king's heart, which gave life to these qualities and passions that were captured in stone by the sculptor

Explorations

First reading

1. The poem is in the form of a narrative or story told by a traveller who had been to 'an antique land'. What suggestions and pictures does this phrase conjure up for you?
2. What did the traveller actually see, as reported in lines 2–4? What is your first reaction to this scene: interesting, pathetic, grotesque, or what? Why do you think he might consider this worth reporting?
3. Where is this scene? What impression of the land do we get?
4. Does the poet tell us the name of the place? Why do you think this is?

Second reading: lines 4–8

5. What do we learn of the king from this sculpture: qualities, character traits, etc.?
6. Do you think Shelley appreciates the sculptor's skill? Explain.
7. Relate lines 4–8 in your own words and as simply as possible.

Third reading: the sextet etc.

8. What was your own reflection on reading the words on the pedestal?

9. Explore the final two-and-a-half lines. What do you see? Really look. What atmosphere is created here? What statement do you think is being made?
10. What do you think this poem is saying about human endeavour and about power? Explain with reference to specific phrases etc.
11. Consider the imagery. Do you think the imagery appropriate to the theme? Explain. What pictures do you find most effective?

Fourth reading

12. How does the poet make use of irony to communicate his theme? Do you find this effective?
13. Would you agree that this poem embodies Shelley's view that the poet should really be a kind of prophet or wise person in society? Discuss this with reference to the text.
14. What features of the sonnet do you notice in the poem? Do you think it is a good sonnet?
15. Do you think this poem was worth reading? Why, or why not?

A Critical Commentary

A reading of the poem

'Ozymandias' explores a common theme of Romantic poetry: the passing of all human creations, the vanity of the works of humankind, and so the pointlessness of life. Perhaps it is also sneering at the arrogance of rulers—a favourite theme of Shelley's. There is a hint here too of the relative superiority of art over life (in that it lasts slightly longer).

Unusually for a sonnet, this poem is structured as a narrative. It tells the story of a traveller who returned from visiting the remains of an ancient civilisation and described what he saw. The place has been reconquered by the desert, and all that remains as an indication of a once-great power are the ruins of an enormous statue—'Two vast and trunkless legs of stone' and some pieces of its shattered face. Yet the shattered head still preserves the king's features, particularly the expression of arrogance and of unchallengeable authority ('frown, | And wrinkled lip, and sneer of cold command'). This shows the perceptiveness of the sculptor, who managed to capture the king's emotions or passions in the stone ('its sculptor well those passions read | which yet survive, stamped on these lifeless things').

The syntax is quite involved here and makes understanding less immediate. In the eighth line, 'hand' refers to the sculptor's hand, and 'the heart that fed' refers to the king's heart, which gave life and energy to all this in the first place. Shelley uses this technique of *synecdoche* (where a part stands for the whole) to reinforce the sculptor's excellence at recording the king's inner emotions. Hand captures heart. The pedestal also survives, ironically still proclaiming its message of arrogant superiority ('Look on my works, ye mighty, and despair!').

In fact it is mainly by the use of irony right through the poem that Shelley reinforces his theme of the vanity of human endeavour. For example, the once-great civilisation is now a desert, and even its precise name is no longer used ('an antique land'). The haughty superiority of the king, while still visible in the sculpture, is nevertheless shattered ('Half sunk, a shattered visage'). The fact that all that remains of a civilisation renowned for its architecture and art is this grotesque piece of statuary ('Two vast and trunkless legs') adds a further twist to the irony. It is now disparagingly referred to as 'that colossal wreck'. The caption on the pedestal too is deeply ironic, as time has made the king's boast a hollow one.

The final statement, by sound and image, reinforces the theme: we see that the works of humans are merely a disfiguring, decaying wreck spoiling the serene emptiness of the natural landscape. The insignificance of human civilisation when compared with the vastness of time is caught in that beautiful image of rolling desert sands, stretching as far as the eye can see and back through history. The long vowel sounds reinforce this sense of the emptiness of time: decay, boundless, bare, lone, far away.

As a sonnet

This poem has been highly praised by critics, who suggest that it displays the best features of sonnet form. Its simplicity is often remarked on. It has a single idea and one simple point to make. The language is simple yet effective (Think of the 'sneer of cold command'). The only change from octave to sextet is a deepening of the tone of irony with the reference to the king's foolish boast. The epigrammatical summary in the final lines reinforces the theme visually and definitively, as we expect from a good final couplet.

The sonnet is structured as a narrative, so the run-on lines are entirely appropriate, the first long sentence holding the atmosphere of the story. Subsequently, the dramatic effect of the single short sentence is all the greater: 'Nothing beside remains.' We hardly notice that the rhyming scheme is slightly irregular, with some off-rhymes (stone—frown; appear—despair) and an unusual rhyming scheme.

20 *Stevie Smith* (1902–1971)

Florence Margaret (Stevie) Smith was born in Yorkshire but reared by her mother and aunt in London in what she described as 'a house of female habitation.' She worked all her life as secretary to the chairman of a publishing firm, where she wrote her famous first novel, *Novel on Yellow Paper* (1936). But she is best known for her witty and strange verse, of which there are eight volumes; 'she came to be recognised as a very special poet of strangeness, loneliness and quirky humour,' as the critic Anthony Thwaite said. 'Deeply Morbid' is taken from the collection *Harold's Leap* (1950). (For fuller information see page 140.)

Deeply Morbid

Deeply morbid deeply morbid was the girl who typed the letters
Always out of office hours running with her social betters
But when daylight and the darkness of the office closed about her
Not for this ah not for this her office colleagues came to doubt her
It was that look within her eye   5
Why did it always seem to say goodbye?

Joan her name was and at lunchtime
Solitary solitary
She would go and watch the pictures
In the National Gallery   10
All alone all alone
This time with no friend beside her
She would go and watch the pictures
All alone.

Will she leave her office colleagues   15
Will she leave her evening pleasures
Toil within a friendly bureau
Running later in her leisure?
All alone all alone
Before the pictures she seems turned to stone.   20

Close upon the Turner pictures
Closer than a thought may go
Hangs her eye and all the colours
Leap into a special glow
All for her, all alone   25
All for her, all for Joan.

First the canvas where the ocean
Like a mighty animal
With a really wicked motion
Leaps for sailors' funeral   30

Holds her panting. Oh the creature
Oh the wicked virile thing
With its skin of fleck and shadow
Stretching tightening over him.
Wild yet captured wild yet captured   35
By the painter, Joan is quite enraptured.

Now she edges from the canvas
To another loved more dearly
Where the awful light of purest
Sunshine falls across the spray,   40
There the burning coasts of fancy
Open to her pleasure lay.
All alone, all alone
Come away, come away
All alone.   45

Lady Mary, Lady Kitty
The Honourable Featherstonehaugh
Polly Tommy from the office
Which of these shall hold her now?
Come away, come away   50
All alone.

The spray reached out and sucked her in
It was a hardly noticed thing
That Joan was there and is not now

(Oh go and tell young Featherstonehaugh)   55
Gone away, gone away
All alone.

She stood up straight
The sun fell down
There was no more of London Town   60
She went upon the painted shore
And there she walks for ever more
Happy quite
Beaming bright
In a happy happy light   65
All alone.

They say she was a morbid girl, no doubt of it
And what befell her clearly grew out of it
But I say she's a lucky one
To walk for ever in that sun   70
And as I bless sweet Turner's name
I wish that I could do the same.

Explorations

First reading: stanzas 1–3

1. From a reading of the first stanza, what are your first impressions of Joan? Consider the evidence of friends, her habits, her looks, etc.
2. Is there anything that would indicate that she is 'deeply morbid'? Is she strange in any way?
3. Explore stanzas 2 and 3. What does she do in her lunchtime? What do you notice about this activity, as described in the poem? What words indicate her state of mind or humour, and what is suggested?

Second reading: stanzas 4–6

4. What do you notice about the Turner pictures Joan is viewing?
5. How is the ocean portrayed? Comment on the relationship between humankind and the ocean here.
6. What are Joan's feelings for the paintings? Comment on her attitude to Turner's art.

7. In stanza 7 Joan moves from the first Turner canvas 'to another loved more dearly.' What features of this does she appreciate in particular? What does she mean by 'the burning coasts of fancy'? How does the painting affect her?

Third reading

8. Explain what happens in stanzas 8, 9, and 10. Are we to take this literally or do you think it is metaphorical? If so, what is the significance?
9. Here, for the first time, we are conscious of the personal voice of the poet. What is revealed of her attitude to and feelings about the happening? Do you think this is an important point in the poem? Why?

Fourth reading

10. Explain your general reaction to this poem. Did you find it strange, odd, weird, daft, or silly, or had it a serious point? If so, what?

11. What impression of city life and work do we get from this poem?
12. Comment on the view of life or philosophy behind this poem.
13. Outline the main themes it deals with.

14. What do you notice about the style of writing? Comment on two of the following: choice of language; the form of the lines and stanzas; the imagery; the metre or rhythms; the sounds of words.

A Critical Commentary

A reading of the poem

This poem treats of the need to escape from the rut of modern living, in particular the tedium of office life ('when daylight and the darkness of the office closed about her') and the shallow socialising with 'social betters' ('Lady Mary, Lady Kitty | The Honourable Featherstonehaugh'). The unsatisfactory nature of that experience is suggested in the simple childish rhythms ('Lady Mary, Lady Kitty') and through the pompous sounds ('The Honourable Featherstonehaugh'). We see the loneliness beneath the glamour as the poem deals with the essential isolation of city living. For instance, Joan drops names of acquaintances but has 'no friend beside her' as she goes alone to the galleries. Art here is a substitute for family, for real relationships, indeed for sexual fulfilment. Her description of the male ocean is breathlessly sensual:

> Oh the creature
> Oh the wicked virile thing
> With its skin of fleck and shadow
> Stretching tightening over him.

The scene 'holds her panting,' 'wild yet captured,' and 'quite enraptured.' Her encounter with art is sensuous and sexual.

There is a sad and depressing philosophy behind the poem. The need to escape the tedium of work and social routine is a universal human problem, but no positive solutions are suggested in this poem. The only escape lines hinted at are through the unreal world of art, the exclusive world of fantasy and madness, or the ultimate escape of death. Joan's translocation into the painting has suggestions of all three modes of escape.

Style

The poem is structured in a very conventional way, as a narrative: a dramatic monologue, as we find out at the end. But the style of language, the metre and rhyme are anything but conventional.

At the obvious level of form we notice the variety of line lengths, from the long, eight-stress lines of trochaic and iambic feet at the opening of the poem to the two-stress lines of 'all alone.' The running lines of the opening stanza, lacking in any punctuation, set up the atmosphere of ceaseless, tedious routine and help us feel the ever-rushing but pointless and unsatisfactory pace of Joan's life. The shorter lines are where the particular insight into her character is given, the oddness emphasised (the 'look within her eye' that 'always seems to say goodbye'). Short lines are also used to create the mood of isolation and loneliness: 'all alone all alone.' Smith manipulates rhythm and can change the pace of the verse dramatically to accommodate different moods.

Consider the drama and excitement created by the run-on lines in:

> First the canvas where the ocean
> Like a mighty animal
> With a really wicked motion
> Leaps for sailors' funeral
> Holds her panting.

We should note also the effect of the sounds of words here: the hollow, echoing sounds of 'all alone all alone' or 'all for her, all for Joan' convey the emptiness of her life. This plaintive refrain echoes through the poem, deflating even the illusory happiness of escape:

> Beaming bright

In a happy light
All alone.

There is a certain childish magical quality to the 'Come away, come away' repetition, reminiscent of the faery call in Yeats's poem, 'Come away, O human child! | To the waters and the wild.' Smith uses rhyme also to draw attention to ideas. The unexpectedness, even the downright daftness of some rhymes creates a bleak humour but also draws the reader in to notice certain things. The startling 'eye'—'goodbye' rhyme at the end of the first stanza focuses the reader on that final word and so introduces the idea of departure, which becomes the main theme. The odd rhyming phrases of the final stanza ('no doubt of it'—'grew out of it') convey the slightly cynical, off-hand tone that pervades the entire poem. We noticed already how the onomatopoeic 'Featherstonehaugh' conveys the shallowness of the social experience. Sounds of words are an important part of the communication of ideas in this poem.

The language has been reduced and refined to a simplicity that is almost childish at times:

Joan her name was and at lunchtime
Solitary solitary
She would go and watch the pictures
In the National Gallery.

But the simplicity does not prevent the distinctive voices of the speaker from coming across. Notice, for example, the shocked yet lustful spinsterish voice of 'Oh the creature | Oh the wicked virile thing.' Or the wistful yearning of 'But I say she's a lucky one | To walk for ever in that sun.' And the language is capable of rising to the complexity of metaphor when she wants to communicate the enticing beauty of the paintings, for example 'the burning coasts of fancy.'

21 *Pauline Stainer (born 1941)*

Pauline Stainer was educated at Oxford and Southampton University. She has produced four collections of poetry: *The Honeycomb* (1989), *Sighting the Slave Ship* (1992), *The Ice-Pilot Speaks* (1994), and *The Wound-Dresser's Dream* (1996). Her poetry is sparked off by a wide range of sources: mediaeval lyrics; sculptures; paintings, ranging from Renaissance to Paul Klee; the music of Erik Satie; and nature. Her imagery and settings are spectacular and varied. Many of her poems are difficult to understand at a first reading. (For fuller information see page 141.)

Sighting the Slave Ship

We came to unexpected latitudes—
sighted the slave ship
during divine service
on deck.

In earlier dog-days   5
we had made landfall
between forests of sandalwood,
taken on salt, falcons and sulphur.

What haunted us later
was not the cool dispensing   10
of sacrament
in the burnished doldrums

but something more exotic—
that sense
of a slight shift of cargo   15
while becalmed.

Notes

[5] **dog-days:** the hottest period of the year, usually coinciding with the rise of the Dog Star, generally regarded as from 3 July to 11 August

[9] **falcon:** a bird of prey, perhaps used to hunt sea-birds; the term can also refer to a small cannon

[9] **sulphur:** a greenish-yellow substance found in volcanic regions or occurring naturally in crystalline form; it has many uses in medicine and chemistry and was an ingredient of gunpowder

[12] **doldrums:** a region near the Equator where there is total calm, because the trade winds neutralise each other; hence 'in the doldrums', becalmed at sea

Explorations

First reading

1. What do you see? On a first reading, describe how you imagine the scene. What type of ships are they? What sounds do you hear? What are people wearing? What is happening?
2. Who do you imagine the speaker to be? What particular activities are listed that might enable us to come to some understanding of the speaker and crew?
3. When do you think the poem is set?

Second reading

4. What contrasts are set up between the speaker's ship and the slave ship?
5. Do you think the timing of the sighting is strange, even ironic? Explain.
6. Normally the dispensing of the sacrament provides a welcome moment in the day. How is this suggested in the imagery? What does this reveal of the speaker's attitude to religion?
7. In this instance the sighting of the slave ships has a much more powerful effect on the watchers ('haunted us later'). The speaker is unclear about the exact nature of how they are affected. How does he communicate their feelings, in the fourth stanza? From this image, how would you describe their feelings?
8. Are you surprised by the description of it as 'something more exotic'? What would the term normally suggest? Do you think it applies here? Does the phrase make the speaker and us rethink attitudes to the slave ship? Reread the poem.

Third reading

9. In your own words, describe the nature of the experience encountered here. Refer to the text.
10. Briefly, set down what you understand to be the theme of the poem.
11. Do you like the way this poem works— through suggestion rather than definite statement? Explain.
12. How would you describe the atmosphere of the poem? What words or phrases lead you to this conclusion?
13. Write a brief diary extract as you imagine the speaker might have written it for the following day.

A Critical Commentary

A reading of the poem

This poem dramatises a moment of profound experience: an encounter, albeit at a distance, with human wickedness and inhumanity.

The poet chooses a historical setting for this experience: the time of the slave trade, probably in the eighteenth century and certainly at a time when sailing-ships were in use. A slave ship is sighted one morning while the speaker is at divine service on deck. This encounter with such a radically different way of life and philosophy has a profound impact on speaker and crew. The shocking difference between the two is registered through the ironic contrasts in the poem. That the slave ship, symbol of the deepest human degradation and of inhumanity, should be sighted during divine service is deeply ironic—a perverse religious vision.

There is also the obvious contrast between the religious philosophy of the speaker's ship and that of the slaver. There is an ironic difference in cargoes. The speaker's ship has just taken on minerals and chemicals that are life-preserving: salt to replace that lost through sweat in the tropical heat, sulphur for cleansing, and the falcon for hunting. It is ironic too that the sight of the slave ship supplants the Eucharist in the impact it made ('haunted us later'). The effect was so disturbing and so difficult to comprehend that it can be adequately communicated only by the paradox of the fourth stanza. He describes it in terms of the unexplainable: the shifting or moving about of cargo while the ship is becalmed. In other words, he is not able to define his reaction but was somehow inexplicably fascinated by the encounter.

What are the unasked questions behind this experience? Does it challenge the speaker's religious way of life? Is there a sudden awareness of the drawing power of evil and a suggestion that the evil has a more profound effect than the good? Why is he fascinated by the sighting?

Tone

Despite the inner turmoil created by the sighting and the lingering effect of it, the event is narrated in a very matter-of-fact tone of voice for the most part. It reads like a log or diary record of the journey:

> We came to unexpected latitudes—
> sighted the slave ship
> during the divine service ...

The ugly frisson of excitement came with the eeriness of the 'shifting cargo' metaphor and the use of the word 'exotic' to describe the experience.

22 *Richard Wilbur* *(born 1921)*

Richard Wilbur was born in New York and educated at Amherst College and Harvard University. He served in the American army during the Second World War and has been a teacher at Harvard and other universities. Among his collections of poetry are *The Beautiful Changes and Other Poems* (1947); *Ceremony and Other Poems* (1950) (from which 'The Pardon' is taken); *Things of This World: Poems,* which won a Pulitzer Prize in 1956; and *New and Collected Poems* (1988). Wilbur believed that one of the main functions of poetry was to examine the inconsistencies and disharmony of modern life. He was made Poet Laureate of the United States in 1987. (For fuller information see page 141.)

The Pardon

My dog lay dead five days without a grave
In the thick of summer, hid in a clump of pine
And a jungle of grass and honeysuckle-vine.
I who had loved him while he kept alive

Went only close enough to where he was   5
To sniff the heavy honeysuckle-smell
Twined with another odour heavier still
And hear the flies' intolerable buzz.

Well, I was ten and very much afraid.
In my kind world the dead were out of range   10
And I could not forgive the sad or strange
In beast or man. My father took the spade

And buried him. Last night I saw the grass
Slowly divide (it was the same scene
But now it glowed a fierce and mortal green)   15
And saw the dog emerging. I confess

I felt afraid again, but still he came
In the carnal sun, clothed in a hymn of flies,
And death was breeding in his lively eyes.
I started in to cry and call his name,   20

Asking forgiveness of his tongueless head.
... I dreamt the past was never past redeeming:
But whether this was false or honest dreaming
I beg death's pardon now. And mourn the dead.

Explorations

First reading

1. Briefly outline the story of this poem.
2. How did the boy first discover that his dog was dead? What did he do then? Can you understand his reaction? Have you any experience of a similar situation?
3. How does he himself rationalise or explain his reaction? Examine stanza 3 in some detail. Can you understand his response? Explain.

Second reading

4. The boy is haunted by this experience. What elements of nightmare do you find in the dream?
5. How is the frightening effect of the dream created? Examine stanzas 4 and 5 in detail. 'But still he came': what is the effect of this? What is suggested by 'the carnal sun'? What does the image 'a hymn of flies' suggest? Do you find this contradictory? Explain your immediate reaction to the phrase. 'And death was breeding in his lively eyes.' Why 'lively'? What does the line mean to you?
6. How does he comprehend death at first—rationally or sensually? Does 'the carnal sun' fit in with his experience of death and of nature generally?
7. In the final stanza he talks about 'asking forgiveness' and begs 'death's pardon'. Can

you explain his feelings? What are the thoughts inside his head at this point?
8. Explain the title of the poem.
9. 'False or honest dreaming': do you think Wilbur considers that dreams have an important function? Explain.

Third reading

10. What does the speaker of this poem learn about himself and about life? Refer to specific phrases to support your assertions.
11. 'Wilbur apprehends the world mainly through the senses.' Could this statement be justified from the evidence of this poem? Explain.
12. Do you think Wilbur's power of description is particularly effective? Examine two examples and say why you think them effective.
13. Would you agree that this is a dramatic poem? Explain two ways in which you think this effect is created. Examine the subject matter; the pace of the narration; the depth of feelings involved; the descriptions.

Fourth reading

14. Outline the main themes you find in the poem.
15. What do you think is the most effective aspect of Wilbur's style of writing? Explain.

A Critical Commentary

A reading of the poem

This poem explores a young boy's experience of death. The aspect of it borne in on him most forcefully is that the dead are so different. 'Sad or strange' are the words from a child's vocabulary used to describe this difference or 'otherness' of death. The sense of distance involved also strikes him: 'In my kind of world the dead were out of range.' The strangeness of death and its completely different nature register strongly on the boy.

The poem also records the boy's inability to cope with it. Straightforward fear is the repeated response: 'I was ten and very much afraid ... I felt afraid again ...' The nightmare images manifest this: 'still he came ... clothed in a hymn of flies, | And death was breeding in his lively eyes.' There is also the inability to comprehend death—inadequately described as 'strange', as we saw. Death is somehow seen as a failing, a hurt, an injury to the living: 'I could not forgive the sad or strange | In beast or man.' And this leads to an inability to mourn.

Consequently the boy is consumed with guilt; but the horror of the dream is cathartic for him and opens the flood-gates of emotion: 'I started in to cry and call his name.' The guilt is faced and named, and so he is free of it.

> Asking forgiveness of his tongueless head.
> ... I beg death's pardon now. And mourn the dead.

There is emotional release in mourning.

Some knowledge of the imperfections of the world and the strange contradictions of life are among the powerful insights gained from this experience. Death and beauty exist side by side: the honeysuckle smell and 'another odour heavier still.' This is a traumatic growing-up experience, a moment of realisation concerning the discordance of the world that Wilbur talks about (see the biographical note, page 141). Death has invaded the child's Eden. Nature shows its other frightening, less beautiful face; and the boy must learn to cope with this less than perfect world.

The poem also explores the power of dreams to communicate truth. The nightmare or vision results in the beneficial release of bottled-up feelings and emotions: 'whether this was false or honest dreaming | I beg death's pardon now.'

Themes and issues

- Coping with the experience of death: the inability to comprehend it; the inability to mourn; the resultant guilt; and finally the release of tears.
- Discovering the discordance of the world and the imperfections of nature.
- A moment of growth and development.
- The function and power of dreams.

Structure

The poem is structured as a first-person narrative, which develops into a reflection on the psychological nature of the experience. In some ways this is a typical Wilbur poem, as he often begins by describing a scene or an object, then goes on to make a moral or philosophical point about it, thereby gaining insight and wisdom from the event. Often, as happens here, the poem grows by drawing him into an emotional relationship with the subject. This poem is framed by the first and final lines: 'My dog lay dead ... And mourn the dead.' In between is the process whereby he came to mourn.

Conventional in form, the poem has regular four-line stanzas with a loose and barely noticeable rhyme. The second and third lines rhyme fully, while the first and fourth often manage a looser off-rhyme (grave—alive, was—buzz, grass—confess), as well as the full head—dead, etc. The general effect is of naturalness, totally appropriate to a narrative reminiscence.

A sensuous poem

One of the most striking features of Wilbur's

style is the sensuous evocation of death. The earliest intimations are through the sense of smell, where the odour of death mingles with the scent of summer honeysuckle. The suggestion is delicately rendered yet real: 'another odour heavier still.' The sounds are more explicit, 'the flies' intolerable buzz' communicating something of the boy's revulsion; further down, the startling combination of the religious and the rotten, 'clothed in a hymn of flies,' communicates something of the discordance of death. It is a sort of bizarre dirge or requiem that evokes all the horror that the boy experiences. Nor is the sense of sight neglected. The nightmare image 'glowed a fierce and mortal green' and 'death was breeding in his lively eyes,' suggesting the horror of maggots without actually mentioning it. Altogether, the boy's memories of the event are powerfully sensuous.

Tone

From the matter-of-fact, conversational opening ('My dog lay dead five days ...') we are swiftly introduced to powerful if still controlled emotions and suggestions of guilty feelings ('I who had loved him while he kept alive | Went only close enough ...'). This reflective tone of the first three stanzas gives way to something verging on panic in the fourth and fifth and to emotional relief in the final stanza; so we can see a growing emotional involvement as the poem progresses.

23 *Judith Wright (born 1915)*

Judith Wright is one of the most important Australian poets of the twentieth century. Her first volume of poetry, *The Moving Image* (1946), dealt with the Aboriginal and convict history of Australia and made an immediate impact. She also writes about the Australian landscape and the solitary figures of Australian rural life, and she is interested in conservationist issues. She also explores the theme of love, and particularly maternal experience, in *Woman to Man* (1949). Her *Collected Poems, 1942–1970* was published in 1972. (For fuller information see page 142.)

Request to a Year

If the year is meditating a suitable gift,
I should like it to be the attitude
of my great-great-grandmother,
legendary devotee of the arts,

who, having had eight children   5
and little opportunity for painting pictures,
sat one day on a high rock
beside a river in Switzerland

and from a difficult distance viewed
her second son, balanced on a small ice-floe,   10
drift down the current towards a waterfall
that struck rock-bottom eighty feet below,

while her second daughter, impeded,
no doubt, by the petticoats of the day,
stretched out a last-hope alpenstock   15
(which luckily later caught him on his way).

Nothing, it was evident, could be done;
and with the artist's isolating eye
my great-great-grandmother hastily sketched the scene.
The sketch survives to prove the story by.   20

Year, if you have no Mother's day present planned;
reach back and bring me the firmness of her hand.

Explorations

First reading

1. Picture the drama in this scene. What do you see? Roughly sketch the outline of the scene and describe what you see. What is happening? Where is each character? Imagine the expression on the face of each.
2. What was the reaction of the great-great-grandmother to the incident? Can you explain her reaction? What is your impression of her?
3. Do you think this poem is meant to be taken seriously? Explain your view.

Second reading

4. Does the poet realise that this scenario is incredible? Where is this indicated?

5. Explore the poet's reaction to the great-great-grandmother. Is it one of horror, indifference, admiration, or what? What quality of the great-great-grandmother's does she respect?
6. Explain the title of the poem.

Third reading

7. How is the humour created? Explore the effect of exaggeration, unexpected behaviour, the language used, and irony. Do you consider this light humour or bleak humour? Why?
8. What statements do you think the poem is making about motherhood, about art, or about childhood?

A Critical Commentary

Some approaches to the poem

Could this poem be read as a sneer at the colonial past, at the slightly dotty Europeans with a logic all of their own? Is it another version of the typical Australian send-up of the 'Poms'? Is this unusual moment deliberately chosen to illustrate how different the colonial ancestors were: tough, logical, and difficult to understand?

It is certainly a cool, calculated, unsentimental look at family ancestry. It is a tongue-in-cheek treatment of ancestral eccentricity, in the woman who, 'having had eight children | and little opportunity for painting pictures ... hastily sketched the scene.' But there is also a certain tone of admiration here for her toughness: 'bring me the firmness of her hand.'

As a portrait of a woman it is unusual in that it subverts the conventional image of the caring mother. Instead we find this almost incredible detachment of the woman painting as her son is in danger of drowning.

Some of the satire is directed at the world of art and artists. We notice the unreality of the scene: art carried to extremes is more important than life. The 'legendary devotee of the arts' is taking this opportunity to paint.

The distressing scene is viewed from an artistic perspective ('from a difficult distance') rather than a human one. It is with 'the artist's isolating eye' rather than the tearful eyes of a mother that the impending disaster is watched. Perhaps it is the cold tyranny and compulsion of the artistic temperament that is being pointed up. Perhaps it is best read as a humorous poem.

Humour

The humour is created chiefly by the incongruities of the scene: the woman sketches while her son drowns. The sense of fun is helped by the minute detailing: she sketched 'hastily'; it was a 'small' ice-floe; and the repeated numbering of the children—'second son' or 'second daughter'—as if she could readily spare one! The use of the clichéd phrase 'struck rock-bottom' to describe the waterfall rings like an embarrassing gaffe. There is a deliberate underplaying of the seriousness of the situation, which adds to the incongruity and creates humour, as in the alpenstock (a long staff) 'which luckily later caught him on his way.' The relaxed feeling is conveyed through the language: 'Nothing, it was evident, could be done' and 'from a difficult distance viewed.' This deliberate emotional distance creates a sense of disbelief, and hence the humour.

Style of language

As befits a narrative poem, the style of narration is conversational. Yet it is slightly formal, a little stuffy. There is a formality about the style of the opening: 'If the year is meditating a suitable gift, | I should like it to be ...' At times the structure of the sentences, the parenthesis in the syntax, gives it a certain long-winded formality. We see this, for example, in 'impeded, no doubt, by the petticoats of the day,' or 'Nothing, it was evident, could be done.' The contrast between the dramatic and frightful scene and the rather stylised formal telling of it is a big element in the creation of the humour of the piece.

24 *William Butler Yeats* (1865–1939)

William Butler Yeats was born in Dublin of a County Sligo family. He was interested in Irish mythology, history, and folklore; it became one of his life's great passions to develop a distinctive, distinguished Irish literature in English. He was one of the founders of the Abbey Theatre in 1904. He published many volumes of poetry, from *Crossways* (1889) to *Last Poems* (1939). 'An Irish Airman Foresees His Death' is taken from the collection *The Wild Swans at Coole* (1919). In 1923 Yeats was awarded the Nobel Prize for Literature. (For further information see page 142.)

An Irish Airman Foresees His Death

I know that I shall meet my fate
Somewhere among the clouds above;
Those that I fight I do not hate,
Those that I guard I do not love;
My country is Kiltartan Cross,   5
My countrymen Kiltartan's poor,
No likely end could bring them loss
Or leave them happier than before.
Nor law, nor duty bade me fight,
Nor public men, nor cheering crowds,   10
A lonely impulse of delight
Drove to this tumult in the clouds;
I balanced all, brought all to mind,
The years to come seemed waste of breath,
A waste of breath the years behind   15
In balance with this life, this death.

Notes

an Irish airman: The speaker in the poem is Major Robert Gregory, the only son of Yeats's friend and mentor Lady Augusta Gregory of Coole Park, near Gort, County Galway. He was a pilot in the Royal Flying Corps in the First World War and at the time of his death, on 23 January 1918, was on service in Italy. It emerged later that he had been accidentally shot down by the Italian allies

[3] **Those that I fight:** the Germans

[4] **Those that I guard:** the English, or possibly the Italians

[5] **Kiltartan Cross:** a crossroads near Robert Gregory's home at Coole Park, Gort, County Galway

Background

This poem was one of a number written by the poet for Robert Gregory, including 'Shepherd and Goatherd' and 'In Memory of Major Robert Gregory'. Yeats saw Gregory as an educated aristocrat and all-round Renaissance man ('Soldier, scholar, horseman, he'). He was also an energetic boxer and hunter and a painter who designed many sets for Yeats's own plays. The poem was written in 1918 and first published in the collection *The Wild Swans at Coole* (1919).

Explorations

Pre-reading

1. Read only the title. What do you expect to find in this poem? Imagine what this man's thoughts might be. How might he visualise his death? How might he feel about it? Jot down, briefly, the thoughts and pictures and feelings you imagine might go through his mind.

First reading

2. Who is the speaker in this poem? If in doubt, consult the note at the end of the poem.

3. Focus on lines 1 and 2. Are you surprised by how definite he is? Can you suggest any reasons why he might be so definite about his coming death? How would you describe his mood?

4. How do you think the speaker would say these first two lines? Experiment with various readings aloud.

5. Taking the first four lines as a unit, are you surprised that they are spoken by a military man, a pilot? In your own words, describe how he views his situation.

Second reading

6. In lines 5–8 the speaker talks about the people of his home area. How does he feel about them? Does he identify with them in any way? Have the people and the speaker anything in common? How does he think his death will affect their lives? Does he feel they will miss him? Do you think his attitude to them is uncaring, or that he feels unable to affect their lives in any way? Discuss these questions and write down the conclusions you come to, together with the evidence from the text.

7. What do you think is the purpose of his mentioning his Kiltartan countrymen in the context of his explanation? How does it fit in to his reasoning?

8. Lines 9 and 10: In your own words, explain these further reasons, which the speaker discounts as having any influence on his decision to volunteer.

9. What is revealed about the character of the speaker in the lines you have explored so far?

Third reading

10. Lines 11 and 12: Here we get to the kernel of his motivation. Examine the language very carefully. 'A lonely impulse of delight': can you understand why he might feel this sense of delight? Explain how you see it. 'Impulse': what does this tell us about the decision? 'A lonely impulse': what does this suggest about the decision and the man? 'Drove': what does this add to our understanding of how he felt and of his decision? 'Tumult in the clouds': in what other contexts might the words 'tumult' or 'tumultuous' be used? Suggest a few. What does the sound of the word suggest? What does it suggest about the speaker's view of flying?

11. In the light of what you have discovered so far, and in the voice of the speaker, write a letter home, explaining your decision to volunteer as a pilot. Try to remain true to the speaker's feelings as outlined in the poem.

12. Lines 13–16: 'In spite of his hint of excitement earlier, the speaker did not make a rash and emotional decision.' On the evidence of these lines, would you agree with that statement? Write a paragraph.

13.

> The years to come seemed waste of breath
> ...
> In balance with this life, this death.

Yet the speaker seemed to want this kind of life very much. Explore how the use of 'breath' and 'death' as rhyming words help to emphasise this.

Fourth reading

14. Having read this poem, what do you find most interesting about the speaker?

15. What appeals to you about the poem? Do you find anything disturbing about it?

16. Thousands of Irishmen fought and died in the British army during the First World War; others could not bring themselves to join that army while Ireland was governed by England. How does the speaker deal with this issue? Is the title significant?

17. As well as being a rhetorical device, the repetition of words and phrases emphasises certain ideas and issues. List the main ideas thus emphasised.

18. What are the principal themes or issues the poem deals with? Write a number of short paragraphs on this.

19. 'The pictures of images are sparsely used but very effective.' Comment on any two images.

20. To whom is this being spoken? Read it aloud. Is the tone more appropriate to a letter or to a public statement or speech? Explain your view with reference to phrases or lines in the text.

A Critical Commentary

At one obvious level of reading, this is a type of elegy in memory of the dead man. But it is a variation on the form, in that it is structured as a monologue by the dead man rather than the more usual direct lament by a poet, praising the person's good qualities and showing how he is much missed, etc.

It makes an interesting contribution to war poetry in its attempt to chart the motivation and psychological state of the volunteer. What strikes one immediately is not just the sense of fatalism—he knows his death is imminent—but the bleakness of his outlook on life, his disenchantment with living, despite his privileged background.

> The years to come seemed waste of breath,
> A waste of breath the years behind ...

In contrast, the war seemed an adventure, an 'impulse of delight,' a 'tumult in the clouds.' The poem captures well the excitement and exhilaration felt by many a volunteer. As Ulick O'Connor put it (in *The Yeats Companion*, 1990), 'there can seldom have been a better summing up of the sense of elation which the freedom to roam the uncharted skies brought to the young men of Gregory's pre-1914 generation.'

Yet the decision to volunteer was not a heady, emotional one. The poem stresses the thought and calculation brought to the decision. The concept of balance is repeatedly stressed:

> I balanced all, brought all to mind
> ...
> In balance with this life, this death.

He was not carried away by the emotion of enlistment meetings ('Nor public men, nor cheering crowds'). He was not moved by any sense of duty or 'patriotism'; neither was there conscription in Ireland ('Nor law, nor duty bade me fight'). These 'nor'—'nor' negatives of the rejected motives are balanced against the excitement of action. The general picture is of a young man who has chosen, after careful consideration, this path of action, almost indeed chosen his death.

This heavy sense of fatalism is most obvious in the opening lines. But there is never a sense in which this fatalism is merely weak surrender or opting out. He accepts his fate, he goes consenting to his death, but more like one of Homer's heroes. Yeats gives Gregory Homeric stature by allowing him to choose a heroic death; and this gives meaning to an otherwise meaningless conflict. The airman feels none of the great passions of war, neither patriotic love nor hatred of the foe:

> Those that I fight I do not hate,
>
> Those that I guard I do not love.

Further, he does not think the war will make a whit of difference to his own countrymen:

> No likely end could bring them loss
>
> Or leave them happier than before.

But it is the self-sacrificing death, 'this death' freely chosen, that raises the young man above the events of his time and confers particular significance on him. The awareness of impending death also brings this moment of insight, this clearness of vision that allowed him to evaluate his past life and contemplate a possible future as a country landowner—all of which he rejects for the 'tumult' of action.

So, as a war poem, this is an interesting personal, even intimate approach charting the thoughts and motivation of this young man. But it has a more general aspect also. Gregory may be seen as representative of all those young men of talent who were cheated of their promise by the slaughter of the First World War.

We have already mentioned that Yeats saw Gregory as the all-round Renaissance man, in other words an educated man and a person of culture as well as a man of action. Yeats had felt that the 'lonely impulse of delight' was what differentiated the artist from others, that the artistic impulse was essentially lonely and solitary. Here we see this artistic impulse motivating a man of action, who is essentially instinctive rather than intellectual. Yeats felt that the impulse was sometimes hampered in the artist who often thought too much. So the later Yeats began to champion the non-intellectual hero and the instinctive man; the sportsman and the adventurer are given the status of mythic figures. The airman Gregory is essentially a solitary figure, like other mythic figures created by Yeats, such as 'The Fisherman'.

Some critics read this poem as a classic statement of Anglo-Irishness as Yeats saw it. In later life he used to talk about the 'Anglo-Irish solitude'. Is there a sense here of not quite fully belonging to either side, of being neither fully committed English nor unreservedly Irish? There is certainly a sense of emotional distance, both from those he guards and those he fights. Though he has an affinity with Kiltartan's poor ('my countrymen'), he is aware that the war and his involvement in it will have no impact on their lives. In general, the feeling one gets is one of some detachment from the events in which he participates, and this could be read as a metaphor for 'Anglo-Irish solitude'.

Biographical
Information on the Poets

Fleur Adcock

Fleur Adcock was born in New Zealand in 1934 but spent much of her childhood in England during the war years, constantly on the move from lodging to lodging and from school to school. She describes her feeling of not belonging in poems such as 'Neston', 'Chippenham' and others in *The Incident Book* (1986).

> Just visiting: another village school
> with a desk for me to fill, while Chippenham
> decided whether it wanted me—too young
> for there, too over-qualified for here.
> ('Neston')

She returned to New Zealand at the age of thirteen and went to Wellington Girls' College (which had been Katherine Mansfield's school also). The poets she remembers enjoying during her teenage years were Blake, Milton, Donne, and T. S. Eliot. She herself was determined to be a poet, despite the fact that all the models she had were male.

> One of the characteristics of the young is their
> conviction of their own uniqueness: it was
> impossible to see myself as the product of my
> time and circumstances; I was me, there would
> never be another exactly the same, I was going
> to *show* them. My poems of that time are full
> not only of adolescent despair and introspection
> but of seething ambition: just you wait, they
> say. Later, with more experience, came more
> humility, but the determination persisted.

When she was eighteen she married the poet Alastair Campbell; by the time she was twenty-four she had two young sons and was divorced. An account of her return to New Zealand and subsequent happenings can be found in her poem 'Going Back', from the collection *The Inner Harbour* (1979).

But she began to find New Zealand stifling and left for England in 1963, and she gradually put aside her antipodean identity until, as she says, 'the country of my birth feels deeply foreign to me after more than twenty years away from it.' She worked in London for many years as a librarian in the civil service.

A prolific poet, her collections include *The Eye of the Hurricane* (1964), *Tigers* (1967), *High Tide in the Garden* (1971), *The Inner Harbour* (1979), *Below Loughrigg* (1979) (a collection of poems on the Lake District), *Selected Poems* (1983), *The Incident Book* (1986), and *Time Zones* (1991).

The critic Andrew Motion has said that Fleur Adcock is very good 'at bed,' that is, at dealing with dreams, illness, and sex. She herself says that she brings dreams into her poems in order to explore elements of the irrational. She also admits an interest in the decay of the body, in getting old and dying. And she tends to write a good deal about intimate private moments, in poems often addressed to husband or lover. In this category she has become famous for what is described as the 'anti-erotic' style of poem; she herself describes these less grandly as poems 'about how horrible men are.' They include poems such as 'Incident' and 'Against Coupling'; the latter she explained as a kick in the teeth for someone she was finished with! But she does write widely about love and its pleasures as well as its transience and unhappiness.

She is regarded as one of the foremost feminist poets of the age, though she herself feels that nationality and travel were also important in her development as a poet.

> The question of my nationality has always
> seemed at least as significant as the question of
> my gender. I write a good deal about places; I
> have passionate relationships with them.
> Wherever I happen to live I have always some
> residual feeling of being an outsider: a fruitful
> position for a writer, perhaps, if it means one
> takes nothing for granted. But now I wonder:

has being a woman contributed to this? Are women natural outsiders? Perhaps my early competitiveness had something to do with being female, as well as being young.' (From *The Bloodaxe Book of Contemporary Women Poets,* edited by Jeni Couzyn, 1985.)

Many of her poems display a personal quality, growing out of personal associations and human encounters. They are intimate poems, often spoken to a son, lover, or husband. So she has become known for poems of a private and domestic nature. But her poetry also shows a broader view of the world. She has been a wanderer ever since childhood and she writes of places and travel. She has quite a few poems on journeys in Ireland.

The Incident Book (1986) contains a diverse range of poems: some London streetscapes, views of life in Thatcher's Britain, poems of family relationships, some of the anti-erotic poems for which she is famous, and a collection of memories from her own childhood in England during the war. The volume is dedicated in part to her god-daughter, Heidi Jackson, and contains the poem 'For Heidi with Blue Hair'.

Fleur Adcock has also translated Greek and mediaeval Latin poetry and edited *The Oxford Book of Contemporary New Zealand Poetry* (1983) and *The Faber Book of Twentieth-Century Women's Poetry* (1987).

W. H. Auden

Wystan Hugh Auden was born at York on 21 February 1907, the youngest of three brothers. In 1925 he won a scholarship to study natural science at Christ Church College, Oxford, but changed to English literature. While at Oxford he developed strong views on poetry and wrote and published it and came to be regarded by his contemporaries as something of an authority on the subject. There he met Stephen Spender, Cecil Day-Lewis, and Louis MacNeice. These four were to become

influential poets of the thirties and were seen as a distinct group, affectionately known as 'MacSpaunday'. The group produced a good deal of poetry on political and social themes; they aimed to rouse the public conscience on issues such as the poverty of people's lives and the dangers of fascism. Auden soon came to be regarded as one of the most talented voices of this generation.

After Oxford he studied German for a year in Berlin, where he was much influenced by the psychology of Sigmund Freud and the drama of Bertolt Brecht, influences that surface in his writings. He worked as a schoolteacher in Scotland and England for a number of years and at the same time wrote poetry prolifically. *Poems* (1930) was followed by *The Orators* (1932) and *Look Stranger* (1936). *Another Time* (1940) contains many of his most famous poems, including 'Sept. 1939' and 'Lullaby'; it also contains 'Funeral Blues'. He wrote dramas for the Group Theatre, whose aim was to produce plays that would have a social impact. Some of these were collaborations with Christopher Isherwood, his friend since schooldays. They include *The Dog Beneath the Skin* (1935) and The *Ascent of F6* (1936). The latter is a type of fable, showing a very bleak view of society and dealing with corruption in high places, flawed heroes, and the hopeless, boring lives of many ordinary people. (A version of 'Funeral Blues' is used as a song in this play.)

In 1936 Auden visited Iceland with Louis MacNeice and they produced *Letters from Iceland* (1937). 1937 saw him in Spain, briefly, as a volunteer ambulance driver in the International Brigade. Commissioned to write a travel book, Auden and Isherwood journeyed to China in 1938, where they witnessed the Japanese invasion. *Journey to a War* (1939) was the outcome. All in all, the thirties were a most prolific decade for Auden, when he demonstrated at the beginning of his career what an energetic and versatile writer he was.

In 1939 Auden and Isherwood left Europe

to live in the United States, where Auden became a citizen in 1946. He taught in many universities there and was showered with prizes for his poetry, including the Pulitzer Prize in 1948. Because of his absence during the war his poetry was not popular in England for a time, but he gradually came back into favour and was professor of poetry at Oxford from 1956 to 1961. He continued to be a prolific and versatile writer. *The Shield of Achilles* (1955) is only one of the more famous of the many volumes of poetry he produced in the forties and sixties. He also wrote librettos and collaborated on many musical compositions, including an opera with Benjamin Britten. He wrote for films (the poem 'The Night Mail' was originally written for the documentary film of that title), edited numerous poetry anthologies, and produced quite a few volumes of literary criticism, the best known of which is *The Dyer's Hand* (1962). It has been said by his critics that he sometimes achieved quantity at the expense of quality.

Over his lifetime, Auden's poetry dealt with a wide range of concerns, from his interest in social issues in the thirties to a concern with Christianity and the spiritual and psychological aspects of human beings—a concern with the mind as well as the heart. He was often concerned with how the individual can maintain a sense of identity and individuality against the pressures of modern society and bureaucracy. He felt that the poet had an important role in society, as a voice of insight and of protest.

Auden was a very skilful poet. He used a great variety of verse forms—ballads, lyrical verse, dramatic monologues, and songs—and a great range of poetic voices and moods, from romantic to satirical. He wrote both light humorous verse and serious poetry.

Elizabeth Bishop

A literary life

Elizabeth Bishop was born on 8 February 1911 in Worcester, Massachusetts. Her parents, Gertrude Bulmer (pronounced and sometimes spelt Boomer) and William Bishop, were both of Canadian origin. Her father died when she was eight months old. Her mother never recovered from the shock and for the next five years was in and out of mental hospitals and moved between Boston, Worcester, and her home town of Great Village in Nova Scotia.

In 1916 Gertrude Bulmer's insanity was diagnosed as permanent and she was institutionalised and separated from her daughter, whom she was never to see again. She died in 1934. Elizabeth was reared for the most part by the Boomer grandparents in Great Village, with occasional long stays at the wealthy Bishop household in Worcester, Massachusetts, which she did not enjoy. As a child she suffered severe lung illnesses, often having to spend almost entire winters in bed, reading. Chronic asthma became a problem for her all her life.

She describes her early days in Nova Scotia from a child's point of view in the autobiographical short story 'In the Village'. The elegy 'First Death in Nova Scotia' also draws on some childhood memories. 'Sestina' too evokes the sadness of this period. These and other snippets from unpublished poems and papers point to an unsatisfactory relationship with an ill and transient mother. Yet in spite of these difficulties her recollections of her Nova Scotia childhood were essentially positive and she had great affection for her maternal grandparents, aunts and uncles in this small agricultural village, many of whose inhabitants, including the Boomers, farmed the local hinterland.

In 1927 she went to Walnut Hill School for girls, a boarding-school in Natick, Massachusetts. She attended Vassar College, a private university in Poughkeepsie, New York, from 1930 to 1934, where her fees were paid by the Bishop family at first and then by the income from a legacy left by her father. She graduated in English literature (but also took

Greek and music), always retaining a particular appreciation for Renaissance lyric poetry and for the works of Gerard Manley Hopkins. It was at Vassar that she first began to publish stories and poems in national magazines and where she met the poet Marianne Moore, who became an important influence on her career as a poet and with whom she maintained a lifelong friendship and correspondence. It was also at Vassar that she formed her first lesbian relationship, and here too, on her own admission, the lifelong problem with alcohol addiction began.

Between 1935 and 1938 she made a number of trips to Europe, travelling to England, Ireland, France, north Africa, Spain and Italy in the company of her friends Louise Crane and Margaret Miller, the latter losing an arm in a road accident on the trip. Bishop dedicated the poem 'Quai d'Orléans' to Miller. In 1939 she moved to Key West, Florida, a place she had fallen in love with over the previous years. 'The Fish' reflects her enjoyment of the sport of fishing at that time. She and Louise Crane bought a house at 624 White Street, now called the Elizabeth Bishop House. Later she lived with Marjorie Carr Stevens, to whom 'Anaphora' was dedicated posthumously after Stevens' death in 1959.

Key West became a sort of refuge and base for Bishop over the next fifteen years. In 1945 she won the Houghton Mifflin Poetry Award, worth $1,000. In 1946 her first book of poetry, *North and South,* was published and was well received by the critics. 'The Fish' is among its thirty poems. She met and began a lifelong friendship and correspondence with the poet Robert Lowell. In 1948 she won a Guggenheim Fellowship worth $2,500.

From 1949 to 1950 she was poetry consultant to the Library of Congress. She was paid $5,000 for supervising the library's stock of poetry and acquiring new works and for providing opinions and advice. The money was important to her, as she had dedicated herself exclusively to her poetry, at which she was a slow and often erratic worker. The years 1945–1951, when her life was centred on New York, were very unsettled. She felt under extreme pressure in a very competitive literary circle and drank heavily. 'The Bight' and 'The Prodigal' reflect this dissolute period of her life. In 1947 she began seeing Dr Amy Baumann, who became her main medical support for her chronic depression, asthma, and alcoholism.

In 1951 she left for South America on the first stage of a writer's trip round the world. She stopped first in Brazil, where she went to visit her old acquaintances Mary Morse and Maria Carlota Costellar de Macedo Soares (Lota Soares). She was fascinated by the country and by Lota Soares, with whom she began a relationship that was to last until the latter's death in 1967. They lived in a new house in the luxurious Brazilian countryside at Samambia, Petrópolis. 'Questions of Travel' and 'The Armadillo' reflect this period of her life.

In 1955 *A Cold Spring,* her second volume of poetry, was published. It contains 'The Bight', 'At the Fishhouses', and 'The Prodigal'. In 1956 she won the Pulitzer Prize.

The Diary of Helena Morley was published in 1957. This was a translation by Bishop of the diary of a girl aged thirteen to fifteen who lived in the Brazilian village of Diamantina in the eighteen-nineties. *Questions of Travel,* her third volume, was published in 1965. Among this selection, as well as the title poem, were 'Sestina', 'First Death in Nova Scotia', and 'Filling Station'.

Bishop was poet in residence at the University of Washington, Seattle, from 1966 to 1967, where she met Suzanne Bowen, who became her secretary, human caretaker, and, after Lota Soares's death, her lover. They lived in San Francisco from 1968 to 1969, where Bishop found the new culture bewildering, and then in Brazil, until the tempestuous ending of the relationship in 1970.

In 1969 the *Complete Poems* was published. Bishop won the National Book Award for Poetry in 1970. She was appointed poet in residence at Harvard, where she taught advanced verse writing and studies in modern poetry for her first year and, later, poets and their letters. She described herself as 'a scared elderly amateur prof'. It was here she met Alice Methfessel, an administrative assistant who became her minder and companion for the remainder of her life. She began to do a good many public readings of her poetry to earn a living, as she had not been able to get much of her money out of Brazil. She continued to teach term courses for the remainder of her years, though she found the work draining and it interfered with the already slow production of poetry. But she needed the money to maintain her style of life and travel.

In the summer of 1972 she went on a cruise through Scandinavia to the Soviet Union. In 1973 she secured a four-year contract from Harvard to teach a term each year, until her retirement in May 1977. She continued to do public readings, punctuated by spells in hospital with asthma, alcoholism, and depression. She managed to visit Mexico in 1975 and went on a trip to Europe in 1976. In 1976 also *Geography III* was published. Among this slim collection of nine or ten poems were 'In the Waiting Room' and 'The Moose'. The poems in this volume show a new, more directly personal style and a return to her past and her sense of self, in search of themes.

Competing with failing health, including a bleeding hiatus hernia, she continued her usual round of readings, travel, and some writing. She died suddenly of a brain aneurysm on 6 October 1979.

William Blake

William Blake was born in 1757. Despite his lack of proper schooling, he became one of the foremost English poets of the Romantic period; but it was as an engraver and illustrator that he made a very inadequate living.

From an early age he was subject to visionary experiences, for example of a tree with angels, or of his dead brother's soul floating up through the ceiling. These experiences ranged from simply seeing things to the entering of deep spiritual states. Blake was consequently regarded with a certain suspicion, as something of a genius and a madman, and was not given much recognition during his lifetime. But the mystical experiences lend a uniquely individual and magical quality to his illustrations and to his writings. His book *The Marriage of Heaven and Hell* (1790) is a record of his complex and unorthodox religious experience. He continued to write prophetic books, such as *The First Book of Urizen* (1794) and *The Book of Los* (1795).

His more well-known writings are the short lyrical poems such as those contained in the volumes *Songs of Innocence* (1789) and *Songs of Experience* (1794). Blake himself described these as 'Showing the Two Contrary States of the Human Soul'. Some poems show scenes of pastoral innocence, some are addressed to children, and some are more sombre poems about the dark side of human nature. A number of the poems are contrasting pairs, for example 'The Lamb' and 'The Tyger', which are often interpreted as representing two aspects of God—the gentle God and the divine power to be feared and only partly understood. 'A Poison Tree' is from *Songs of Experience*.

The Romantics stressed the importance of feelings, of emotions and sensations, often at the expense of the rational. Dreams and psychological states of mind were regarded as worth writing about. The imagination was considered one of the noblest of the human faculties. Nature was thought to have an important formative and healing influence on humans; and the focus was on the individual and on personal values rather than on community or society. Blake was one of the most distinctive and individual of the Romantics. He was particularly interested in the emotional, psychological and spiritual side of the human being, and he believed that childhood experiences were significant. But above all he believed in the transfiguring power of the imagination.

William Blake died in poverty on 12 August 1827 and was buried in a common grave at Bunhill Fields. The exact spot is unknown.

Eavan Boland

Eavan Boland was born in Dublin in 1944, daughter of the painter Frances Kelly and the diplomat Frederick Boland. She was educated at Holy Child Convent, Killiney, and Trinity College, Dublin. For some years she lectured there in the English Department, before becoming a literary journalist, chiefly with the *Irish Times* but also with RTE, where she produced award-winning poetry programmes for radio. She married the novelist Kevin Casey, exchanging the Dublin literary scene for family life in the suburbs, where she wrote prolifically.

New Territory (1967) was her first volume of poetry. 'The War Horse' (1975) deals with the Northern Ireland 'troubles' and with how violence encroaches on our domestic lives. The poem 'Child of Our Time' is taken from this volume. Her third volume, *In Her Own Image* (1980), explores the darker side of female identity, 'woman's secret history'; it deals with real but taboo issues such as anorexia, infanticide, mastectomy, menstruation, and domestic violence. 'Night Feed' (1982) celebrates the ordinary, everyday domestic aspect of woman's identity. 'The Journey' (1986) and 'Outside History' (1990) consider the image of woman in Irish history, in painting and in literature—a tale of exploitation and repression, of being marginalised and kept from the centre of influence. 'In a Time of Violence' (1994) deals with specifically Irish national and historical issues, such as the Famine, agrarian violence, and the Easter Rising. It also focuses on the

theme of women as mothers and the relationship between mothers and daughters. The poem 'This Moment' is taken from this volume.

The place of the woman writer in Irish literature, mythology and history is a prominent theme in Boland's poetry and other writings. Her pamphlet *A Kind of Scar* (1989) examines this issue. Her collection of autobiographical prose, published in 1995, is entitled *Object Lessons: The Life of the Woman and the Poet in Our Time*. In 1980 she was joint founder of Arlen House, a feminist publishing company.

Emily Dickinson

An enigmatic life

Emily Dickinson was born in Amherst, Massachusetts, on 10 December 1830 to Emily Norcross Dickinson and Edward Dickinson. She was the middle child in the family, between an older brother, Austin (born 1829), and a younger sister, Lavinia (born 1833).

The Dickinsons were prominent public figures. Edward Dickinson was a well-known lawyer, with a great interest in education. For a time he was treasurer of Amherst College, which had been founded by Emily's grandfather, Samuel Fowler Dickinson. He is described by Emily's biographers as a somewhat severe and remote father, an interpretation based on her own letters, though she appears to have loved him, and she was devastated when he died.

The relationship between child and mother does not appear to have been a very warm one either, as Emily mentioned in a letter to her literary guide and friend Thomas Wentworth Higginson: 'I never had a mother. I suppose a mother is one to whom you hurry when you are troubled.' In later life, however, she did become closer to her mother. It is worth remembering that the remoteness of parents was a feature of much nineteenth-century child-rearing practice with the middle and upper classes; and Emily's childhood experiences may not have been that much out of the ordinary.

The family lived in half of the Homestead, an imposing brick house in Main Street, Amherst, built by Edward's father, who occupied the other half. In 1840 the grandfather sold out and moved away. Edward and his family moved to another part of Amherst until 1855, when he managed to buy back the entire house, and there Emily lived for the rest of her life.

Education

In 1840 Emily Dickinson was sent to Amherst Academy, a co-educational school offering a wide range of subjects, from the classics to modern sciences. The principal, Rev. Edward Hitchcock, was a well-known scientist. Emily developed a particular interest in biology and botany, which might account for the precision of her observations and the prevalence of natural imagery in many of her poems.

In 1847 she went to Mount Holyoke Female Seminary for further education but was withdrawn after two terms because of poor health and possibly because of the overpowering religious ethos of the school. She had been expressing religious doubts even before she went there. Though she was a believer in God, she remained aloof from the religious fervour, in the form of religious revival meetings, that was sweeping through Amherst about this time.

Life in Amherst

After her formal education finished in 1847, Dickinson seems to have lived a fairly normal life in Amherst, with some excursions to the cities (Boston in 1851, Washington and Philadelphia in 1855).

In 1855 her mother, who had been in declining health, became seriously disabled. Emily and Lavinia, with the support of domestic servants, took over the running of the household; and Emily began to develop that missing relationship with her mother,

though with roles reversed, as she explained: 'We were never intimate Mother and Children while she was our Mother—but Mines in the same Ground meet by tunnelling and when she became our Child, the Affection came.'

In those days her life was ordinary, her behaviour unremarkable. She went to church; walked her dog, Carlo; wrote letters; did housework; and supported community events. In October 1856 she won a prize for her bread at the local cattle show and served as a member of the produce committee during the following year. In her garden she had the reputation of having 'green fingers'. Perhaps it was here that she first saw 'a Bird' come 'down the Walk' or that she encountered 'A narrow Fellow in the Grass', though that was more likely to have occurred in the Dickinson meadow across the street.

In 1856 Austin joined the First Church of Christ, and also that year he married Emily's closest friend, Susan Gilbert. They built a house, the Evergreens, next door to the Homestead, and this was, at least at first, a place of much gaiety and entertainment, in contrast to the sombre austerity of Emily's own home. The happiness experienced by the young people was referred to by Kate Scott Anthon, a mutual friend, writing to Susan: 'Those happy visits to your house! Those celestial evenings in the library—The blazing wood fire—Emily—Austin—The music—The rampant fun—The inextinguishable laughter, The uproarious spirits of our chosen—our most congenial circle.'

Dickinson was not short of friends and advisers at this time, though the relationships, particularly with her women friends, did not always remain untrammelled. The friendship with Susan Gilbert became somewhat strained after a number of years. In 1859 Emily met Kate Scott Anthon, a friend of Susan's, and considered her a close friend until 1866. Nor was she devoid of male company. Ben Newton, a law student of her father's, encouraged her reading and was considered by her 'a gentle, yet grave Preceptor'. Rev.

Charles Wadsworth was her spiritual adviser for many years. Samuel Bowles, editor of the *Springfield Daily Republican,* was also a close friend. The names of one or two other young men (such as George Gould and Edward Hunt) have been mentioned by scholars as possible recipients of her affections.

After 1862 Thomas Wentworth Higginson became Dickinson's literary guide and critic. There was Judge Otis Lord, a widower who wanted to marry her and for whom she seems to have cared deeply in the early eighties until his death in 1884. And there was the unidentified man addressed as 'Master' in her letters and poems, whom she loved and who may or may not have been one of her acquaintances known to us.

As to her appearance, it is interesting to note how she described herself when asked by Higginson for a portrait: 'I had no portrait, now, but am small, like the Wren, and my Hair is bold, like the Chestnut Bur—and my eyes, like the Sherry in the Glass, that the Guest leaves.'

Crisis and withdrawal

There seems to have been some kind of emotional crisis in her personal life about 1861–63, the nature of which we can only guess at. The speculation is that she may have been rejected by, or herself rejected, the man she loved, perhaps the 'Master' of the letters and poems. Though the exact nature and cause of the experience are open to speculation and argument, Dickinson seems to have undergone a psychological crisis in her early thirties, which resulted in a great outpouring of poetry (four to five hundred estimated in 1862 and 1863) and led to her withdrawal from normal social life.

Her behaviour became noticeably more odd and eccentric. She developed into 'the myth' of Amherst, a single woman dressed all in white who didn't meet strangers or even visitors, who spoke to friends from behind a half-closed door or shrouded in shadow at the head of the stairs. Yet she sent them in wine or fruit on a tray.

She refused to go out. 'I do not Cross my Father's ground to any House or town,' she replied to Higginson's invitation to attend a lecture in Boston in 1869. But he made a trip to Amherst to see her in August 1870 and has left us (in a letter to his wife) an interesting impression of the poet.

I shan't sit up tonight to write you all about E.D. dearest but if you had read Mrs. Stoddard's novels you could understand a house where each member runs his or her own selves. Yet I only saw her.

A large county lawyer's house, brown brick, with great trees and a garden—I sent up my card. A parlour dark & cool & stiffish, a few books & engravings & an open piano—Malbone [Higginson's novel] & O.D. [Outdoor] Papers among other books.

A step like a pattering child's in entry & glided a little plain woman with two smooth bands of reddish hair & a face a little like Belle Dove's; not plainer—with no good feature—in a very plain & exquisitely clean white pique & a blue net worsted shawl. She came to me with two day lilies which she put in a sort of childlike way into my hand & said 'These are my introduction' in a soft frightened breathless childlike voice—& added under her breath Forgive me if I am frightened; I never see strangers & hardly know what I say—but she talked soon & thenceforward continuously—& deferentially—sometimes stopping to ask me to talk instead of her—but readily recommencing. Manner between Angie Tilton & Mr. Alcott—but thoroughly ingenuous & simple which they are not & saying many things which you would have thought foolish & I wise—& somethings you wd. hv. liked. I add a few over the page.

In 1883 she visited her dying nephew, Gilbert, next door at the Evergreens and was ill for months afterwards. When she died on 15 May 1886, on her own instructions her white coffin was carried across the fields to the churchyard, rather than by the usual route of funeral processions. She was found to have left almost two thousand poems and fragments, in which she explored love, pain, absence and loss, doubt, despair, hope, mental anguish, and other universal themes.

Paul Durcan

Paul Durcan was born in Dublin in 1944. Both his parents were from County Mayo, where Durcan spent many school holidays and which features prominently in his poetry. The contrast between the magical land of Mayo and the barren, empty Dublin landscape is the most striking feature of the poem 'Going Home to Mayo, Winter, 1949'.

Durcan was educated at Gonzaga College, Dublin. The nineteen-sixties saw him work at a succession of poor jobs in Dublin and London. He survived a stay in a mental hospital, became an acquaintance and admirer of the poet Patrick Kavanagh, taught for a time in Barcelona, and married Nessa O'Neill, with whom he had two children, before settling in Cork in the early seventies and taking a degree in archaeology and mediaeval history at University College, Cork.

He is the author of sixteen collections of poetry, from *Endsville,* written jointly with Brian Lynch in 1967, to *Christmas Day* (1996). Among the more notable collections he has published are *O Westport in the Light of Asia Minor* (1975), *The Berlin Wall Café* (1985), *Going Home to Russia* (1987), and *Daddy, Daddy* (1990). His poetry has won many prizes, including the Patrick Kavanagh Award in 1974 and the Whitbread Poetry Prize in 1990.

A glance at some of his titles, which read like tabloid newspaper headlines, suggests the uniqueness of Durcan's poetry: 'Diarrhoea Attack at Party Headquarters in Leningrad'; 'Irish Hierarchy Bans Colour Photography'; 'Making Love outside Áras an Uachtaráin'; 'The Married Man who Fell in Love with a Semi-State Body'. He is a popular poet, a storyteller who writes accessible poetry often with a zany twist to it. He has an eye for the odd, the quaint, the bizarre, and the downright surreal; but there is always a core of sharp wisdom and insight in his verse, a quality akin to what Kavanagh called 'the laughter of wise innocence.'

He focuses on contemporary Ireland, particularly the west, and also on themes of political violence, love and marriage, and religion. He is well known for his satires directed at church and state. He writes elegies for the dead, such as the late President Cearbhall Ó Dálaigh, Micheál Mac Liammóir, Sid Vicious, the murdered members of the Miami Showband, and others. He has a particular love for Russia, which he visited a number of times in the eighties, and for its writers. Recently he has produced two volumes on paintings in the National Gallery of Ireland (*Crazy About Women,* 1991) and the National Gallery, London (*Give Me Your Hand,* 1994). But much of his most moving poetry springs from his own life experience. There is a fine sequence of poems in *The Berlin Wall Café* (1985) dealing with the break-up of his marriage. *Daddy, Daddy* (1990) charts the story of his relationship with his father, a judge and president of the Circuit Court, from their early closeness through the father-son 'divorce' during his teenage years to a re-established intimacy at the time of the father's impending death.

Durcan is famous for his public poetry readings, which are more performances than readings in the usual sense. For him the poet is as much orator and public commentator as writer.

Robert Graves

The descendant of a distinguished Anglo-Irish family that produced generations of well-known doctors, poets, scholars, diplomats, and clergymen, Robert von Ranke Graves was born in England in 1895 and educated at Charterhouse and Oxford. Though his first poetry was published when he was serving as an officer in the British army in the First World War, he was not regarded primarily as one of the war poets. It is in his prose that the war is most powerfully evoked: his autobiography, *Goodbye to All That* (1929), not only tells of his unhappy schooldays and the breakdown of his first marriage but also recalls the horrors of the trenches and the post-war disillusionment.

During his lifetime Graves produced an enormous volume of writing: essays, novels, biography, and songs for children, as well as a great many volumes of poetry, which he considered his main vocation. Of his historical novels, *I, Claudius* and *Claudius the God*, about imperial Rome, are the most famous. *The White Goddess*, a book on mythology, is probably his best-known non-fiction work. Volumes of his collected poems appeared regularly during his lifetime and he was continuously rewriting or deleting poems. Graves is not identified with any particular poetic movement (though some critics view him as a Modernist and others as a later Romantic). He was not given to experimenting but wrote conventional, well-crafted verse. His favourite theme was love, which he explored in volume after volume. He felt that all love involved suffering.

'Hedges Freaked with Snow' is the third part of 'Three Songs for the Lute', from *New Poems, 1962*. Most of the poems in the collection are quite bleak, recording Graves's despondency at the perpetual cycle of death and rebirth; but it does contain a few hopeful poems about love, and he went on to write about these positive aspects of love in the years that followed. 'Hedges Freaked with Snow' is among the last of his bleak love poems of that period. He died in 1985.

Michael Hartnett

Born in Croom, County Limerick, in 1941, Michael Hartnett lived for a time in London, Madrid and Dublin (where he was curator of 'Joyce's Tower' in Sandycove) before returning to Newcastle, County Limerick, in 1974.

Anatomy of a Cliché (1968) is a book of love poems to his wife. His *Selected Poems* was published in 1970. A poet in Irish and English, Hartnett announced his decision to write only in Irish in the volume *A Farewell to English* (1975, enlarged 1978). 'Death of an Irishwoman' is taken from this volume. His collections after this include *Adharca Broic* (1978), *An Phurgóid* (1983), *Do Nuala: Foidhne Chrainn* (1984), and *An Lia Nocht* (1985). Some of the poems in these collections are dark, sombre explorations into the psyche. There are poems of self-doubt, caused, some would say, by critical neglect and financial troubles. *Inchicore Haiku* (1985), set in working-class Dublin, marked a return to English and to the city. There followed some lighter, more hopeful and humorous poems in collections such as *Poems to Younger Women* (1989) and *The Killing of Dreams* (1992).

In some ways a poet of the local community, Hartnett finds inspiration in his own environment, whether the rural Ireland of his upbringing or urban Dublin, the small farm or Fairview Park. He considers celebration of the local to be one of the main functions of the poet.

> A poet's not a poet until the day he
> Can write a few songs for his people.

But he also looked outside Ireland, to Continental rather than to English literature, and has done a considerable body of translation. As well as *Tao* (1963), he has translated the Spanish poet and dramatist Lorca (*Gipsy Ballads*, 1972) and the Hungarian poet Ferenc Juhász (*An Damh-Mhac*, 1987).

Séamus Heaney

Early life

Séamus Heaney was born on 13 April 1939 on the family farm at Mossbawn, near Bellaghy, County Derry, the eldest of nine children.

From 1945 to 1951 he attended Anahorish primary school; from 1951 to 1957 he was educated at St Columb's College in Derry and from 1957 to 1961 at Queen's University, Belfast, where he got a first-class degree in English language and literature. In 1961 and 1962 he took a teacher training diploma at St Joseph's College of Education in Belfast. He taught at St Thomas's Intermediate School in Belfast, 1962–63, before becoming a lecturer in English at St Joseph's. In 1966 he was appointed lecturer in English at Queen's University.

'Death of a Naturalist'
Heaney's first volume of poetry, *Death of a Naturalist,* was published in 1966. Filled mostly with the characters, scenes, customs, flora and fauna of the countryside that formed him, this volume explores Heaney's cultural and poetic origins. Poems such as 'Digging', 'Follower', 'Churning Day', 'Ancestral Photograph' and 'The Diviner' honour his rural roots as they celebrate ancestral and family skills, as diggers of turf, makers of butter, ploughers of fields and diviners of water and show a people living in a close and almost spiritual relationship with the earth. Dominant among these is the larger-than-life heroic figure of his father. In describing them, and keenly aware that he is breaking with this tradition, Heaney seems to be at the same time defining his own space as a writer.

> But I've no spade to follow men like them.
> Between my finger and my thumb
> The squat pen rests.
> I'll dig with it.
> ('Digging')

'Door into the Dark'
Door into the Dark, Heaney's second volume, was published in 1969. While the first collection dealt in the main with childhood, coming of age, and the poet's relationship with the somewhat heroic figure of his father, this volume deals with more adult relationships. It focuses in particular on the joys, griefs and social role of women as mothers and partners, in such poems as 'The Wife's Tale', 'Cana Revisited', and 'Elegy for a Still-born Child'. A series of poems—'Rite of Spring', 'Undine', 'Outlaw', and 'A Lough Neagh Sequence'— celebrate the teeming fertility of nature. A couple of poems—'The Forge' and 'Thatcher'—hark back to the style of the first volume in the celebration of local skills and in the poet's discovery in them of metaphors for his own craft. But the poet's Irish focus broadens out from local considerations to a more general awareness of geography, history and archaeology in such poems as 'The Peninsula', 'Whinlands', 'The Plantation', 'Shoreline', and 'Bogland'.

'Wintering Out'
Heaney's third volume of poetry, *Wintering Out*, was published in 1972. The terms 'wintering out' and 'winterage' are used in farming to describe the custom of putting mature cattle onto a sheltered area of dry land with relatively good grass; this is often at some distance from the main farm, where they would be expected to survive the winter with no extra feeding and with little supervision. It was a sort of seasonal exile for animals. The term 'wintering out' was also used in connection with the seasonal movement of migrant farm labourers, and it is in this context that the term is used in the poem 'Servant Boy'. 1969 saw riots, bombs and sectarian killings. The Provisional IRA became a powerful force, and the British army was deployed on the streets. Yet Heaney hardly ever addresses these contemporary political issues directly. Instead he makes a journey back into the past, exploring Ireland's past and also the remote past of prehistoric humankind. So he focuses on the origins of the conflict: the sense of linguistic and cultural difference; the history of conflicting classes; and an exploration of the traditions, history and sense of identity of his own community, the Northern Catholics. In 'Bog Oak', through the metaphor of the title, he can revisit the native

dispossessed of the seventeenth century. In 'Gifts of Rain' he tries to forge links with the watery landscape of his birth and to establish a sense of his own identity. 'The Last Mummer' points up the clash of cultures and signals the death of the old ways. And there are many poems exploring the original meaning of place-names and in so doing exemplifying the linguistic dispossession of the native Irish, poems such as 'Anahorish', 'Broach', 'Toome', and 'Traditions'.

'The Other Side' is one of the few poems in *Wintering Out* that deals directly and personally with the present-day issue of religious and cultural difference. Directness and immediacy are achieved by dramatising the issues and objectifying them in the uneasy relationship between the poet's family and a Presbyterian neighbour. Once again Heaney is focusing in on the local scene, the small picture; but by examining the microcosm he gives us an insight into the larger scene, the relationship between the two cultures in Northern Ireland. Differences in outlook, self-image and modes of language, as well as in religion, are explored.

In 'The Tollund Man' Heaney finds an oblique way of examining the sacrificial killings, the power of religion and the deadly demands of myth in our society. But this examination is carried out at one remove, with the voice of the anthropologist, or historian, for the most part. It is as if the present is too raw to be viewed directly.

Part 2 contains some more personal and emotive poems: exploring the sadness behind the celebration in 'Wedding Day', recording painful separation in 'Mother of the Groom', and a string of poems featuring isolated, unappreciated, tragically unhappy female figures: 'A Winter's Tale', 'Shore Woman', 'Maighdean Mara', 'Limbo', and 'Bye-child'.

The move south

Heaney spent the academic year 1970/71 as guest lecturer at the University of California in Berkeley and found it difficult to settle back into life in Northern Ireland when he returned, a transition he described as 'like putting an old dirty glove on again.' He found the daily ritual of road-blocks, arrests, vigilante patrols, explosions and killings deeply disturbing. There were many flash-points and multiple killings at that time, such as 'Bloody Sunday' in January 1972, when British soldiers opened fire during a Civil Rights Association march, killing thirteen people and wounding others. Soon afterwards the internal system of government operating from Stormont was abolished and direct rule from London instituted in its place.

Whatever the background reasons, whether political, family, or artistic, Heaney decided that it was time to leave Belfast and devote himself entirely to his writing. He resigned his post as lecturer in English at Queen's University and moved with his family to a cottage at Glanmore, County Wicklow, during the summer of 1972, determined to go it alone as a poet and freelance writer.

The Heaney family lived a fairly insular rural existence in County Wicklow from 1972 until 1976. 'I wanted the kids to have that sort of wild animal life that I had,' Heaney said in an interview. 'They were like little rodents through the hedges ... I wanted that eye-level life with the backs of ditches, the ferns and the smell of cow dung, and I suppose I didn't want to lose that in myself.' Isolated, the family was forced back on its own resources, a process not without its rewards. The children's enjoyment of this simple life enabled Heaney to re-imagine his own childhood and rural values; the isolation also forced husband and wife to rediscover each other. These issues surfaced as themes in his lyrics.

Heaney went back to full-time teaching in the English Department of Carysfort Teacher Training College, Blackrock, County Dublin, from 1975 to 1981. And, chiefly to facilitate their growing family, in 1976 the Heaneys abandoned their rural retreat for the convenience of a house in Sandymount, Dublin.

'North'

Heaney's fourth volume of poetry, *North*, was published in 1975. The publisher's blurb gives an accurate overview: 'Here the Irish experience is refracted through images drawn from different parts of the Northern European experience, and the idea of the north allows the poet to contemplate the violence on his home ground in relation to memories of the Scandinavian and English invasions which have marked Irish history so indelibly.'

In part I he ranges over three thousand years of European civilisation, from the myths of Classical Greece to nineteenth-century Irish history, examining stories of conquest, cultural conflict and deeds of violence in an effort to understand the present-day Irish conflict, attempting to illuminate the present through focusing on the past. In part II the focus narrows to the individual human being caught in this vortex. A sequence of six poems entitled 'Singing School' marks milestones in his development as a poet and member of his tribe: the Northern Catholic. 'A Constable Calls' is of this sequence. Here he recalls, from a child's perspective, his fear of an alien law.

This collection of conflict poems is prefaced by two poems of a totally different sort, two peaceful poems outside the stream of history and time, recalling the security of childhood, the holistic nature of the old ways of life, the peacefulness of the countryside, and the stability and certainty provided by family love and values. These are 'Mossbawn: Two Poems in Dedication'. 'Sunlight' is the first of these.

'Field Work'

Field Work, Heaney's fifth collection, was published in 1979. In the meantime the violence in Northern Ireland had continued to increase, and in this volume Heaney examines a number of incidents directly. But he returns to the domestic for reassurance, notably in the ten 'Glanmore Sonnets', in which he celebrates married life and love.

'Station Island'

Published in 1984, *Station Island* is a complicated and sophisticated work, which uses a great range of myth, legend, and literary and historical allusion. These come from both Irish and Continental culture, ancient, mediaeval, and modern, and Heaney uses them as entry points, or sometimes as parallels, in order to examine his own culture. Heaney has often been accused of not 'tackling' the Northern violence directly, of lack of passionate involvement. However, he does deal with the situation: indeed this volume is full of allusions and references to prisons, cells, compounds, policemen, punishments, informers, betrayals, and victims of violence. But Heaney is happier exploring the situation at one remove, using myth, legend, literature and history as an intermediary, a glass through which it is viewed.

'The Haw Lantern'

The Haw Lantern, published in 1987, is chiefly a book about loss, emptiness, and absence. The most accessible and moving poems in the book are elegies: 'The Summer of Lost Rachel', for a niece who died in an accident; 'The Wishing Tree' for his wife's late mother; a poem for Robert Fitzgerald, a deceased colleague at Harvard; and 'The Stone Verdict', an elegy for his father. But the most powerful of all are 'Clearances', a sequence of eight sonnets, elegies in memory of his mother, who died in 1984. Some deal simply and movingly with ordinary, everyday experiences, such as peeling potatoes together or folding sheets; another deals with the scene at the death-bed; yet another is written from the vantage-point of the house of the dead, drawn with mundane realism, which gives it a surreal quality. Altogether they are a moving series of poems on the relationship between mothers and sons.

'Seeing Things'

Seeing Things, published in 1991, in some

ways sees a return to the concerns of the early Heaney. It deals with personal vision and personal history rather than with politics or historical issues. He returns to poems of childhood memories: football, fishing, sailing, skating; memories of an old bicycle, of fair-days, of rat poison in an outhouse, of first firing a gun; memories of Glanmore, revisited in a sequence of seven sonnets. He is going back, making a 'journey back into the heartland of the ordinary.' But here Heaney is interested in seeing the ordinary in a different way, looking more deeply into things, as in 'Field of Vision'. He is still the observer whom we met in the early Heaney but now also the visionary, exploring the significance of these observations. This results in a new, fresh 'seeing', a new excitement, as in 'Fosterling'.

> Me waiting until I was nearly fifty
> To credit marvels.

Prose

Séamus Heaney has lectured and written widely about poets and poetry. These collected prose pieces were published in *Preoccupations: Selected Prose, 1968–78* (1980) and *The Government of the Tongue* (1988).

In 1988 Heaney was elected professor of poetry at the University of Oxford, and in 1995 his lectures were published as *The Redress of Poetry*. In 1995 he was awarded the Nobel Prize for Literature.

John Hewitt

John Hewitt was born in Belfast in 1907, of devout Methodist ancestry; he had a grandfather who boasted that 'no Hewitt ever married a Papist or kept a public-house.' Educated at Methodist College, Belfast, and Queen's University, the young Hewitt turned out to be of more liberal mind and more independent of spirit. Perhaps it was a symbolic omen that, through some family disagreement, he was not baptised into the Methodist Church. As he himself rationalised

it (in *The Bell*, autumn 1953),

> this has given me a sense of liberation, spiritually I have felt myself to be my own man, the ultimate Protestant. And when to this I add the fact that since our family doctor, a friendly old man in a frock-coat and with a pointed beard, had no great belief in vaccination, and going through the secular ritual with me, deliberately used an innocent concoction, which left no scar, I have often felt doubly free from the twin disciplines of organised religion and science. In argument this has been advantageous, as I can quite honestly cry plague on both their houses, and, unimplicated, set up my own mythology and magic in opposition to either.

But his religious upbringing made him suspicious of Catholicism and of the influence of Rome in politics. Though he was not bigoted in a personal sense—as is revealed in the poems about his Catholic friends and his awakening interest in Irish history and stories through these boyhood acquaintances— nevertheless he is a product of his particular tradition, as 'The Green Shoot' shows. His own political ideas were influenced, particularly in the nineteen-thirties, by the notion of 'regionalism'. This was the idea that in modern states, with remote, centralised government and increased bureaucracy, loyalty to one's local region, with its history, traditions, and culture, was all that was necessary for a sense of political identity.

This loyalty to Ulster is paramount in his understanding of his own identity.

> I'm an Ulsterman, of planter stock. I was born in the island of Ireland, so secondly I'm an Irishman. I was born in the British archipelago and English is my native tongue, so I am British. The British archipelago consists of offshore islands to the continent of Europe, so I'm European. This is my hierarchy of values and so far as I am concerned, anyone who omits one step in that sequence of values is falsifying the situation. (*Irish Times*, 4 July 1974)

All his life, Hewitt was devoted to Ulster

culture and to understanding the rights and wrongs of its history. His social views were radical, influenced by Marx and by English radical thinkers such as the Chartist movement and William Morris. The influence of his nonconformist father—a devout Methodist but also a liberal thinker—had some part in his development. There were photographs of Keir Hardie and Jim Larkin in the Hewitt kitchen when he was growing up. In the thirties Hewitt and his wife, Roberta, were active in left politics and in the Labour Party. Indeed he always believed that his left-wing politics were instrumental in denying him promotion to the directorship of the Belfast Museum and Art Gallery, where he worked from 1930 to 1957, eventually becoming deputy director; so he moved to England in 1957, as director of the Herbert Art Gallery, Coventry, but returned to Belfast on his retirement in 1972.

Hewitt managed a considerable output of writing during his working life and in retirement. As well as literary criticism and books on art and artists he published fourteen volumes of poetry. These range from *Conacre* (1943) to *Freehold* (1986) and include *The Planter and the Gael* (1970)—a collection he shared with John Montague and in which the two poets are seen as speaking for the two different traditions. In the main, Hewitt's poems deal with the culture and heritage of Ireland; the political and religious divisions in Ulster; childhood memories and personal themes; and his justly famous keen-eyed nature poetry capturing the life of the Glens of Antrim. He died in 1987.

John Keats

A brief view of a brief life

John Keats was born at Finsbury, near London, on 31 October 1795, the eldest child of Frances Jennings Keats and Thomas Keats, a livery-stable keeper. Two brothers, George and Thomas, were born in 1797 and 1799, respectively, and a sister, Frances (Fanny), in

1803. A fifth child, Edward, was born in 1801 but died in 1802.

From 1803 to 1811 John and his brothers attended Rev. John Clarke's school in an old Georgian country house at Enfield, north London. John Keats was a small boy (fully grown he was only five feet tall) but he was athletic and liked sports, and, though he had a quick temper, he was generally popular.

Clarke's was a liberal, progressive boarding-school, which did not allow the flogging or 'fagging' (junior boys acting as servants to the older boys) common at the time. The pupils, who were mostly of middle-class background and destined for the professions, received a well-rounded education. They had their own garden plots to cultivate; interest in music and the visual arts was also encouraged, as well as the usual study of history, geography, arithmetic, grammar, French, and Latin. Keats received a particularly good classical Latin education. He was able to compose a prose version of the *Aeneid*, Virgil's long epic poem. Classical mythology is used in Keats's own poetry, particularly in the long narrative poems *Endymion, Hyperion,* and *The Fall of Hyperion,* and also in 'Ode on a Grecian Urn'.

Keats was both helped and befriended by the headmaster's son, Charles Cowden Clarke, now a young assistant master, who lent him books such as Spenser's *The Faerie Queene.* He also introduced him to the *Examiner,* a weekly paper that advocated reform both in politics and poetry, edited by Leigh Hunt, a supporter of romantic poets, especially Shelley and Byron, and later to become an influence on Keats's poetic career.

In 1804 Keats's father died in a riding accident. Frances Keats married again, to William Rawlings, but the marriage was unhappy. The children went to live with their grandparents, John and Alice Jennings, at Enfield. John Jennings died in 1805, leaving about £8,000 to the Keats children. This was a substantial sum (£50 was a typical annual wage for a worker at that time); but the will was complicated and led to legal disputes.

In 1810 Frances Keats, who had left William Rawlings some years earlier and had begun to drink heavily, returned to look after the children, but she died from tuberculosis in March. Two guardians were appointed for the children, one of them Richard Abbey, a tea merchant and respected public figure. Both George and Tom later worked for a time as clerks in his office, and, apart from four years at school, Fanny Keats lived with the Abbeys until she was twenty-one. It was a strict household and she was discouraged from visiting her brothers. Abbey proved notoriously mean about money, and Keats had great difficulty getting funds from his inheritance.

Keats left school in 1811 to begin an apprenticeship as a surgeon with Thomas Hammond. This was then the manual side of the medical profession, involving bone-setting, tooth-pulling, and amputation and was considered socially inferior to becoming a physician, which would have entailed expensive university education. After some years as an apprentice, in 1815 Keats registered as a student at Guy's Hospital, London, and attended lectures in anatomy, physiology, and chemistry.

In May 1816 the sonnet 'O Solitude' was the first of Keats's poems to be published, by Hunt in the *Examiner*. In June, Keats wrote 'To One Long in City Pent'.

He qualified in July 1816 and was licensed to practise as a surgeon and apothecary; but by now he had developed an aversion to surgery (then performed without anaesthetic, in primitive conditions), and he devoted more of his time to writing poetry. His early poems reflect liberal attitudes and a rebellious outlook on life. He celebrated in verse Hunt's release from prison (he had called the Prince Regent, the future King George IV, 'a fat Adonis of forty,' among other things).

Some of Keats's poems show a romantic idealisation of women. He also formed a strong aversion to Christianity, as a poem of December 1816, 'Written in Disgust of Vulgar Superstition', demonstrates. In October he composed 'On First Looking into Chapman's Homer'. He made a number of important acquaintances and friendships, including Benjamin Haydon, an unsuccessful painter, John Reynolds, a fellow-poet, with whom he exchanged many letters, and Joseph Severn, a poet and painter, who became a supporter and friend.

In December 'Sleep and Poetry' was written. Keats told Abbey, who was not best pleased, that he was gong to be a poet, not a surgeon.

In March 1817 Haydon took Keats to see the Parthenon Marbles (called the 'Elgin Marbles' in England) at the British Museum—huge fragments of classical sculpture taken by Thomas Bruce, Earl of Elgin, from the ruins of the Parthenon, with the permission of the Turks after they had conquered Athens. (Their return is now being demanded by the Greeks.) Keats was fascinated by the imagery. Perhaps the 'heifer lowing at the skies' in 'Ode on a Grecian Urn' may have been suggested by a procession in one of the marbles.

Keats's first book, *Poems,* was published in 1817 but did not sell well, even though it was favourably received. In April, Keats left London to work on *Endymion*. In September he met Charles Armitage Brown, a wealthy educated man who became a friend and patron. The 4,000-line poem *Endymion* was completed by the autumn. It tells the story of Endymion, a typical romantic hero, who achieves perfect love and immortality through loving and being loved by the goddess of the moon, Cynthia. There are two main themes: the search for love and the quest for poetic achievement. The opening lines of the poem are famous:

> A thing of beauty is a joy for ever:
> Its loveliness increases; it will never
> Pass into nothingness

Keats began to express his ideas on poetry. From his letter to Benjamin Bailey of 22 November 1817 we get some idea of the value he placed on the imagination, the importance of feelings, and the central place of beauty in poetry.

> I am certain of nothing but of the holiness of the Heart's affections and the truth of Imagination—What the imagination seizes as Beauty must be truth—whether it existed before or not—for I have the same Idea of all our Passions as of Love, they are all in their sublime, creative of essential Beauty … the Imagination may be compared to Adam's dream—he awoke and found it truth … O for a Life of Sensations rather than of Thoughts!

In a letter to George and Tom Keats the following month Keats talked about the essential attitude or operational mode necessary to be a great poet, which he called 'negative capability', 'that is when man is capable of being in uncertainties, Mysteries, doubts, without any irritable reaching after fact and reason.' He began to denigrate the current classical tradition of correctness.

In December he met William Wordsworth and Charles Lamb at a dinner given by Haydon. He greatly admired Wordsworth, though the feeling was not reciprocated.

Some time in January or February 1818 Keats wrote 'When I have fears that I may cease to be', a sonnet dealing with three major concerns in his life—love, death, and his poetry. In April *Endymion* was published, to very hostile reviews, in particular from the influential *Blackwood's Magazine* and the *Quarterly Review*. In May his brother Tom became ill with tuberculosis; George lost his job and was forced to emigrate to America.

In the spring of 1818 Keats wrote 'Isabella', a poetic translation of a story from Boccaccio's *Decameron*. It is a gruesome story of love and death with an unhappy ending. Isabella's brothers murder her lover, Lorenzo; he appears to her in a dream and tells her where he is buried. She digs up his head, hides it in a pot of basil, and weeps over it every day. Eventually her brothers find it and take it away and she dies of a broken heart.

From June to August, Keats toured the Lake District and Scotland with Brown. Then he returned to nurse Tom, who died on 1

December. During this winter of nursing, Keats worked on *Hyperion,* an epic story from classical mythology featuring the overthrow of the old gods by the young Olympians. Its themes are change, progress, and the victory of youth and beauty. But he abandoned it after Tom's death, and it was published unfinished in 1820 as *Hyperion: A Fragment.* It was much praised by Keats's contemporaries, including Byron and Shelley.

In September 1818 Keats met Fanny Brawne. She and her mother rented part of Wentworth Place, Hampstead, where Keats's friends Charles and Maria Dilke lived. She became the great love of his life, and they became engaged in the autumn of 1819. When Keats was dying he wrote to Brown: 'I can bear to die—I cannot bear to leave her.'

1819 was an extraordinary year, the most productive of Keats's career. He was writing mature poems, sometimes dashing them off at great speed. In January he composed 'The Eve of St Agnes', a long narrative about the carrying off of a girl by her lover. This incorporated the legend of St Agnes, patron saint of young virgins, which stated that girls would dream of their future husband on 20 January, the Eve of St Agnes, provided certain ritual ceremonies were carried out.

In February he worked on 'The Eve of St Mark', an unfinished poem set in the Middle Ages. In April 'La Belle Dame sans Merci' was written. Between April and May the five great odes were written, also known as the Spring Odes: 'Ode to Psyche', 'Ode to a Nightingale', 'Ode on a Grecian Urn', 'Ode on Melancholy', and 'Ode to Indolence'. Keats's poetic reputation today chiefly rests on these, though their power was scarcely noticed when they were written, even by critics like Lamb and Shelley, as the long poem was then in fashion.

Keats was deeply in love with Fanny Brawne, as we can see from his letters. But, paradoxically, he tried to stay away from her, perhaps fearing that conflict between the real and the ideal that he deals with in his great poetry.

If I were to see you today it would destroy the half comfortable sullenness I enjoy at present into downright perplexities. I love you too much to venture to Hampstead, I feel it is not paying a visit, but venturing into a fire ... Knowing well that my life must be passed in fatigue and trouble, I have been endeavouring to wean myself from you.

From June to September Keats worked on 'Lamia', a long narrative poem, his third attempt at the theme of the sexual encounter between mortal man and immortal woman. This union symbolises the human being's desire to perpetuate eternally the moment of passion, the experience of love. Here, as in 'La Belle Dame sans Merci', the human hero ends up alone and abandoned; Lamia, the enchanter, is forced to return to her original state of being—a serpent—and Lycius, the lover, pines and dies. Of the three such poems, only *Endymion* has a happy ending.

Keats then returned to the theme of Hyperion, composing *The Fall of Hyperion*, which he also had to abandon unfinished. He worked on two plays, *Otho the Great* and *King Stephen*, which were undertaken because of financial need, since Keats could not get his hands on enough of his inheritance to enable him to marry Fanny Brawne. He talked of going to sea as a ship's doctor in order to make money. With the famous actor Edmund Kean in mind for the principal role, Brown and Keats collaborated on *Otho the Great*, a Gothic story of deception, unhappy love, and death, involving the family of the tenth-century ruler who became Holy Roman Emperor. Drury Lane Theatre had accepted it, but when Kean left to perform in America they refused to go ahead with it. In the meantime Keats had begun work on *King Stephen*, another mediaeval play dealing with courage and chivalry. But he abandoned it after the disappointment of *Otho the Great*.

'Bright Star', the sonnet to Fanny Brawne, dates from this time, as does the ode 'To Autumn', considered by some critics to be the best of the year's work.

In 1820 Keats's brother George returned briefly from America, as he had had a financial setback and needed to raise some money. It is suspected that John Keats put himself further into debt on George's account.

In February Keats suffered a severe lung haemorrhage, the significance of which was apparent to him, as he wrote to Brown: 'I know the colour of that blood;—it is arterial blood;—I cannot be deceived in that colour;—that drop of blood is my death-warrant.' Indeed, it was the beginning of the end. That summer he spent being cared for by, and falling out with, various friends, including Brown and the Hunts, and eventually he ended up in the care of Mrs Brawne and Fanny, who nursed him in their home at Wentworth Place.

In July a volume of his poetry, *Poems, 1820,* was published, which included 'Lamia', 'Isabella', 'The Eve of St Agnes', and other poems.

The Shelleys invited him to Pisa, and, as the doctors were urging him to avoid the English winter, he agreed to go. But Abbey refused him funds, and he was forced to sell the copyright of his poems. In September he set sail on the *Maria Crowther*, accompanied by his friend Thomas Severn as companion and nurse. After a violent stormy passage and quarantine at Naples, they finally reached Rome in November and took rooms at 26 Piazza di Spagna. Though ably nursed by Severn, Keats deteriorated throughout the winter, and he died on 23 February 1821, aged twenty-five. He is buried in the Protestant cemetery in Rome, having requested as an inscription for his tombstone: *Here lies one whose name was writ in water.*

Philip Larkin

Philip Arthur Larkin was born in Coventry in 1922, the son of Eva Larkin and Sydney Larkin, the city treasurer. He attended King Henry VIII High School, where he was an avid reader and had some poems and humorous prose printed in the school magazine. In 1940 he went to study English at St John's College, Oxford. He is remembered as a shy, introverted person with a speech impediment. He was a prominent member of the Jazz Club and the English Society. As it was wartime, Larkin expected to be called up, but he failed his medical and so managed to spend a full three years at Oxford. Among his contemporaries were John Wain and Kingsley Amis.

In 1943 Larkin was awarded a first-class degree in English language and literature and the same year had three poems included in *Oxford Poetry, 1942–43*. From 1943 to 1946 he was librarian at Wellington, Shropshire, where he reorganised the library and managed to write a good deal. It was here that he first became involved in a relationship with Ruth Bowman.

Some of his poems were included in the anthology *Poetry from Oxford in Wartime*, published in 1945 by Fortune Press, which also brought out Larkin's first collection, *The North Ship*, the same year. In 1946 his first novel, *Jill*, was published. In September that year he took up a position as assistant librarian at the University College of Leicester. There he met Monica Jones, a lecturer in the English Department, with whom he began a relationship that was to last, on and off, for the rest of his life.

His second novel, *A Girl in Winter*, was published in 1947. In 1948 his father died, and Larkin went back to live with his mother. He became engaged to Ruth Bowman, but the engagement was broken off in 1950. In that year Larkin went to Belfast to become sub-librarian at Queen's University. He enjoyed living in Belfast, and he wrote a good deal.

In April 1951 Larkin had twenty of his early poems privately printed as *XX Poems*. These included 'Wedding-Wind' and 'At Grass' (both included in his later volume, *The Less Deceived*). His emotional life became a bit of a tangle. He developed particular relationships with Patsy Strang and with Winifred Arnott,

who worked in the library. And Monica Jones came to visit.

In 1955 his collection *The Less Deceived* was published. This included the poem 'Toads', a protest against the daily grind of work. Going for interview for the job of librarian at the University of Hull later that year, Larkin feared the board would have seen his poem as representative of his attitude to his job; but he was appointed, and, with brief absences, he spent the rest of his life in this position. Here he met Maeve Brennan.

In 1964 *The Whitsun Weddings* was published, and in 1965 Larkin was awarded the Queen's Gold Medal for Poetry. *All That Jazz*, a selection of his jazz reviews, was published in 1970. He was a visiting fellow at All Souls College, Oxford, for the academic year 1970/71, and he edited *The Oxford Book of Twentieth-Century Verse* (1973).

In 1974 *High Windows* was published, and Larkin bought his first house, opposite the university, where he lived for the rest of his life. His mother died in 1977. In 1982 Monica Jones became ill, and Larkin brought her to live at his home.

Required Writing: Miscellaneous Pieces, 1955–82 was published in 1983. In 1984 Larkin refused the offer of appointment as Poet Laureate. He died on 2 December 1985.

Michael Longley

Michael Longley was born in Belfast on 27 July 1939, of English parents. His father, Richard, who features in the poems 'Wounds', 'Wreaths', and 'Last Requests', fought in the trenches in the First World War and was gassed, wounded, decorated, and promoted to the rank of captain.

Between the wars the Longleys moved to Belfast, where Richard was a commercial traveller for an English firm of furniture manufacturers. He enlisted again in the Second World War, ending with the rank of major. In *Tuppenny Stung*, a short collection of autobiographical chapters published in 1994, Longley described the events of his childhood; his twin brother, Peter, and older sister, Wendy; his ingenious and versatile father ('that rare thing, an Englishman accepted and trusted by Ulstermen'); his crippled and temperamental mother ('It has taken me a long time to forgive her that atmosphere of uncertainty, its anxieties, even fears'); his irrepressible English grandfather, 'Grandpa George'; and the usual menagerie of eccentric relatives we all accumulate. He describes his primary and secondary education and the forces of his early cultural formation: Protestant schoolboy fears of the dark savageries supposedly practised by Catholics, an English education system dismissive of Irish culture and history, and Protestant Belfast's fear and resentment of the Republic. His early education and local socialisation made him aware of conflicting classes and religions and of the duality of Irish identity.

Later he was educated at the Royal Belfast Academical Institution and in 1958 went to Trinity College, Dublin, where the student population at the time consisted in the main of southern and northern Protestants, middle and upper-class English, and a scattering of southern Catholics who defied the Catholic Church's ban on attendance. He studied classics and wrote poetry but felt very under-read in English literature until taken in hand by his friend and young fellow-poet Derek Mahon.

> We inhaled with our untipped Sweet Afton cigarettes MacNeice, Crane, Dylan Thomas, Yeats, Larkin, Lawrence, Graves, Ted Hughes, Stevens, Cummings, Richard Wilbur, Robert Lowell, as well as Rimbaud, Baudelaire, Brecht, Rilke—higgledepiggledy, in any order. We scanned the journals and newspapers for poems written yesterday. When Larkin's 'The Whitsun Weddings' first appeared in *Encounter*, Mahon steered me past the documentary details, which as an aspiring lyricist I found irritating, to the poem's resonant, transcendental moments. He introduced me to George Herbert who thrilled

me as though he were a brilliant contemporary published that very week by the Dolmen Press. Herbert, thanks to Mahon, is a beneficent influence in my first collection and provides the stanzaic templates for two of its more ambitious poems.

Longley first worked as a teacher in Dublin, London, and Belfast. From 1964 he became one of the group of young writers fostered by Philip Hobsbaum at Queen's University, Belfast, though Longley felt that his poetry didn't fit in particularly well.

> From the beginning Hobsbaum made it clear that his stars were Séamus Heaney and Stewart Parker, who was teaching in the States at this time. Hobsbaum's aesthetic demanded gritty particularity and unrhetorical utterance. Heaney's work fitted the bill especially well: at the second or third meeting which I attended a sheet of his poems was discussed—'Digging' and 'Death of a Naturalist' (it was called 'End of a Naturalist' then).
>
> By this time I was beginning to enjoy what was for me as a lapsed Classicist a new experience—practical criticism. But I didn't much care for The Group aesthetic or, to be honest, the average poem which won approval. I believed that poetry should be polished, metrical and rhymed; oblique rather than head-on; imagistic and symbolic rather than rawly factual, rhetorical rather than documentary. I felt like a Paleface among a tribe of Redskins. Although I have since modified my ideas, I still think that despite the rigours of practical criticism and the kitchen heat of the discussions, many Group poems tended to be underdone.

Longley worked for the Arts Council of Northern Ireland between 1970 and 1991, when he took early retirement. His work for the arts was driven by a number of guiding principles, among which were the nurturing of indigenous talent (he used to ask 'How much of what we are doing differentiates us from Bolton or Wolverhampton?'), support for the artists, not just the arts, and the need to transcend class barriers and bring the arts, at an affordable price, to the working class. He was a champion of cultural pluralism, fostering the artistic expression of both sides of the religious and political divide. In fact the first event Longley organised for the Arts Council was 'The Planter and the Gael', a poetry reading tour by John Hewitt and John Montague, in which each poet read poems exploring his particular experience of Ulster. So it was not surprising that Michael Longley should be invited to join the Cultural Traditions Group at its launch in 1988. Its aims are, as he has written, 'to encourage in Northern Ireland the acceptance and understanding of cultural diversity; to replace political belligerence with cultural pride.'

His vision of Ulster culture has always sought to include its many different strands and influences and so to encourage a unique hybrid rather than separate, antagonistic cultures. As he wrote elsewhere, 'imaginative Ulstermen (and by extension, Irishmen) could be the beneficiaries of a unique cultural confluence which embraces the qualities of the Irish, the Scottish, the English and the Anglo-Irish.'

In his time Longley fostered a great range and diversity of artists, from traditional singers and fiddlers to painters, drama groups, and photographers. For the last nine years of his career with the Arts Council he was combined arts director, overseeing traditional arts, youth arts, and community arts, while concentrating on his chief preoccupation—literature. Here he directed Arts Council money towards publication, attempting to ensure that as many writers as possible got into print.

No Continuing City (1969), Longley's first collection, is known for its technically accomplished and learned poetry. Among its concerns are poets and poetry and nature, but it is best known for the erudite, witty and sophisticated love poetry, almost in the metaphysical tradition. *An Exploded View* (1973) continues to deal with poetry and poetic issues. Nature is also a major preoccupation. ('Badger' is from this volume.) The collection does respond briefly to the upsurge of violence in Northern Ireland around this time. In 'Wounds' the violence is seen in the broad perspective of international conflict. A great number of the poems focus on an alternative life in the west of Ireland. 'Carrigskeewaun' and 'Poteen' are among these. This attachment of Longley's for County Mayo forms the central focus of his third volume, *Man Lying on a Wall* (1976).

The Echo Fate (1979) demonstrates Longley's now-established bifocal view: on Belfast and Mayo. He confronts the political violence in its stark everyday settings in 'Wreaths' and explores the war experiences of his father as a perspective on this violence in 'Last Requests'. He also explores the folklore, ethos and culture of the west of Ireland and finds a bleak unconscious parallel between its crude violence and that of Belfast in 'Self-Heal'.

Gorse Fires (1991) is centred on Longley's adopted second home of Carrigskeewaun in County Mayo. But it also includes poems on the Holocaust, the Second World War, and the Spanish Civil War. Interspersed with these are some free translations from Homer's *Odyssey*, focusing on Odysseus' return to his home and interpreted by some critics as having strong if oblique relevance to Longley's own home province. 'Laertes' is from this sequence.

The Ghost Orchid (1995), Longley's sixth volume, continues with translations from Homer and the Roman love poet Ovid. He continues to write perceptively and sensitively about the delicacy of nature, and constructs exquisite Larkin-type poems about elements of Chinese and Japanese culture. Northern Ireland does not feature here directly, though some poems have relevant resonances of conflict. 'Ceasefire' is from this volume.

Tuppenny Stung (1994) is a collection of autobiographical chapters, previously published in periodicals or delivered as lectures and dated variously from 1976 to 1992.

Michael Longley is a fellow of the Royal Society of Literature and a member of Aosdána. He is married to the critic and academic Edna Longley.

John Montague

John Montague was born in New York in 1929, the third son of Mary Carney and James Montague, both of whom had recently emigrated from Ireland. In 1933 John and his older brothers were sent back to live with relatives, John to his aunts on the remainder of the family farm at Garvaghy, County Tyrone. The poem 'The Cage' features these two poles of his early experience, New York and Garvaghy.

Montague was a good student, winning scholarships to St Patrick's College, Armagh, and University College, Dublin, where he obtained an MA in Anglo-Irish literature. His youth in County Tyrone and his Dublin education are described in some of the autobiographical pieces in *The Figure in the Cave and Other Essays* (1989). Between 1953 and 1956 he travelled widely in the United States, attending postgraduate school at Yale and the universities of Indiana, Iowa, and California. During this period he became acquainted with many well-known American writers, such as Robert Lowell, John Crowe Ransom, Richard Wilbur, and Allen Ginsberg.

Montague has worked as a teacher and writer for most of his life. He has taught in the University of California at Berkeley and the State University of New York, at the University of Paris, at University College, Dublin, and from 1972 to 1988 at University College, Cork. A prolific poet, his first collection of verse, *Forms of Exile*, was published in 1958. He is best known for his work on the history, traditions and problems of Northern Ireland. Poems on that subject can be found in his collections *Poisoned Lands* (1961), *A Chosen Light* (1967), and *The Dead Kingdom* (1984); but his most famous collection on that theme is *The Rough Field* (1972), where he investigates his personal and historical experience of Northern Ireland. He examines the disintegration of rural life and traditions, continuity and change, and the colonial history of the region. On this subject he toured with John Hewitt in 1970 and 1971 in a joint poetry-reading show entitled 'The Planter and the Gael', with Montague as the voice of the Gael.

But he writes of other subjects too: about nature in *A Slow Dance* (1975) and about love in *The Great Cloak* (1978). His poetry has won many prizes. He edited *The Faber Book of Irish Verse* (1974) and has also written two works of fiction, *Death of a Chieftain* and *The Lost Notebook*.

Eiléan Ní Chuilleanáin

Born in Cork, daughter of the children's writer Éilis Dillon and the veteran republican and academic Cormac Ó Cuilleanáin, Eiléan Ní Chuilleanáin was educated at University College, Cork, and the University of Oxford. She is a fellow of Trinity College, Dublin, where she teaches mediaeval and renaissance English.

Her first collection of poems, *Acts and Monuments* (1972), won the Patrick Kavanagh Award. Many of the poems focus on the relationship between human beings and the natural world, showing human fragility against the uncaring Earth, and depict nature, in particular the sea, callously obliterating human endeavours. The poems feature many voyages, symbolic journeys such as those of Noah and Odysseus, and the soul's journey. So the prevailing image of the human being that comes across from this volume is that of the isolated wanderer, a searcher on a quest, constantly at the mercy of greater powers. With this elemental view of the world it is no surprise that myths feature prominently in the poems: Odysseus, Theseus, Fionn, and Christian and pagan stories—a blend of classical, biblical and Irish myths. In this collection there is little enough on the theme of female identity, which comes to be developed in her later poetry. Yet we do meet in these poems isolated female characters, strong women of courageous and independent nature.

And by contrast there are some confused and inept men, as if Ní Chuilleanáin is attempting to overturn our accepted presumptions about sex roles or at least blur the distinctions between the sexes. 'Swineherd' is from this volume.

Ní Chuilleanáin's other volumes of poetry are *Site of Ambush* (1975), *The Second Voyage*, a volume of selected poems (1977 and 1986), *The Rose Geranium* (1981), and *The Magdalene Sermon* (1984). She is the editor of *Irish Women: Image and Achievement* (1985).

Siegfried Sassoon

Siegfried Sassoon was born in England in 1886 and educated at Marlborough and the University of Cambridge.

He enlisted on the first day of the First World War; he was awarded the Military Cross for bravery, which he later threw away. The changes in his poetry during this period serve as a barometer of his thinking on the war. His early poetry, like that of Rupert Brooke, welcomed with excitement the challenge of war; but after his experience of the fighting at the front he adopted a more realistic attitude and recorded with sympathy the real misery of mutilation and death. This attitude later turned to bleak satire, displaying his contempt for the war leadership and for the patriotic cant that encouraged young men to make this sacrifice. He is best known for these satirical poems of disillusionment, such as 'The Hero', 'They', 'Base Details', and 'The General'.

In July 1917 he made a now-famous public protest to his commanding officer, that the war was being 'deliberately prolonged by those who had the power to end it.' Sent home as shell-shocked, he was sent to hospital to recover. There he organised a public protest against the war; there too he met and encouraged Wilfred Owen. But the tone of Sassoon's poetry did not make it popular at that time. Despite his protests he was sent

back to the war, first to the Middle East, where he was promoted captain, and then back to the Western Front in May 1918. He suffered a head wound and was again returned home, one of the few poets to survive the First World War.

It is this escape, this sense of freedom, that is celebrated in 'Everyone Sang'. The poem was written in April 1919, and Sassoon, in *Siegfried's Journey*, describes how it came to be written.

> One evening in the middle of April I had an experience which seems worth describing for those who are interested in methods of poetic production. It was a sultry spring night. I was feeling dull-minded and depressed, for no assignable reason. After sitting lethargically in the ground-floor room for about three hours after dinner, I came to the conclusion that there was nothing for it but to take my useless brain to bed. On my way from the arm-chair to the door I stood by the writing-table. A few words had floated into my head as though from nowhere. In those days I was always on the look-out for a lyric—I wish I could say the same for my present self—so I picked up a pencil and wrote the words on a sheet of note-paper. Without sitting down, I added a second line. It was as if I were remembering rather than thinking. In this mindless, recollecting manner I wrote down my poem in a few minutes. When it was finished I read it through, with no sense of elation, merely wondering how I had come to be writing a poem when feeling so stupid. I then went heavily upstairs and fell asleep ...

In 1919 Sassoon became literary editor of the *Daily Herald* and continued to write poetry. Volumes published in the twenties finally began to make him a reputation. His later poetry of the forties and sixties shows an attachment to nature and an interest in religion. His reputation was further enhanced with three semi-autobiographical books, *Memoirs of a Fox-Hunting Man* (1928), *Memoirs of an Infantry Officer* (1930), and *Sherston's Progress* (1936). In 1938 he published *The Old Century and Seven More Years,* the story of his youth. *The Weald of Youth* (1942) and *Siegfried's Journey* (1945) brought this story up to about 1920. He died in 1967.

William Shakespeare

A brief overview of a literary life

William Shakespeare was born in April 1564 in Stratford-upon-Avon, Warwickshire, the son of Mary Arden, daughter of a gentleman-farmer, and John Shakespeare, a glover. John Shakespeare became a man of some importance in Stratford, eventually becoming the equivalent of mayor and achieving considerable wealth and property in the fifteen-seventies but losing it again in the eighties, when his fortunes took a downturn for some unknown reason.

William Shakespeare probably attended the local grammar school; he never went to university but was self-educated to a very high standard. He was an avid reader. There is a tradition, which cannot be substantiated, that he was for a time an assistant country schoolmaster. Certainly he was familiar with Latin authors used in the grammar schools of his time: Plautus, Ovid, and Seneca.

> Lucius, what book is that she tosseth so?
> Grandsire, 'tis Ovid's *Metamorphoses*
> (*Titus Andronicus,* IV, i)

However, Shakespeare was also an 'out-of-doors' man. From the evidence of his writing it seems he was addicted to sports of all kinds: deer-hunting, hare-coursing, hawking, bowls, and archery.

> I do follow here in the chase, not like a hound
> that hunts, but one that fills up the cry.
> (*Othello,* II, iii)

> When the wind is southerly, I know a hawk
> from a handsaw
> (*Hamlet,* II, ii)

In November 1582, at the age of eighteen, Shakespeare married Anne Hathaway, eight or nine years his senior, and six months later their first daughter, Susanna, was born. In 1585 a twin son and daughter, Hamnet and Judith, were born. Hamnet died, aged eleven, in August 1596; Shakespeare wrote his grief for his only son into the play he was composing at the time, *King John* (III, iv):

> Grief fills the room up of my absent child,
> Lies in his bed, walks up and down with me,
> Puts on his pretty looks, repeats his words,
> Remembers me of all his gracious parts ...

Shakespeare left Stratford to follow a career in acting and the theatre, though there is no definite information about which company he was with or exactly when he went to London. But we know that he was working with Lord Strange's company in London in 1592. In 1595, when the company was renamed the Chamberlain's Men and organised on a shareholding basis, Shakespeare was wealthy enough to become one of the eight shareholders.

His early attempts at comedy, tragedy, and history—*The Comedy of Errors, Titus Andronicus,* and *Henry VI*—were popular successes. But, more importantly, he had acquired a patron in the young Henry Wriothesley, Earl of Southampton, to whom he dedicated his narrative poems, *Venus and Adonis* (1593) and *The Rape of Lucrece* (1594). It was rumoured that Wriothesley's financial bequest of a thousand pounds for this gesture enabled Shakespeare to buy into the Chamberlain's Men, thereby securing his financial future, as it was the acting company that generally held the copyright in a play. This meant that Shakespeare had continuous remuneration for both writing and performance. And write he did, at least thirty-seven plays in about twenty years, among them *Romeo and Juliet, The Merchant of Venice,* and *Julius Caesar,* as well as the tragedies *Hamlet, Othello, King Lear,* and *Macbeth.* He also wrote the long narrative poems and over 150 sonnets. So he was a prolific writer as well as an actor and producer.

Shakespeare achieved fame as well as fortune in his lifetime, performing twice as frequently as any other company at court. With his wealth he bought up property in his home town, to which he retired in 1613. But his retirement was brief, and he died in April 1616.

Percy Bysshe Shelley

Shelley was born on 4 August 1792, the son of a country gentleman and member of Parliament. He was educated at Stow, where he was very unhappy, bullied, and known as 'Mad Shelley', and then at the University of Oxford. Still unhappy and rebellious, he was expelled for jointly writing a pamphlet *The Necessity of Atheism*. In August 1811 he eloped with and married the sixteen-year old friend of his sister, Harriet Westbrook, with whom he had two children.

The period 1811–14 saw Shelley embark on a period of frantic travelling, speaking and writing on the need for radical social and political reforms. He spoke at public meetings in Dublin and published *An Address to the Irish People* (1812) and *Proposals*. He also agitated for land reclamation in Wales and campaigned for a free press and other democratic reforms. He published a pamphlet on vegetarianism. A revolutionary in thought, he was anti-religion and anti-monarchy. His early thinking on politics and poetry is contained in his poem *Queen Mab* (1813), which became a very popular text among the radical working-class movement, the Chartists.

His marriage failed, and in 1814 he eloped with Mary Godwin (who later wrote *Frankenstein*). Accompanied by Mary's fifteen-year-old step-sister, Claire Clairmont, they fled to Switzerland for a time. This trio became the nucleus of the unconventional Shelley family.

During the period 1814–18 Shelley wrote numerous pamphlets, essays, and poems, of which 'Alastor' and 'Laon and Cythna' (published as 'The Revolt of Islam') are

perhaps the best known. He met and developed friendships with Keats, Hazlitt and other literary figures and visited Byron in Switzerland.

In 1816 his wife, Harriet, committed suicide. Shelley immediately married Mary but was devastated on being refused custody of his children. Constantly in debt, despite a fortune left him by his grandfather, and dogged by poor health, he emigrated with his wife to Italy in 1818, 'leaving behind his sonnet "Ozymandias" and a mass of unpaid bills' (as the *Oxford Companion to English Literature* puts it).

The next two years were the most traumatic and yet the most creative of his life. He endured extraordinary family misfortune. In the summer of 1818 his one-year-old daughter, Clara, died of dysentery at Venice. The family spent the winter at Naples, where he wrote the unhappy 'Stanzas Written in Dejection near Naples'. In June 1819 their three-year-old son William died at Rome, and Mary had a nervous breakdown. They lived for a time at Florence, where 'Ode to the West Wind' was begun, before finally settling at Pisa in January 1820. It was here that some of Shelley's best-known lyrics were written, such as the ode 'To a Skylark' and 'The Cloud'. *Prometheus Unbound,* the poetic drama that is one of his chief claims to fame, was finished. Inspired by the Peterloo massacres in England, he wrote a satire condemning the government, *The Mask of Anarchy*. He mourned the death of Keats in the elegy 'Adonais' (1821). These titles are but a small representative sample of his fluid creativity at this time.

From his famous essay 'Defence of Poetry' (1821) can be gleaned some idea of Shelley's theory of poetry. Taking a sort of religious view of nature, he literally believed that there was a spirit in nature, transforming the world. It is to this spirit he appeals in 'Ode to the West Wind'. He understood the role of the poet in society to be that of prophet or visionary; he felt that poetry had to do with feelings rather than the intellect and that spontaneity rather than planning was the key to creating good poetry, as the mind works best in flashes of spontaneity. His critics would complain that he is too spontaneous and too emotional, that he verges at times on sentimentality and depressed self-pity.

In July 1822 Shelley, at the age of thirty, was drowned when caught in a storm at sea near La Spezia.

Stevie Smith

Florence Margaret Smith was born in Hull, Yorkshire, in 1902 to a somewhat feckless father who soon exchanged his young family for a life at sea, for which the poet never forgave him. In 1906, with her mother, her sister, and her Aunt Margaret (called 'Lion Aunt' by Stevie), she moved to Palmers Green, London, setting up what she described as 'a house of female habitation'. There she lived the rest of her life, being cared for and eventually looking after 'Lion Aunt'.

She was educated at Palmers Green High School and North London Collegiate School for girls in Camden Town. She acquired the nickname 'Stevie', liked it, and began to use it.

Not considered university material, she did a secretarial course and in 1923 became secretary to Sir Neville Pearson, chairman of Pearson's publishing firm, a position she held for the remainder of her working life, until she retired at the age of fifty-one. The work was not particularly onerous and she found time for her own writing while at the office. In fact her first work of fiction, *Novel on Yellow Paper* (1936), was typed on the office paper used at Pearson's for making carbon copies. She wrote two other novels, *Over the Frontier* (1938) and *The Holiday* (1949).

But she is better known for her witty and seriously strange verse, of which she composed eight volumes, many with her own unusual line drawings. Her first book of poetry, *A Good Time Was Had by All*, was published in 1937 and introduced the subjects that were to

fascinate her during her poetic life: childhood, adolescence, the relationship between the sexes, parents and children, animals, God and religion, and of course death. Her second collection, *Tender Only to One* (1938), is concerned primarily with death and parting. The title poem of *Harold's Leap* (1950) praises the bravery of a suicide, a theme that forms a major element of that collection. The romantic allure of death is featured in many poems, for example in the well-known 'Do Take Muriel Out', where we find out at the end that the boy being invited to take her out is Death.

Many other poems feature lonely or entrapped women in unsatisfactory relationships. Escape is a significant theme in both *Harold's Leap* and the collection *Not Waving But Drowning* (1957): the need to escape from boring middle-class suburban life, to run away from family and marriage, to flee the tedious, unsatisfactory office job, even to escape life itself. 'Deeply Morbid' is from the *Harold's Leap* collection.

She had at least two serious love affairs but always resisted marriage. 'I love life, I adore it, but only because I keep myself well on the edge,' she said. 'I won't commit myself to anything.'

Stevie Smith approached her subjects in a very original manner, using a simple, even childish language that disguises the seriousness of the themes. The tone is frequently offhand: we might notice, for instance, her 'jolly hockey-sticks' approach to death. Critics have drawn attention to three different voices or personas that she uses: that of an innocent child or adolescent girl, a lonely, cynical woman, and a wise stoical philosopher. Her poetry is quite distinctive. As Anthony Twaite said (*Poetry Today: A Guide to British Poetry, 1960–1984*, 1985), 'gradually she came to be recognised as a very special poet of strangeness, loneliness and quirky humour.'

Her popularity waned in the war years, but she became popular again in the nineteen-sixties, when she was in great demand as a reader. She was an unusual figure: a small, middle-aged woman, often dressed like a schoolgirl with ankle socks and a straight clipped fringe, who read in a sing-song voice. But her agnosticism, her sprightly approach to death and her views on love, war and male power gave her something of a cult status among hippies, radicals, and educated young people. She died of a brain tumour on 7 March 1971.

Pauline Stainer

Pauline Stainer was born in 1941 and studied English at St Anne's College, Oxford, and took a master's degree in philosophy at Southampton University. She has worked at a variety of jobs—in a mental hospital, a pub, and a library, for example—and is now a freelance writer and lecturer. She lives in Saffron Walden, Essex.

Pauline Stainer has published four volumes of poetry: *The Honeycomb* (1989), *Sighting the Slave Ship* (1992), *The Ice-Pilot Speaks* (1994), and *The Wound-Dresser's Dream* (1996). Her poetry is sparked off by a wide range of sources: mediaeval lyrics; sculptures; paintings, ranging from Renaissance to Paul Klee; the music of Erik Satie and others; and nature (as in the bee poems of *The Honeycomb*). Her imagery and settings are spectacularly varied and international: medicine, the Christian liturgy, scientific data and historical references all feature regularly. But at heart she is interested in human beings and why they do what they do.

Many of her poems are difficult to understand at a first reading and only gradually yield up their wisdom. Some resist being explained, as she herself says of 'The Ice-Pilot Speaks':

> It isn't a poem that can be 'explained'. The images reflect off one another like those high glass buildings designed to mirror one another. It should be read intuitively. I went to a school recently where the pupils had done drawings to illustrate 'The Ice-Pilot Speaks'. I remember thinking 'that's how the poem should be read!'

Perhaps 'Sighting the Slave Ship' should be 'read' in a similar way.

Richard Wilbur

Richard Wilbur was born in New York in 1921 and educated at Amherst College and Harvard University. He served in the Second World War and has been a teacher at Harvard and other universities.

His first collection of poetry, *The Beautiful Changes and Other Poems* (1947), examines the subjects of war, art, the uniqueness of nature, conscience, and love. *Ceremony and Other Poems* (1950), from which 'The Pardon' is taken, explores the tension between the actual world and one that can only be imagined. Very often scenes described have symbolic significance, and dreams are a means of insight and knowledge. There are also poems in this collection about heroic figures; poems about human failings; and some based on the experiences of the poet. Among Wilbur's many other collections are *Things of This World: Poems,* which won a Pulitzer Prize in 1956, and *New and Collected Poems,* which was published in 1988.

Wilbur believed that one of the main functions of poetry was to examine the inconsistencies and disharmony of modern life. 'Poetry could not be honest, we thought, unless it began by acknowledging the full discordancy of modern life ... I still believe this to be the true view of poetry.' And he felt that this discord must be structured in a formal framework in the poem. In that sense he was quite traditional. 'As regards technique, a critic has called me one of the 'New Formalists', and I will accept the label provided it be understood that to try to revive the force of rhyme and other formal devices, by reconciling them with the experimental gains of the past decades, is itself sufficiently experimental.' He put the same case for form and structure in a colourful and memorable phrase when he said, 'The strength of the genie comes of his being confined in a bottle.'

Richard Wilbur was made Poet Laureate of the United States in 1987.

Judith Wright

Judith Wright, born in 1915, is one of the most significant Australian poets of the twentieth century. She contributed to the development of a literature that is distinctly Australian, a literature that no longer takes its themes or style from England and, while neither rejecting nor slavishly following a colonial past, forges a new Australian consciousness. As she said (in *Preoccupations in Australian Poetry,* 1965), 'we are beginning to write, no longer as transplanted Europeans, nor as rootless men who reject the past and put their hopes only in the future, but as men with a present to be lived in and a past to nourish us.'

Her first volume of poetry, *The Moving Image,* was published in 1946 and had an immediate impact. It deals with Australian history (convict and Aboriginal), war and the post-war period and considers the present and the future of the country. She is fascinated by landscape, particularly the New England tablelands, which is the territory of her own pioneering family; by the native animals; by the original inhabitants, the Aboriginals; and by solitary figures of Australian rural life that are symbolic of the nation, shepherds and drovers such as 'The Bullocky'.

Woman to Man (1949) explores the theme of love, particularly maternal experience. *The Gateway* (1953) is concerned in a big way with time and eternity. *The Two Fires* (1955) deals with the destructive forces in the world, both outside (such as the hydrogen bomb) and inside humankind, and searches for positive forces of renewal against this darkness. The journeys here are spiritual as well as geographical.

Judith Wright is a prolific writer, with many volumes of poetry to her name, including *Birds* (1966) and *Collected Poems, 1942–1970* (1972), and is also the author of many volumes of critical studies, mostly on Australian poets and poetry.

In general, her own poetry deals with many conservationist issues: the encroachment of the cities on natural life; the desecration of the landscape (some of her later works are protest poems); the Australian past, both convict and Aboriginal; the loneliness and isolation of rural people; the native wisdom and insights of simple people; the significance of landscape and animals; love; the impact of war; and issues of the human psyche—affairs of the mind and heart of Australia.

W. B. Yeats

William Butler Yeats was born in Dublin in 1865 of a County Sligo family. His grandfather had been rector of the Church of Ireland at Drumcliff. His father, the portrait-painter John Butler Yeats, had married Susan Pollexfen, who belonged to a family of substantial traders and ship-owners from County Sligo. His brother, Jack B. Yeats, was to become one of Ireland's best-known painters.

William Yeats was educated intermittently at the Godolphin School, London, the High School, Dublin, and the Dublin Metropolitan School of Art. He was interested in mysticism and the supernatural and developed a great curiosity for Irish mythology, history, and folklore. It became one of his life's great passions to develop a distinctive, distinguished Irish literature in English. His first long poem, 'The Wanderings of Oisin' (1889), established the tone of what became known as the 'Celtic Twilight'. His early volumes of poetry— *Crossways* (1889), *The Rose* (1893), *The Wind among the Reeds* (1899), and *In the Seven Woods* (1904)—reflect his interest in mysticism, theosophy and mythology but also deal with his hopeless love affairs, most notably that with Maud Gonne. In 1889 he had met and fallen in love with her; and though she would not marry him, he remained obsessed with her for most of his life. With Lady Gregory of Coole Park, Gort, County Galway, and John Millington Synge he founded the Irish Literary Theatre Society in 1899 and later the Abbey Theatre in 1904.

By the end of the century Yeats had changed his decorative, symbolist style of poetry and began to write in a more direct style. From *The Green Helmet* (1910) onwards he shows a more realistic attitude to love and also begins to write about everyday cultural and political affairs. *Responsibilities* (1914) contains satires on the materialism of Dublin's middle class. 'An Irish Airman Foresees his Death' is taken from *The Wild Swans at Coole* (1919).

Among the major themes of his mature years are the need for harmony in life, the search for perfection in life and art, and the mysteries of time and eternity. These are to be found particularly in the poems of the later volumes, *The Tower* (1928), *The Winding Stair* (1933), and *Last Poems* (1936–39).

Yeats was made a senator in 1922 and was very active in public life; he supervised the design of the new coinage in 1926. He was awarded the Nobel Prize for Literature in 1923.

He died in Rome in 1939, but his body was not brought back to Ireland until after the war, when it was buried at Drumcliff. In the poem 'Under Ben Bulben' he had composed his own famous three-line epitaph, which is inscribed on the tombstone.

> Under bare Ben Bulben's head
> In Drumcliffe churchyard Yeats is laid.
> An ancestor was rector there
> Long years ago, a church stands near,
> By the road an ancient cross.
> No marble, no conventional phrase;
> On limestone quarried near the spot
> By his command these words are cut:
> > *Cast a cold eye*
> > *On life, on death.*
> > *Horseman, pass by!*

2
Unseen Poetry

Reading, thinking and writing about poems

An approach to a poem

Like any other work of art, such as a painting, sculpture, film, or building, a poem needs many viewings or readings before we come to appreciate it fully. All the usual techniques we employ when viewing any new or unusual object can be of use here: first noticing the particularly striking or unusual features; focusing in on a small area of it; drawing back and trying to see the whole structure; circling around it; finding words to describe it to ourselves; asking ourselves what we like about it; and so on. And so by circling the object and zooming in and out to examine interesting features, gradually we pick up more and more of the detail, until the entire object makes sense for us. *Many readings are the key to understanding.*

Here are some possible questions you might ask yourself as you read and re-read.

What do I see?
- What do I notice on a first reading? List them.
- Where is it set? What scene or scenes are featured?
- What pictures strike me as interesting? Focus on a location or an image. What are my thoughts on it?
- Follow the images through the poem. Is there a sequence, or a pattern?
  Have the images anything in common?
- Do the images or locations suggest anything about the *themes* or *issues* the poem might be dealing with?
- What *atmosphere* or *mood* is suggested by the visual aspects?

Is there a story?
- Is there a narrative structure to this poem? If so, what is happening? Trace the sequence of events.
- If the poem is divided into stanzas, perhaps each stanza should be treated as a paragraph and examined separately and in sequence. Am I clear about the story?
- What is my reaction to the story?
- Is there a main idea or *theme* behind the narrative?

What is the poet describing?
- If it is not a story, then what is the poet describing—a scene? or recalling a mood or recapturing a moment of experience? Can I describe what the poem is doing?
- How does the poet want me to feel? What *mood* is created in the poem? What words, phrases etc. help to create this mood?

The speaker, the poet?
- Who is the speaker in the poem? What kind of person do I imagine him or her to be? What state of mind is the speaker in? What words or phrases reveal most about the attitude and state of mind of the speaker? How do I think he or she would say this poem (*tone*)?
- To whom is the poet speaking—a particular person? the world in general? me? If to a particular person, who is involved, and what does that add to my understanding of the poem?
- What *point of view* is being put across in the poem? Am I in sympathy with it?

How does the poet write?

● What do I notice about the poet's style?
● Does the poet rely on *images*? If so, what do I notice about them?
● Does the poet use the *musical sounds of words—alliteration, assonance, onomatopoeia,* etc.?
● Does the poet like to *rhyme*?
● Does the poet use regular *metre* (rhythm or regular beat in the lines), or do the lines sound more like ordinary conversation or a piece of prose writing?
● What do I notice about the type of words (*diction*) most frequently used—ordinary, everyday? difficult and technical? long, with many syllables, or short and brief, etc.?
● Are any of these features particularly noticeable or effective? What do I like?

What is my reaction to it?

● What seems most important about the poem?
● How do I react to it? Do I find it amusing, interesting, exciting, frightening, revolting, thought-provoking, or what?
● Can I identify with the experience in this poem? Is it like my own experience in any way?
● What does it add to my understanding of people, places, feelings, life, etc.?
● What does it make me think about?

A short selection

A Blessing
James Wright

Just off the highway to Rochester, Minnesota,
Twilight bounds softly forth on the grass.
And the eyes of those two Indian ponies
Darken with kindness.
They have come gladly out of the willows   5
To welcome my friend and me.
We step over the barbed wire into the pasture
Where they have been grazing all day, alone.
They ripple tensely, they can hardly contain their happiness
That we have come.   10
They bow shyly as wet swans. They love each other.
There is no loneliness like theirs.
At home once more,
They begin munching the young tufts of spring in the darkness.
I would like to hold the slenderer one in my arms,   15
For she has walked over to me
And nuzzled my left hand.
She is black and white,
Her mane falls wild on her forehead,
And the light breeze moves me to caress her long ear   20
That is delicate as the skin over a girl's wrist.
Suddenly I realise
That if I stepped out of my body I would break
Into blossom.

A Call

Séamus Heaney

'Hold on,' she said, 'I'll just run out and get him.
The weather here's so good, he took the chance
To do a bit of weeding.'

                So I saw him
Down on his hands and knees beside the leek rig,   5
Touching, inspecting, separating one
Stalk from the other, gently pulling up
Everything not tapered, frail and leafless,
Pleased to feel each little weed-root break,
But rueful also ...   10

                  Then found myself listening to
The amplified grave ticking of hall clocks
Where the phone lay unattended in a calm
Of mirror glass and sunstruck pendulums ...

And found myself then thinking: if it were nowadays,   15
This is how Death would summon Everyman.

Next thing he spoke and I nearly said I loved him.

Leinster Street

Dermot Bolger

I

Let us wake in Leinster Street,
   Both of us still twenty six,
On a December Monday in 1985.
   We lie on, relaxed, illicit,
Listening to the melody below   5
   Of friends cooking breakfast.

Flaking paint on the lattice,
   Old wire, crumbling stone,
The silos of the abandoned mill
   Framed by windows which open   10
Onto flowers that are lodged
   Between bricks in the lane.

And no need for us to rise
   For one more drowsy hour:
Lie on with me in that moment   15
   When you were still too shy
To dress yourself while I watched
   Your limbs garbed in light.

II

In those rooms five years passed
   In a single drawn-out breath   20
Before we plunged into new lives.
   Remember how the ceiling wept
Beneath each rafter in the winter,
   The rustle of cards that crept

Up unlit stairways after midnight.   25
   May some tenant of the future
Turn when switching out his light
   And, framed by the doorway, glimpse
The phosphorescence of our lives
   Still glowing with this happiness.   30

Anseo
Paul Muldoon

When the Master was calling the roll
At the primary school in Collegelands,
You were meant to call back Anseo
And raise your hand
As your name occurred.   5
Anseo, meaning here, here and now,
All present and correct,
Was the first word of Irish I spoke.
The last name on the ledger
Belonged to Joseph Mary Plunkett Ward   10
And was followed, as often as not,
By silence, knowing looks,
A nod and a wink, the Master's droll
'And where's our little Ward-of-court?'

I remember the first time he came back   15
The Master had sent him out
Along the hedges
To weigh up for himself and cut
A stick with which he would be beaten.
After a while, nothing was spoken;   20
He would arrive as a matter of course
With an ash-plant, a salley-rod.
Or, finally, the hazel-wand
He had whittled down to a whip-lash,
Its twist of red and yellow lacquers   25
Sanded and polished,
And altogether so delicately wrought
That he had engraved his initials on it.

I last met Joseph Mary Plunkett Ward
In a pub just over the Irish border.   30
He was living in the open,
In a secret camp
On the other side of the mountain.
He was fighting for Ireland,
Making things happen.   35
And he told me, Joe Ward,
Of how he had risen through the ranks
To Quartermaster, Commandant:
How every morning at parade
His volunteers would call back Anseo   40
And raise their hands
As their names occurred.

Anything Is Better Than Emptying Bins

Rita Ann Higgins

(For Jessie)

I work at the Post Office.
I hate my job,
but my father said
there was no way
I could empty bins   5
and stay under his roof.

So naturally,
I took a ten week
extra mural course
on effective stamp licking;   10
entitled
'More lip and less tongue'.

I was mostly unpleasant,
but always under forty
for young girls   15
who bought stamps with hearts
for Valentine's Day.

One day a woman asked me
could she borrow a paper clip,
she said something about   20
sending a few poems away
and how a paper clip
would make everything so much neater.
But I've met the make-my-poems-neater type before;
give in to her once,   25
and she'll be back in a week asking
'Have you got any stamps left over?'

Well I told her where to get off.
'Mrs Neater-poems,' I said,
'this is a post office   30
not a friggin' card shop,
and if you want paper clips
you'll get a whole box full
across the street for twenty pence.'

Later when I told my father,   35
he replied,
'Son, it's not how I'd have handled it,
but anything is better than emptying bins.'

'As the team's head-brass flashed out'
Edward Thomas

As the team's head-brass flashed out on the turn
The lovers disappeared into the wood.
I sat among the boughs of the fallen elm
That strewed an angle of the fallow, and
Watched the plough narrowing a yellow square   5
Of charlock. Every time the horses turned
Instead of treading me down, the ploughman leaned
Upon the handles to say or ask a word,
About the weather, next about the war.
Scraping the share he faced towards the wood,   10
And screwed along the furrow till the brass flashed
Once more.

       The blizzard felled the elm whose crest
I sat in, by a woodpecker's round hole,
The ploughman said. 'When will they take it away?'   15
'When the war's over.' So the talk began—
One minute and an interval of ten,
A minute more and the same interval.
'Have you been out?' 'No.' 'And don't want to, perhaps?'
'If I could only come back again, I should.   20
I could spare an arm. I shouldn't want to lose
A leg. If I should lose my head, why, so,
I should want nothing more ... Have many gone
From here?' 'Yes, a good few.
Only two teams work on the farm this year.   25
One of my mates is dead. The second day
In France they killed him. It was back in March,
The very night of the blizzard, too. Now if
He had stayed here we should have moved the tree.'
'And I should not have sat here. Everything   30
Would have been different. For it would have been
Another world.' 'Ay, and a better, though
If we could see all all might seem good.' Then
The lovers came out of the wood again:
The horses started and for the last time   35
I watched the clods crumble and topple over
After the ploughshare and the stumbling team.

Backside to the Wind

Paul Durcan

A fourteen-year-old boy is out rambling alone
By the scimitar shores of Killala Bay
And he is dreaming of a French Ireland,
Backside to the wind.

What kind of village would I now be living in?   5
French vocabularies intertwined with Gaelic
And Irish women with French fathers,
Backsides to the wind.

The Ballina Road would become the Rue de Humbert
And wine would be the staple drink of the people;   10
A staple diet of potatoes and wine,
Backsides to the wind.

Monsieur O'Duffy might be the harbour-master
And Madame Duffy the mother of thirteen
Tiny philosophers to overthrow Maynooth,   15
Backsides to the wind.

Father Molloy might be a worker-priest
Up to his knees in manure at the cattle-mart;
And dancing and loving on the streets at evening
Backsides to the wind.   20

Jean Arthur Rimbaud might have grown up here
In a hillside terrace under the round tower;
Would he, like me, have dreamed of an Arabian Dublin,
Backside to the wind?

Garda Ned MacHale might now be a gendarme   25
Having hysterics at the crossroads;
Excommunicating male motorists, ogling females,
Backside to the wind.

I walk on, facing the village ahead of me,
A small concrete oasis in the wild countryside;   30
Not the embodiment of the dream of a boy,
Backside to the wind.

Seagulls and crows, priests and nuns,
Perch on the rooftops and steeples,
And their Anglo-American mores asphyxiate me,   35
Backside to the wind.

Not to mention the Japanese invasion:
Blunt people as serious as ourselves
And as humourless; money is our God,
Backsides to the wind.   40

The medieval Franciscan Friary of Moyne
Stands house-high, roofless, by;
Past it rolls a vast asphalt pipe,
Backside to the wind,

Ferrying chemical waste out to sea   45
From the Asahi synthetic-fibre plant;
Where once monks sang, wage-earners slave,
Backsides to the wind.

Run on, sweet River Moy,
Although I end my song; you are   50
The scales of a salmon of a boy,
Backside to the wind.

Yet I have no choice but to leave, to leave,
And yet there is nowhere I more yearn to live
Than in my own wild countryside,   55
Backside to the wind.

Christmas in the West
Noel Monahan

The night smells of whiskey,
Clouds of cigarette smoke rise
Above the beads of Christmas lights
On aslant streets. Mothertown, bride
To the wind and rain   5
Is mad with people home for Christmas.

Pint glasses chime in The Green Piano,
Phatic conversations, every word
A fairy light in the dark lounge,
Body curves touch, hands hoop familiar waists,   10
Drink comes with ice.
High-stoolers, elbows on the counter,
Vacate their metal thrones to trot to the Men's.

It's two a.m.
Everyone ignores the coloured TV,   15
Laughing doors open into alleyways,
Taxi doors slam in the holly berry dawn
Of Christmas morn.

Candles flicker on linen,
Bare hands, fingers twisted in fire,   20
Three camels eat silage outside,
Weather-prophets stand on their heads
Looking for a star in the East.

It's a bungee jump, a quick splash
For Christmas and they're gone,   25
Ferrying their dreams
As far as they care to go.
January takes a bite out of the town,
It's all peaceful again,
Silent nights ... Holy nights ...   30

Claudy

James Simmons
(For Harry Barton, a song)

The Sperrins surround it, the Faughan flows by,
at each end of Main street the hills and the sky,
the small town of Claudy at ease in the sun
last July in the morning, a new day begun.

How peaceful and pretty if the moment could stop,   5
McIlhenny is straightening things in his shop,
and his wife is outside serving petrol, and then
a girl takes a cloth to a big window pane.

And McCloskey is taking the weight off his feet,
And McClelland and Miller are sweeping the street,   10
and, delivering milk at the Beaufort Hotel,
young Temple's enjoying his first job quite well.

And Mrs McLaughlin is scrubbing her floor,
and Artie Hone's crossing the street to a door,
and Mrs Brown, looking around for her cat,   15
goes off up an entry—what's strange about that?

Not much—but before she comes back to the road
that strange car parked outside her house will explode,
and all of the people I've mentioned outside
will be waiting to die or already have died.   20

An explosion too loud for your eardrums to bear,
and young children squealing like pigs in the square,
and all faces chalk-white and streaked with bright red,
and the glass and the dust and the terrible dead.

For an old lady's legs are ripped off, and the head   25
of a man's hanging open, and still he's not dead.
He is screaming for mercy, and his son stands and stares
and stares, and then suddenly, quick, disappears.

And Christ, little Katherine Aiken is dead,
and Mrs McLaughlin is pierced through the head.   30
Meanwhile to Dungiven the killers have gone,
and they're finding it hard to get through on the phone.

Dawn Walkers
Jenny Joseph

Anxious eyes loom down the damp-black streets
Pale staring girls who are walking away hard
From beds where love went wrong or died or turned away,
Treading their misery beneath another day
Stamping to work into another morning.   5

In all our youths there must have been some time
When the cold dark has stiffened up the wind
But suddenly, like a sail stiffening with wind,
Carried the vessel on, stretching the ropes, glad of it.

But listen to this now: this I saw one morning.   10
I saw a young man running, for a bus I thought,
Needing to catch it on this murky morning
Dodging the people crowding to work or shopping early.
And all heads stopped and turned to see how he ran
To see would he make it, the beautiful strong young man.   15
Then I noticed a girl running after, calling out 'John'.
He must have left his sandwiches I thought.
But she screamed 'John wait'. He heard her and ran faster,
Using his muscled legs and studded boots.
We knew she'd never reach him. 'Listen to me John.   20
Only once more' she cried. 'For the last time, John, please wait, please listen.'
He gained the corner in a spurt and she
Sobbing and hopping with her red hair loose
(Made way for by the respectful audience)
Followed on after, but not to catch him now.   25
Only that there was nothing left to do.

The street closed in and went on with its day.
A worn old man standing in the heat from the baker's
Said 'Surely to God the bastard could have waited'.

Death Bed

Thomas Kinsella

Motionless—his sons—
we watched his brows draw together with strain.
The wind tore at the leather walls of our tent;
two grease lamps fluttered
at the head and foot of the bed.   5
Our shadows sprang here and there.

At that moment our sign might
have coursed across the heavens,
and we had spared no one to watch.

Our people are most vulnerable to loss   10
when we gather like this to one side,
around some death,

and try to weave it into our lives
—who can weave nothing but our ragged
routes across the desert.   15

And it is those among us
who most make the heavens their business
who go most deeply into this death-weaving.

As if the star might
spring from the dying mouth   20
or shoot from the agony of the eyes.

'We must not miss it,
however it comes.'
—If it comes.

He stretched out his feet   25
and seemed to sink deeper in the bed,
and was still.

Sons no longer,
we pulled down his eyelids
and pushed the chin up gently to close his mouth,   30
and stood under the flapping roof.
Our shelter sheltered under the night.

Hides, furs and skins,
are our shelter and our garments.

We can weave nothing.   35

Down by the Salley Gardens
W. B. Yeats

Down by the salley gardens my love and I did meet;
She passed the salley gardens with little snow-white feet.
She bid me take love easy, as the leaves grow on the tree;
But I, being young and foolish, with her would not agree.

In a field by the river my love and I did stand,   5
And on my leaning shoulder she laid her snow-white hand.
She bid me take life easy, as the grass grows on the weirs;
But I was young and foolish, and now am full of tears.

Dream of a Black Fox
Brendan Kennelly

The black fox loped out of the hills
And circled for several hours,
Eyes bright with menace, teeth
White in the light, tail dragging the ground.
The woman in my arms cringed with fear,   5
Collapsed crying, her head hurting my neck.
She became dumb fear.

The black fox, big as a pony,
Circled and circled,
Whimsical executioner,   10
Torment dripping like saliva from its jaws.
Too afraid to show my fear,
I watched it as it circled;
Then it leaped across me,
Its great black body breaking the air,   15
Landing on a wall above my head.

Turning then, it looked at me.

And I saw it was magnificent,
Ruling the darkness, lord of its element,
Scorning all who are afraid,   20
Seeming even to smile
At human pettiness and fear.

The woman in my arms looked up
At this lord of darkness
And as quickly hid her head again.   25
Then the fox turned and was gone
Leaving us with fear
And safety—
Every usual illusion.

Quiet now, no longer trembling,   30
She lay in my arms,
Still as a sleeping child.

I knew I had seen fear,
Fear dispelled by what makes fear
A part of pure creation,   35
Some incomparable thing,
A thing so utterly itself
It might have taught me
Mastery of myself,
Dominion over death,   40
But was content to leap
With ease and majesty
Across the valleys and the hills of sleep.

Driving Home at Dusk with Donal, 4
Don Byrne

As if you were born again,
your question, about headlights,
and my reply about other cars
needing to see, brought us
together, your smile   5
in the mirror, that 'Ah, yeah'
bonding us just as much
as the night they handed you over
into my cradled arms.

Your surefooted arrival,   10
just two days after
your grandfather's funeral,
tears of two kinds
rising in me, and you
taking it in silently,   15
steadily, as if
to secure me.

Much of our lives now
twin orbits,
catching the odd glimpse   20
in the rear mirror,
the snug feel of you
into my armpit at night
at storytime.

Always that sure sense   25
that you and he passed
each other in soul flight,
touched hands for just
long enough for him to say,
'Look after your father,   30
he's all yours now.'

Easter-Wings
George Herbert

Lord, who createdst man in wealth and store,
    Though foolishly he lost the same,
        Decaying more and more,
           Till he became
             Most poor: 5
            With thee
         O let me rise
      As larks, harmoniously,
    And sing this day thy victories:
Then shall the fall further the flight in me.   10

My tender age in sorrow did begin:
    And still with sicknesses and shame
        Thou didst so punish sin,
           That I became
             Most thin.   15
            With thee
         Let me combine,
      And feel this day thy victory:
    For, if I imp my wing on thine,
Affliction shall advance the flight in me.   20

Notes

[10] **the fall etc.:** the fall of humankind from grace paradoxically leads us closer to Heaven, because it made the birth and death of Christ necessary to atone for our sins

[19] **I imp my wing:** imping was a technique used by falconers, in which they grafted feathers onto the wings of birds to repair damage and so restore or improve their flying ability; here the poet says that the weaker we are the more we need Christ's help, and so the higher our spirits fly towards God

First Calf
Séamus Heaney

It's a long time since I saw
The afterbirth strung on the hedge
As if the wind smarted
And streamed bloodshot tears.

Somewhere about   5
The cow stands with her head
Almost outweighing her tense sloped neck,
The calf hard at her udder.

The shallow bowls of her eyes
Tilt membrane and fluid.   10
The warm plinth of her snout gathers
A growth round moist nostrils.

Her hide stays warm in the wind,
Her wide eyes read nothing:
Those gay semaphores of hurt   15
Swaddle and flap on a bush.

The Flea
John Donne

Mark but this flea, and mark in this,
How little that which thou deny'st me is;
Me it sucked first, and now sucks thee,
And in this flea, our two bloods mingled be;
Confess it, this cannot be said   5
A sin, or shame, or loss of maidenhead,
    Yet this enjoys before it woo,
    And pampered swells with one blood made of two,
    And this, alas, is more than we would do.

Oh stay, three lives in one flea spare,   10
Where we almost, nay more than married are.
This flea is you and I, and this
Our marriage bed, and marriage temple is;
Though parents grudge, and you, we are met,
And cloistered in these living walls of jet.   15
    Though use make you apt to kill me,
    Let not to this, self murder added be,
    And sacrilege, three sins in killing three.

Cruel and sudden, has thou since
Purpled thy nail, in blood of innocence?   20
In what could this flea guilty be,
Except in that drop which it sucked from thee?
Yet thou triumph'st, and say'st that thou
Find'st not thyself, nor me the weaker now;
   'Tis true, then learn how false, fears be;   25
   Just so much honour, when thou yield'st to me,
   Will waste, as this flea's death took life from thee.

Notes

[6] **maidenhead:** virginity

[15] **walls of jet:** the flea's body is black, like jet

[20] **purpled thy nail:** fleas were usually killed by cracking them with a fingernail

Harvest Hymn

John Betjeman

We spray the fields and scatter
The poison on the ground
So that no wicked wild flowers
Upon our farm be found.
We like whatever helps us   5
To line our purse with pence;
The twenty-four-hour broiler-house
And neat electric fence.

All concrete sheds around us
And Jaguars in the yard,   10
The telly lounge and deep-freeze
Are ours from working hard.

We fire the fields for harvest.
The hedges swell the flame,
The oak trees and the cottages   15
From which our fathers came.
We give no compensation.
The earth is ours today,
And if we lose on arable,
Then bungalows will pay.   20

All concrete sheds around us
And Jaguars in the yard,
The telly lounge and deep-freeze
Are ours from working hard.

Hearts and Flowers

Roger McGough

Aunty Marge,
Spinster of the parish, never had a boyfriend.
Never courted, never kissed.
A jerrybuilt dentist and a smashed jaw
Saw to that.   5

To her,
Life was a storm in a holy-water font
Across which she breezed
With all the grace and charm
Of a giraffe learning to windsurf.   10

But sweating
In the convent laundry, she would iron
Amices, albs and surplices
With such tenderness and care
You'd think priests were still inside.   15

Deep down,
She would like to have been a nun
And talked of missing her vocation
As if it were the last bus home:
'It passed me by when I was looking the other way.'   20

'Besides,'
She'd say, 'What Order would have me?
The Little Daughters of the Bingo?
The Holy Whist Sisters?' A glance at the ceiling.
'He's not that hard up.'   25

We'd laugh
And protest, knowing in our hearts that He wasn't.
But for the face she would have been out there,
Married, five kids, another on the way.
Celibacy a gift unearned, unasked for.   30

But though
A goose among grown-ups,
Let loose among kids
She was an exploding fireworks factory,
A runaway pantomime horse.   35

Everybody's
Favourite aunt. A cuddly toy adult
That sang loud and out of tune.
That dropped, knocked over and bumped into things,
That got ticked off just like us.   40

Next to
A game of cards she liked babysitting best.
Once the parents were out of the way
It was every child for itself. In charge,
Aunt Marge, renegade toddler-in-chief.   45

Falling
Asleep over pontoon, my sister and I,
Red-eyed, would beg to be taken to bed.
'Just one more game of snap,' she'd plead,
And magic two toffees from behind an ear.   50

Then suddenly
Whooshed upstairs in the time it takes
To open the front door. Leaving us to possum,
She'd tiptoe down with the fortnightly fib:
'Still fast asleep, not a murmur all night. Little angels.'   55

But angels
Unangelic, grew up and flew away. And fallen,
Looked for brighter toys. Each Christmas sent a card
With kisses, and wondered how she coped alone.
Up there in a council flat. No phone.   60

Her death
Was as quick as it was clumsy. Neighbours
Found the body, not us. Sitting there for days
Stiff in Sunday best. Coat half-buttoned, hat askew.
On her way to Mass. Late as usual.   65

Her rosary
Had snapped with the pain, the decades spilling,
Black beads trailing. The crucifix still
Clenched in her fist. Middle finger broken.
Branded into dead flesh, the sign of the cross.   70

From the missal
In her lap, holy pictures, like playing cards,
Lay scattered. Five were face-up:
A full House of Sacred Hearts and Little Flowers.
Aunty Marge, lucky in cards.   75

He Wishes for the Cloths of Heaven
W. B. Yeats

Had I the heavens' embroidered cloths,
Enwrought with golden and silver light,
The blue and the dim and the dark cloths
Of night and light and the half-light,
I would spread the cloths under your feet: 5
But I, being poor, have only my dreams;
I have spread my dreams under your feet;
Tread softly because you tread on my dreams.

Inniskeen Road: July Evening
Patrick Kavanagh

The bicycles go by in twos and threes—
There's a dance in Billy Brennan's barn to-night,
And there's the half-talk code of mysteries
And the wink-and-elbow language of delight.
Half-past eight and there is not a spot   5
Upon a mile of road, no shadow thrown
That might turn out a man or woman, not
A footfall tapping secrecies of stone.

I have what every poet hates in spite
Of all the solemn talk of contemplation.   10
Oh, Alexander Selkirk knew the plight
Of being king and government and nation.
A road, a mile of kingdom, I am king
Of banks and stones and every blooming thing.

Innocence
Patrick Kavanagh

They laughed at one I loved—
The triangular hill that hung
Under the Big Forth. They said
That I was bounded by the whitethorn hedges
Of the little farm and did not know the world.   5
But I knew that love's doorway to life
Is the same doorway everywhere.

Ashamed of what I loved
I flung her from me and called her a ditch
Although she was smiling at me with violets.   10

But now I am back in her briary arms
The dew of an Indian summer morning lies
On bleached potato-stalks—
What age am I?

I do not know what age I am,   15
I am no mortal age;
I know nothing of women,
Nothing of cities,
I cannot die
Unless I walk outside these whitethorn hedges   20

Minding Ruth

Aidan Carl Mathews
(For Séamus Deane)

She wreaks such havoc in my library,
It will take ages to set it right—
A Visigoth in a pinafore

Who, weakening, plonks herself
On the works of Friedrich Nietzsche,   5
And pines for her mother.

She's been at it all morning,
Duck-arsed in my History Section
Like a refugee among rubble,

Or, fled to the toilet, calling   10
In a panic that the seat is cold.
But now she relents under biscuits

To extemporise grace notes,
And sketch with a blue crayon
Arrow after arrow leading nowhere.   15

My small surprise of language,
I cherish you like an injury
And would swear by you at this moment

For your brisk chatter brings me
Chapter and verse, you restore   20
The city itself, novel and humming,

Which I enter as a civilian
Who plants his landscape with place-names.
They stand an instant, and fade.

Her hands sip at my cuff. She cranes,   25
Perturbedly, with a book held open
At plates from Warsaw in the last war.

Why is the man with the long beard
Eating his booboos? And I stare
At the old rabbi squatting in turds   30

Among happy soldiers who die laughing,
The young one clapping: you can see
A wedding band flash on his finger.

Mirror in February
Thomas Kinsella

The day dawns with scent of must and rain,
Of opened soil, dark trees, dry bedroom air.
Under the fading lamp, half dressed—my brain
Idling on some compulsive fantasy—
I towel my shaven jaw and stop, and stare,   5
Riveted by a dark exhausted eye,
A dry downturning mouth.

It seems again that it is time to learn,
In this untiring, crumbling place of growth
To which, for the time being, I return.   10
Now plainly in the mirror of my soul
I read that I have looked my last on youth
And little more; for they are not made whole
That reach the age of Christ.

Below my window the awakening trees,   15
Hacked clean for better bearing, stand defaced
Suffering their brute necessities,
And how should the flesh not quail that span for span
Is mutilated more? In slow distaste
I fold my towel with what grace I can,   20
Not young and not renewable, but man.

Morning Song
Sylvia Plath

Love set you going like a fat gold watch.
The midwife slapped your footsoles, and your bald cry
Took its place among the elements.

Our voices echo, magnifying your arrival. New statue
In a draughty museum, your nakedness   5
Shadows our safety. We stand round blankly as walls.

I'm no more your mother
Than the cloud that distils a mirror to reflect its own slow
Effacement at the wind's hand.

All night your moth breath   10
Flickers among the flat pink roses. I wake to listen:
A far sea moves in my ear.

One cry, and I stumble from bed, cow-heavy and floral
In my Victorian nightgown.
Your mouth opens clean as a cat's. The window square   15

Whitens and swallows its dull stars. And now you try
Your handful of notes
The clear vowels rise like balloons.

My Mother
Medbh McGuckian

My mother's smell is sweet or sour and moist
like the soft red cover of the apple.
She sits among her boxes, lace and tins
And notices the smallest of all breezes,
As if she were a tree upon the mountain   5
Growing away with no problem at all.

Her swan's head quivers like a light-bulb:
Does she breed in perfect peace, a light sleep,
Or smothered like a clock whose alarm
Is unendurable, whose featureless   10
Straight face is never wrong?
No-one knows what goes on inside a clock.

North Wind: Portrush

Derek Mahon

I shall never forget the wind
On this benighted coast.
It works itself into the mind
Like the high keen of a lost
Lear-spirit in agony   5
Condemned for eternity

To wander cliff and cove
Without comfort, without love.
It whistles off the stars
And the existential, black   10
Face of the cosmic dark:
We crouch to roaring fires.

Yet there are mornings when,
Even in midwinter, sunlight
Flares, and a rare stillness   15
Lies upon roof and garden,
Each object eldritch-bright,
The sea scared but at peace.

Then, from the ship we say
Is the lit town where we live   20
(Our whiskey-and-forecast world).
A smaller ship that sheltered
All night in the restless bay
Will weigh anchor and leave.

What did they think of us   25
During their brief sojourn?
A string of lights on the prom
Dancing mad in the storm—
Who lives in such a place?
And will they ever return?   30

But the shops open at nine
As they have always done,
The wrapped-up bourgeoisie
Hardened by wind and sea.
The newspapers are late   35
But the milk shines in its crate.

Everything swept so clean
By tempest, wind and rain!
Elated, you might believe
That this was the first day—   40
A false sense of reprieve,
For the climate is here to stay.

So best prepare for the worst
That chaos and old night
Can do to us. Were we not   45
Raised on such expectations,
Our hearts starred with frost
Through countless generations?

Elsewhere the olive grove,
Le déjeuner sur l'herbe   50
Poppies and parasols,
Blue skies and mythic love.
Here only the stricken souls
No spring can unperturb.

Prospero and his people never   55
Came to these stormy parts:
Few do who have the choice.
Yet, blasting the subtler arts,
That weird, plaintive voice
Choirs now and for ever   60

No Second Troy
W. B. Yeats

Why should I blame her that she filled my days
With misery, or that she would of late
Have taught to ignorant men most violent ways,
Or hurled the little streets upon the great,
Had they but courage equal to desire?   5
What could have made her peaceful with a mind
That nobleness made simple as a fire,
With beauty like a tightened bow, a kind
That is not natural in an age like this,
Being high and solitary and most stern?   10
Why, what could she have done, being what she is?
Was there another Troy for her to burn?

O Friend! I know not
William Wordsworth

O Friend! I know not which way I must look
For comfort, being, as I am, opprest,
To think that now our life is only drest
For show; mean handy-work of craftman, cook,
Or groom!—We must run glittering like a brook   5
In the open sunshine, or we are unblest:
The wealthiest man among us is the best:
No grandeur now in nature or in book
Delights us. Rapine, avarice, expense,
This is idolatry; and these we adore: 10
Plain living and high thinking are no more:
The homely beauty of the good old cause
Is gone; our peace, our fearful innocence,
And pure religion breathing household laws.

One Flesh
Elizabeth Jennings

Lying apart now, each in a separate bed,
He with a book, keeping the light on late,
She like a girl dreaming of childhood,
All men elsewhere—it is as if they wait
Some new event: the book he holds unread,   5
Her eyes fixed on the shadows overhead.

Tossed up like flotsam from a former passion,
How cool they lie. They hardly ever touch,
Or if they do it is like a confession
Of having little feeling—or too much.   10
Chastity faces them, a destination
For which their whole lives were a preparation.

Strangely apart, yet strangely close together,
Silence between them like a thread to hold
And not wind in. And time itself's a feather   15
Touching them gently. Do they know they're old,
These two who are my father and my mother
Whose fire from which I came, has now grown cold?

Oranges
Gary Soto

The first time I walked
With a girl, I was twelve,
Cold, and weighted down
With two oranges in my jacket.
December. Frost cracking   5
Beneath my steps, my breath
Before me, then gone,
As I walked toward
Her house, the one whose
Porch light burned yellow   10
Night and day, in any weather.
A dog barked at me, until
She came out pulling
At her gloves, face bright
With rouge. I smiled,   15

Touched her shoulder, and led
Her down the street, across
A used car lot and a line
Of newly planted trees,
Until we were breathing   20
Before a drugstore. We
Entered, the tiny bell
Bringing a saleslady
Down a narrow aisle of goods.
I turned to the candies   25
Tiered like bleachers,
And asked what she wanted—
Light in her eyes, a smile
Starting at the corners
Of her mouth. I fingered   30
A nickel in my pocket,
And when she lifted a chocolate
That cost a dime,
I didn't say anything.
I took the nickel from   35
My pocket, then an orange,
And set them quietly on
The counter. When I looked up,
The lady's eyes met mine,
And held them, knowing   40
Very well what it was all
About.

Outside,
A few cars hissing past,
Fog hanging like old   45
Coats between the trees.
I took my girl's hand
In mine for two blocks,
Then released it to let
Her unwrap the chocolate.   50
I peeled my orange
That was so bright against
The grey of December
That, from some distance,
Someone might have thought   55
I was making a fire in my hands.

Penance
John F. Deane

They leave their shoes, like signatures, below;
above, their God is waiting. Slowly they rise
along the mountainside where rains and winds go
hissing, slithering across. They are hauling up

the bits and pieces of their lives, infractions   5
of the petty laws, the little trespasses and
sad transgressions. But this bulked mountain
is not disturbed by their passing, by this mere

trafficking of shale, shifting of its smaller stones.
When they come down, feet blistered, and sins   10
fretted away, their guilt remains, and that black
mountain stands against darkness above them.

The Planter's Daughter
Austin Clarke

When night stirred at sea
And the fire brought a crowd in,
They say that her beauty
Was music in mouth
And few in the candlelight   5
Thought her too proud,
For the house of the planter
Is known by the trees.

Men that had seen her
Drank deep and were silent,   10
The women were speaking
Wherever she went—
As a bell that is rung
Or a wonder told shyly
And O she was the Sunday   15
In every week.

Portrait of a Young Girl Raped at a Suburban Party

Brian Patten

And after this quick bash in the dark
You will rise and go
Thinking of how empty you have grown
And of whether all the evening's care in front of mirrors
And the younger boys disowned   5
Led simply to this.

Confined to what you are expected to be
By what you are
Out in this frozen garden
You shiver and vomit—   10
Frightened, drunk among trees,
You wonder at how those acts that called for tenderness
Were far from tender.

Now you have left your titterings about love
And your childishness behind you   15
Yet still far from being old
You spew up among flowers
And in the warm stale rooms
The party continues.

It seems you saw some use in moving away   20
From that group of drunken lives
Yet already ten minutes pregnant
In twenty thousand you might remember
This party
This dull Saturday evening   25
When planets rolled out of your eyes
And splashed down in suburban grasses.

Prayer before Birth
Louis MacNeice

I am not yet born; O hear me.
Let not the bloodsucking bat or the rat or the stoat or the
   club-footed ghoul come near me.

I am not yet born, console me.
I fear that the human race may with tall walls wall me,   5
   with strong drugs dope me, with wise lies lure me,
      on black racks rack me, in blood-baths roll me.

I am not yet born; provide me
   With water to dandle me, grass to grow for me, trees to talk
      to me, sky to sing to me, birds and a white light   10
         in the back of my mind to guide me.

I am not yet born; forgive me
   For the sins that in me the world shall commit, my words
      when they speak me, my thoughts when they think me,
         my treason engendered by traitors beyond me,   15
            my life when they murder by means of my
               hands, my death when they live me.

I am not yet born; rehearse me
   In the parts I must play and the cues I must take when
      old men lecture me, bureaucrats hector me, mountains   20
         frown at me, lovers laugh at me, the white
            waves call me to folly and the desert calls
               me to doom and the beggar refuses
                  my gift and my children curse me.

I am not yet born; O hear me,   25
Let not the man who is beast or who thinks he is God
   come near me.

I am not yet born; O fill me
With strength against those who would freeze my
   humanity, would dragoon me into a lethal automaton,   30
      would make me a cog in a machine, a thing with
         one face, a thing, and against all those
            who would dissipate my entirety, would
               blow me like thistledown hither and
                  thither or hither and thither   35
                     like water held in the
                       hands would spill me.

Let them not make me a stone and let them not spill me.
Otherwise kill me.

Ravens

Ted Hughes

As we came through the gate to look at the few new lambs
On the skyline of lawn smoothness,
A raven bundled itself into air from midfield
And slid away under hard glistenings, low and guilty.
Sheep nibbling, kneeling to nibble the reluctant nibbled grass.   5
Sheep staring, their jaws pausing to think, then chewing again,
Then pausing. Over there a new lamb
Just getting up, bumping its mother's nose
As she nibbles the sugar coating off it
While the tattered banners of her triumph swing and drip from her rear-end. 10
She sneezes again and again, till she's emptied.
She carries on investigating her new present and seeing how it works.
Over here is something elsc. But you are still interested
In that new one, and its new spark of voice,
And its tininess.   15
Now over here, where the raven was,
Is what interests you next. Born dead,
Twisted like a scarf, a lamb of an hour or two,
Its insides, the various jellies and crimsons and transparencies
And threads and tissues pulled out   20
In straight lines, like tent ropes
From its upward belly opened like a lamb-wool slipper,
The fine anatomy of silvery ribs on display and the cavity,
The head also emptied through the eye-sockets,
The woolly limbs swathed in birth-yolk and impossible   25
To tell now which in all this field of quietly nibbling sheep
Was its mother. I explain
That it died being born. We should have been here, to help it.
So it died being born. 'And did it cry?' you cry.
I pick up the dangling greasy weight by the hooves soft as dogs' pads 30
That had trodden only womb-water
And its raven-drawn strings dangle and trail,
Its loose head joggles, and 'Did it cry?' you cry again.
Its two-fingered feet splay in their skin between the pressures
Of my finger and thumb. And there is another,   35
Just born, all black, splaying its tripod, inching its new points
Towards its mother, and testing the note
It finds in its mouth. But you have eyes now
Only for the tattered bundle of throwaway lamb.
'Did it cry?' you keep asking, in a three-year-old field-wide   40
Piercing persistence. 'Oh yes' I say 'it cried.'

Though this one was lucky insofar

As it made the attempt into a warm wind
And its first day of death was blue and warm
The magpies gone quiet with domestic happiness 45
And skylarks not worrying about anything
And the blackthorn budding confidently
And the skyline of hills, after millions of hard years,
Sitting soft.

Requiescat, 1854–1900

Oscar Wilde

Tread lightly, she is near
Under the snow,
Speak gently, she can hear
The daisies grow.

All her bright golden hair 5
Tarnished with rust,
She that was young and fair
Fallen to dust.

Lily-like, white as snow,
She hardly knew 10
She was a woman, so
Sweetly she grew.

Coffin-board, heavy stone
Lie on her breast,
I vex my heart alone, 15
She is at rest.

Peace, Peace, she cannot hear
Lyre or sonnet,
All my life's buried here,
Heap earth upon it. 20

Seed
Paula Meehan

The first warm day of spring
and I step out into the garden from the gloom
of a house where hope had died
to tally the storm damage, to seek what may
have survived. And finding some forgotten   5
lupins I'd sown from seed last autumn
holding in their fingers a raindrop each
like a peace offering, or a promise,
I am suddenly grateful and would
offer a prayer if I believed in God   10
But not believing, I bless the power of seed,
It's casual, useful persistence,
and bless the power of sun,
its conspiracy with the underground,
and thank my stars the winter's ended.   15

Spring
Gerard Manley Hopkins

Nothing is so beautiful as Spring—
  When weeds, in wheels, shoot long and lovely and lush;
  Thrushes' eggs look little low heavens, and thrush
Through the echoing timber does so rinse and wring
The ear, it strikes like lightnings to hear him sing;   5
  The glassy peartree leaves and blooms, they brush
  The descending blue; that blue is all in a rush
With richness; the racing lambs too have fair their fling.

What is all this juice and all this joy?
  A strain of the earth's sweet being in the beginning   10
In Eden garden.—Have, get, before it cloy,
  Before it cloud, Christ, lord, and sour with sinning,
Innocent mind and Mayday in girl and boy,
  Most, O maid's child, thy choice and worthy the winning.

Notes

[3] **Thrushes' eggs look little low heavens:** thrushes' eggs are light blue in colour

Sunny Side Plucked
Rita Ann Higgins

We met outside
the seconds chicken
van at the market.

He was very American,
I was very married.   5

We chatted about
the home-made marmalade
I bought two miles
from home.

He said the eggs were big,   10
I said he'd been eating
his carrots.

'Do you always buy
seconds chickens?'

'Only when I come late.'   15

The witch in me
wanted to scramble
his eggs.

The devil in him
wanted to pluck   20
my chicken.

We parted
with an agreement
written by the eyes.

The Meadow
Peter Fallon

We have welded the towbar
and turned the mower's eighteen blades—
the mower, the meadow reiver.
We'll work all night, by the last
and first light and, in between, by the minutes   5
of moonlight. This is hay fever.

For weeks we've watched smudged fields
weighed down by mean July.
We've heard them broadcast
brightness and woken to wet weather.   10
We'd be better off watching Billy McNamee
than paying heed to the radio forecast.

When meadows grow he finds a way.
We say we'll trust our own translation
of the sky and start to mow   15
this evening. We'll be racing the rain.
Tomorrow we'll turn and turn again.
Midweek we'll set the bob to row.

Then we'll bale. We did that then,
headed the stacks with loose hay   20
from the headlands. We thought we'd won
until we heard of loss that rotted in rows
and stopped aftergrass. Insult to injury.
Talk everywhere of fusty fodder, self-combustion.

Ten years ago we built ten thousand bales,   25
two of us, and climbed the mountain
afterwards to rest in forestry that mearns
sheep pasture, a famine field
of lazy beds. We gazed down from
a cemetery of thirty cairns   30
across a stonewalled country.
Stacks of bales in circles—our work
stood out like harvest monoliths.
A thousand stones, standing,
speaking, leaning, lying stones,   35
the key—and cornerstones of myths ...

Our farms began in those.
It was as if we tried to read the signs
of Newgrange from the moon. A thistle splinter
brought us back to earth   40
knowing that we'd gathered of its plenty
enough to fortify our care against the winter.

The Redemptorist

Austin Clarke

'How many children have you?' asked
The big Redemptorist.
'Six, Father.'
'The last,
When was it born?'   5
'Ten months ago.'
'I cannot absolve your mortal sin
Until you conceive again. Go home,
Obey your husband.'
She whimpered: 10
'But
The doctor warned me ...'
Shutter became
Her coffin lid. She twisted her thin hands
And left the box.   15
The missioner,
Red-bearded saint, had brought hell's flame
To frighten women on retreat:
Sent on his spiritual errand,
It rolled along the village street   20
Until Rathfarnham was housing smoke
That sooted the Jesuits in their castle.
'No pregnancy. You'll die the next time,'
The doctor had said.
Her tiredness obeyed   25
That Saturday night:
Her husband's weight
Digging her grave. So, in nine months, she
Sank in great agony on a Monday.
Her children wept in the orphanage,   30
Huddled together in the annexe,
While, proud of the Black Cross on his badge,
The Liguorian, at Adam and Eve's,
Ascended the pulpit, sulphuring his sleeves
And setting fire to the holy text.   35

The Smile
Michael O'Loughlin

Late summer. A Dublin Sunday,
hushed and heavy
my soles scrape the pavement

There was a smell
of burning rubber   5
from the park behind the flats

A policeman on a motorbike
zigzagged
the afternoon streets

a remote-control toy   10
smudging the air
with demon voices

A young man with a Mexican moustache
stood casual guard
as two children played in the gutter   15

I approached from a long way off
to ask him the way;
he answered slowly

as I watched the phoenix
sketched   20
on the chest of his T-shirt

'Never heard of it. But
I'll tell you this much.
It's nowhere near this kip.'

And we smiled   25
like the future regarding the past
or vice versa.

Theme for English B

Langston Hughes

The instructor said,

> *Go home and write*
> *a page tonight.*
> *And let that page come out of you—*
> *Then, it will be true.*   5

I wonder if it's that simple?
I am twenty-two, coloured, born in Winston-Salem.
I went to school there, then Durham, then here
to this college on the hill above Harlem.
I am the only coloured student in my class.   10
The steps from the hill lead down into Harlem,
through a park, then I cross St Nicholas,
Eighth Avenue, Seventh, and I come to the Y.
The Harlem Branch Y, where I take the elevator
up to my room, sit down, and write this page: 15

It's not easy to know what is true for you or me
at twenty-two, my age. But I guess I'm what
I feel and see and hear. Harlem, I hear you:
hear you, hear me—we two—you, me, talk on this page.
(I hear New York, too) Me—who?   20
Well, I like to eat, sleep, drink, and be in love.
I like to work, read, learn, and understand life.
I like a pipe for a Christmas present,
or records,—Bessie, bop or Bach.
I guess being coloured doesn't make me not like   25
the same things other folks like who are other races.

So will my page be coloured that I write?
Being me, it will not be white.
But it will be
a part of you, instructor.   30
You are white—
yet a part of me, as I am a part of you.
That's American.
Sometimes perhaps you don't want to be a part of me.
Nor do I often want to be a part of you.   35
But we are, that's true!
As I learn from you,
I guess you learn from me—
although you're older—and white—
and somewhat more free.   40

This is my page for English B.

The Telephone Call
Fleur Adcock

They asked me 'Are you sitting down?
Right? This is Universal Lotteries'
they said. 'You've won the top prize,
the Ultra-super Global Special.
What would you do with a million pounds?   5
Or, actually, it's more than a million—
not that it makes a lot of difference
once you're a millionaire.' And they laughed.

'Are you OK?' they asked—'Still there?
Come on, now, tell us, how does it feel?'   10
I said 'I just ... I can't believe it!'
They said 'That's what they all say;
What else? Go on, tell us about it.'
I said 'I feel the top of my head
has floated off, out through the window,   15
revolving like a flying saucer.'

'That's unusual' they said. 'Go on.'
I said 'I'm finding it hard to talk.
My throat's gone dry, my nose is tingling.
I think I'm going to sneeze—or cry.'   20
'That's right' they said, 'don't be ashamed
of giving way to your emotions.
It isn't every day you hear
you're going to get a million pounds.

Relax, now, have a little cry;   25
we'll give you a moment ...' 'Hang on!' I said.
'I haven't bought a lottery ticket
for years and years. And what did you say
the company's called?' They laughed again.
'Not to worry about a ticket.   30
We're Universal. We operate
a Retrospective Chances Module.

Nearly everyone's bought a ticket
in some lottery or another,
once at least. We buy up the files,   35
feed the names into our computer,
and see who the lucky person is.'
'Well, that's incredible' I said.
'It's marvellous. I still can't quite ...
I'll believe it when I see the cheque.'   40

'Oh', they said, 'there's no cheque.'
'But the money?' 'We don't deal in money.
Experiences are what we deal in.
You've had a great experience, right?
Exciting? Something you'll remember?   45
That's your prize. So congratulations
from all of us at Universal.
Have a nice day!' And the line went dead.

Unknown Girl in the Maternity Ward

Anne Sexton

Child, the current of your breath is six days long.
You lie, a small knuckle on my white bed;
lie, fisted like a snail, so small and strong
at my breast. Your lips are animals; you are fed
with love. At first hunger is not wrong.   5
The nurses nod their caps; you are shepherded
down starch halls with the other unnested throng
in wheeling baskets. You tip like a cup; your head
moving to my touch. You sense the way we belong.
But this is an institution bed.   10
You will not know me very long.

The doctors are enamel. They want to know
the facts. They guess about the man who left me,
some pendulum soul, going the way men go
and leave you full of child. But our case history   15
stays blank. All I did was let you grow.
Now we are here for all the ward to see.
They thought I was strange, although
I never spoke a word. I burst empty
of you, letting you learn how the air is so.   20
The doctors chart the riddle they ask of me
and I turn my head away. I do not know.

Yours is the only face I recognise.
Bone at my bone, you drink my answers in.
Six times a day I prize   25
your need, the animals of your lips, your skin
growing warm and plump. I see your eyes
lifting their tents. They are blue stones, they begin
to outgrow their moss. You blink in surprise
and I wonder what you can see, my funny kin,   30
as you trouble my silence. I am a shelter of lies
Should I learn to speak again, or hopeless in
such sanity will I touch some face I recognise?

Down the hall the baskets start back. My arms
fit you like a sleeve, they hold   35
catkins of your willows, the wild bee farms
of your nerves, each muscle and fold
of your first days. Your old man's face disarms
the nurses. But the doctors return to scold
me. I speak. It is you my silence harms.   40
I should have known; I should have told
them something to write down. My voice alarms
my throat. 'Name of father—none.' I hold
you and name you bastard in my arms.

And now that's that. There is nothing more   45
that I can say or lose.
Others have traded life before
and could not speak. I tighten to refuse
your owling eyes, my fragile visitor.
I touch your cheeks, like flowers. You bruise   50
against me. We unlearn. I am a shore
rocking you off. You break from me. I choose
your only way, my small inheritor
and hand you off, trembling the selves we lose.
Go child, who is my sin and nothing more.   55

Vergissmeinicht

Keith Douglas

Three weeks gone and the combatants gone,
returning over the nightmare ground
we found the place again, and found
the soldier sprawling in the sun.

The frowning barrel of his gun   5
overshadowing. As we came on
that day, he hit my tank with one
like the entry of a demon.

Look. Here in the gunpit spoil
the dishonoured picture of his girl   10
who has put: *Steffi. Vergissmeinicht*
in a copybook gothic script.

We see him almost with content
abased, and seeming to have paid
and mocked at by his own equipment   15
that's hard and good when he's decayed.

But she would weep to see today
how on his skin the swart flies move;
the dust upon the paper eye
and the burst stomach like a cave.   20

For here the lover and killer are mingled
who had one body and one heart.
And death who had the soldier singled
has done the lover mortal hurt.

A Visit to the Village
Michael Smith

No ancestral bones of ours
roll like ivory dice
in that black sea

No father of ours
drew his boat   5
across these barren fields
out under that sky
bulging with grey rain

We have no roots here
are not recorded   10
in parochial lore
of fairdays and fights
and reciprocated help

We are strangers here
come from the impersonal city   15
where rain hits concrete
with the shatter of glass

We have come here
to observe local rites
learn new words for things   20
and once again take note
of human sameness

Such roots as we have
we carry with us
in suitcases.   25

Walking in Autumn

Frances Horovitz
(For Diana Lodge)

We have overshot the wood.
The track has led us beyond trees
to the tarmac edge. Too late now
at dusk to return a different way,
hazarding barbed wire or an unknown bull.   5
We turn back onto the darkening path.
Pale under-leaves of whitebeam, alder
gleam at our feet like stranded fish
or Hansel's stones.
A wren, unseen, churrs alarm: 10
each tree drains to blackness.
Halfway now, we know
by the leaning crab-apple,
feet crunching into mud
the hard slippery yellow moons.   15
We hurry without reason
stumbling over roots and stones.
A night creature lurches, cries out,
crashed through brambles.
Skin shrinks inside our clothes;   20
almost we run
falling through darkness to the wood's end,
the gate into the sloping field.
Home is lights and woodsmoke, voices—
and, our breath caught, not trembling now,   25
a strange reluctance to enter within doors.

Wife who Smashed Television Gets Jail
Paul Durcan

'She came home, my Lord, and smashed-in the television;
Me and the kids were peaceably watching Kojak
When she marched into the living-room and declared
That if I didn't turn off the television immediately
She'd put her boot through the screen;   5
I didn't turn it off, so instead she turned it off
—I remember the moment exactly because Kojak
After shooting a dame with the same name as my wife
Snarled at the corpse—Goodnight, Queen Maeve—
And then she took off her boots and smashed-in the television;   10
I had to bring the kids round to my mother's place;
We got there just before the finish of Kojak;
(My mother has a fondness for Kojak, my Lord);
When I returned home my wife had deposited
What was left of the television into the dustbin,   15
Saying—I didn't get married to a television
And I don't see why my kids or anybody else's kids
Should have a television for a father or mother,
We'd be much better off all down in the pub talking
Or playing bar-billiards—   20
Whereupon she disappeared off back down again to the pub.'
Justice Ó Brádaigh said wives who preferred bar-billiards to family television
Were a threat to the family which was the basic unit of society
As indeed the television itself could be said to be a basic unit of the family
And when as in this case wives expressed their preference in forms of violence   25
Jail was the only place for them. Leave to appeal was refused.

When I was 15
Michael Rosen

Ken said to me,
'You know your trouble,
you don't hold your bag right.'
'What's wrong with it?' I said.
'It's the way you put it down.   5
You've got to look at it as if you hate it.
Watch me.'

He went out
he walked back in

shoulders back   10
elbows out
bag balanced in his hand.

'Watch me.'

He stopped walking.
His arm froze   15
and the bag flew out of his hand
as if he'd kicked it.
'Now you try,' he said.
'I'll show you where you've gone wrong.'
I went out the door,   20
I rambled back in again with my bag.
I stopped walking
My arm froze—just like his,
but the bag fell out of my hand
and flopped on to the floor   25
like a fried egg.

'Useless,' he said.
'You don't convince—that's your trouble.'
'So?' I said.
'I'm a slob. I can't change that.'   30

I didn't say that I would try and change
in case that would show I was giving in to him.
But secretly
on my own,
in my room,   35
in front of the mirror
I spent hours and hours
practising bag-dropping.
Walking in,
freeze the arm,   40
let the bag drop.
Walk in
arm freeze
bag drop.
Again and again   45
till I thought I had got it right.

I don't suppose any girl noticed.
I don't suppose any girl ever said to herself,
'I love the way he drops his bag ...'

Language and Writing Skills

Introductory note

The aim of the following sections is to offer guidelines on how to become a proficient and effective writer. A series of examples and exercises is set out, all of which are designed to test and improve the basic skills of writing. Sample exercises, paragraphs and compositions from actual pupils' work are examined and assessed. The approach throughout is a practical one and will help you to become more competent and confident in a variety of writing genres.

Since the new syllabus in English offers an opportunity to explore and write in many different styles and genres, the exercises and guidelines given here are structured in such a way as to make you familiar with all writing styles, from practical writing (writing reports, memos, or letters) to writing a short story, a narrative, or a discursive or imaginative composition.

1
Comprehension

Comprehension means understanding clearly a passage. It means grasping the gist of a piece of writing. To understand *what* is being said, you must pay attention to *how* it is being said.

The word **text** means the content of any type of written communication. Letters, reports, political speeches, film scripts, poems—all are texts, and they may also be treated as examples of a specific genre or a combination of different genres.

A *genre* is the particular form in which language can be structured. For example, a song, a piece of dialogue, a business report or a discursive composition are all examples of different genres.

Look at the following features in any piece of written communication to determine the genre or genres to which the writing belongs:

- the **register**—the vocabulary or kind of words that are used
- the **syntax**—the particular way in which the words are organised in a text
- the **style** of writing of the piece
- the **tone** or 'voice' of the writer
- the **structure** or layout of the writing
- the **format** or external form of the writing—whether it is written in verse or prose, or another form.

Examine the *theme*, the *intention* and the *tone* in comprehension. A writer has a particular intention in his or her writing. The writing itself will be the subject matter or theme. The writer will adopt a particular tone or tones to convey this intention more effectively.

Theme

It is important to identify the theme or subject matter of the prose passage. The writer has something to say: this is the theme. Themes can be profound and serious, or light-hearted and entertaining.

Intention

This is the *purpose* underlying the writing. A writer may have one of many different

intentions; some of these are:

- **to inform.** The writer may wish to inform the reader of particular facts or a particular situation, or to give instructions.

- **to persuade.** Persuasive writing—unlike informative or factual writing—means that the writer is advancing a particular viewpoint.

- **to teach, instruct, or moralise.** While these words are not strictly the same, sometimes a writer who wants to teach or impart some lesson may moralise or use a moralising tone.

— **to warn or alert** the reader to some danger.

— **to mock or satirise** somebody or something, for example an institution such as the Government or the Church.

— **to attack** somebody or something.

— **to amuse or entertain.**

— **to provoke a reaction.** The writer may wish to make the reader indignant or angry about something.

Tone

Tone is the relationship the writer establishes with the reader: *how* they are saying what they are saying. It is the voice of the writer.

The tone used will depend on the writer and on the purpose in writing. The writer could adopt a humorous, a satirical or an ironic tone to communicate the same ideas. On the other hand, the tone could simply be factual and informative.

All these characteristics—theme, tone, and intention—are intimately related. Comprehension can be characterised as well written when the style, tone and feeling are all suited to the message the writer wishes to convey.

Structure and form

A comprehension passage is constructed on the basis of *sentences* and *paragraphs*.

Sentences

A sentence is a self-contained combination of words that makes complete sense.

The particular structure of sentences can also be a method of communicating what the writer wants to say in a more effective fashion. A series of terse sentences can give an impression of movement, tension or excitement in a piece of writing. Look at the following example.

> As we drove through the suburbs of Dachau our car stereo became silent. My German girl-friend began to cry. We did not know what to expect. The tension in the car was overwhelming. We passed through the gates. It is a place without precedent. There is a bleakness and a silence which is indescribable. Maybe the birds do sing in these places but you never notice. The silence drowns their song.

Paragraphs

Examine the structure and paragraphing in a comprehension passage. A 'tabloid' style can consist of very short sentences, perhaps with every sentence constituting a new paragraph.

Examine how the paragraphs are linked. Paragraphs can be linked through the repetition of key words and phrases or through transitional devices such as 'Nevertheless,' 'Therefore,' 'Furthermore,' and so on.

Style and language

Style

Style means presenting the subject in a way that is best suited to achieving the writer's aim.

It is important to be able to identify the different styles used by a writer. The writer's particular use of language will add up to what is known as their style.

Language

Language and the different ways in which it can be used may be classified under the following headings:

(a) the language of *information*

(b) the language of *argument*

(c) the language of *persuasion*

(d) the language of *narration*

(e) the *aesthetic* use of language.

Language forms can overlap and intermingle. The use of language will not always be clear-cut and obvious. For example, a newspaper or television report may include a mixture of argument and persuasion. Similarly an advertisement, though essentially persuasion, may also contain information.

The language of information

This type of language is generally terse, brief and clear in approach. It forms the basis of business reports and correspondence, textbooks, newspaper and television accounts of events, and documentary films.

The following newspaper extracts could be described as informative writing. Read them carefully, then answer the questions that follow.

French tourists drown as overloaded excursion boat sinks in Catalan lake

Twenty French pensioners drowned and more than forty were injured yesterday when a pleasure boat sank on a lake in Catalunya, officials said.

Some of the victims were trapped inside when the electric-powered boat, carrying 141 passengers, went down just twenty-five metres from the dock as it began a cruise on Lago Banyoles, a popular tourist site in the province of Girona.

The boat was heavily overloaded, the Minister for the Interior, Xavier Pomes, said. The boat, the *Anna,* had 141 people on board when it broke in two. It was licensed to carry a maximum of eighty people.

Mr Pomes said it sank in eight metres of water after the captain realised there was a problem and tried to reverse direction moments after the vessel left the shore.

The sudden change of direction caused a panic on board the *Anna.* Dozens of panic-stricken passengers leaped into the cold waters. Some swam to safety, but others drowned.

Rescue crews rushed to the scene to pick up survivors, and scuba divers scoured the lake.

A spokesperson for the emergency services said that twenty passengers were confirmed dead, forty-four were injured, and everyone else on board had been accounted for. The victims all belonged to a French tour group from the port of La Rochelle.

'The cause of the accident could be an overload of the boat or a mechanical fault when it was built,' the mayor of Banyoles, Joan Solana, said. 'We don't really know yet.'

Duffy debut delight but Power failure agonising

Theresa Duffy made a memorable debut in yesterday's Dublin City Marathon, battling her way against strong winds to take the £5,000 first prize by a margin of over eight minutes.

But it was heartbreak for Séamus Power, whose brave run was eventually ended less than half a mile from the finish as he lost his battle against cramp and exhaustion.

But Duffy spoke of her delight at running the twelfth-fastest time by an Irish woman. 'I could not be happier about the way it has worked out for me, and it's just such a thrill to master the distance and win this great race,' she said.

The 29-year-old woman, who has run for Ireland in the world cross-country championships on eight occasions and hopes to make it nine in her home city next March, came home in 2 hours 39 minutes 56 seconds.

Duffy pulled away from last year's winner, Carol Galea of Malta, over the last ten miles, and Galea crossed the line in a time of 2:48.08.

The marathon also marked Power's debut over the classic distance, but he learnt the hard way how cruel such an event can be as he struggled through the closing stages, having actually taken the lead at twenty-one miles.

Power was forced to pull out almost within sight of the finishing-line in O'Connell Street, and his withdrawal ended the last challenge to the Kenyans, who were left to celebrate in style with their runners sweeping the top three places.

Questions

1. Sum up the main points in these two articles.
2. Write out the facts clearly.
3. What type of reader is addressed in each article?
4. Discuss the layout of each article. How does this contribute to the impact of the message being communicated?

The language of argument

Comprehension writing can also be structured on *argument*. Argument may be defined as a way of presenting information so as to convince or persuade the reader of some point of view. It is a type of informative writing, but it has persuasion as the basis of its structure.

You must learn to distinguish between a fact and an opinion. A fact is a statement of something that actually exists. The following statements are all facts:

> London is the capital city of England.
>
> The dog is an animal.
>
> Ireland has a wet climate.

Facts may be true in a particular context but false in another. 'With the growth in prosperity, poverty has rapidly disappeared in Ireland.' This statement may be true in some parts of Ireland, or for some people, but not for others. 'Access to the computer and the internet has made children more mature and literate.' This may be true in regions where technology is more accessible, but it is not true for all parts of the world.

An *opinion* is a judgment or a belief that is held by someone: it goes beyond a fact to make a judgment on the fact. For example, 'The dog is a lovely animal' and 'London is a dirty city' are opinions.

To test factual statements we must examine the evidence. To test statements of opinion we must do two things:

(a) examine the evidence of fact;

(b) examine the inferences drawn from it.

Identify the facts in the following extract:

> Smoking cannabis has valuable medical uses. Cannabis is an immensely complex drug that has over four hundred compounds, including more than sixty chemical derivatives— cannabinoids—which, when ignited, convert to two thousand chemicals.
>
> It is these cannabinoids that have provided relief from pain, nausea and weight loss in some people with multiple sclerosis, cancer, and AIDS. As Peter Cardy, chief executive of the Multiple Sclerosis Society says, 'other sufferers have had unpleasant side effects.'

> Doctors agree that the other toxic constituents in smoked cannabis could actually increase the risk of pneumonia and weaken the immune system in AIDS and cancer patients.

In analysing writing, and particularly writing that is based on argument, it is important to distinguish between valid evidence and false evidence.

Argument is *valid* when the conclusion follows logically from the premise. To test the validity of an argument,

(a) assess the truth of the premise or main statement.

(b) assess the truth of each argument,

(c) assess the truth of each sub-argument.

Look at the following remarks on the subject of dangerous driving. Distinguish the arguments that are made; assess what is fact and what is opinion.

> A few years ago I gave a lift to a French acquaintance who had been in Ireland for a couple of weeks. As I manoeuvred the car through the sea of people who had ignored the red pedestrian light at O'Connell Bridge, my passenger became animated.
>
> Had Irish people some kind of death wish? he asked: they push buggies with children from between parked cars onto busy streets; they see the amber light as a signal not to stop but to accelerate; they park on street corners and on double yellow lines.
>
> I had to agree with his thesis: that there is a widespread disregard for the rules of the road.
>
> If asked I could have added a number of other misdemeanours: allowing children to put their heads through the sunroofs of cars while the car is moving, or to bounce around on the back or front seats unrestrained; or to see any half-decent stretch of road as an opportunity to put the foot down; or to try to square off parking or speeding offences with a Garda friend; or to drive with one hand holding a mobile phone to the ear; or, most despicable, to climb into a car after a night's drinking in the pub.
>
> The point, though, is that Irish people do not treat potential road traffic offences as seriously as other areas of law.

Somehow drivers choose to ignore the potential consequences of their actions: drink-driving and speeding are the main contributory factors behind the high accident rate in this country. Last year 472 people died on the roads and a further 13,000 were injured.

Processes of argument

There are two different processes of argument or reasoning:

- deductive reasoning
- inductive reasoning.

Generally speaking, coherent opinions will use either deductive or inductive reasoning in their development of the argument.

The process of placing a general statement first and following it with supporting details is knows as the *deductive* method of reasoning. Reversing this procedure—opening a paragraph and making a statement with particular details that lead to a broad statement—is known as *inductive* reasoning. The inductive method is useful for leading the reader through a series of persuasive details to a conclusion.

Deductive reasoning

Deduction means 'moving away from'. It begins with a general law and moves to a particular case. 'All men are mortal; John is a man; therefore John is mortal.'

'All Irishmen are alcoholics; John is an Irishman; therefore John is an alcoholic.' The structure here is correct but the reasoning process and conclusion drawn are false. This is because the first premise is not true.

Look at the following statements. 'All animals are dangerous; our pet cat is an animal; therefore our cat is dangerous.' This appears to be a logical structure; the reasoning is false, however, because again the first premise is not a fact. 'All Irish people are friendly; Máire is friendly; therefore Máire is Irish.' The reasoning here is false because the first assertion is not a fact and because the conclusion does not logically follow from the preceding statements.

Inductive reasoning

Induction means 'leading into'. This kind of reasoning begins by observing individual phenomena and then arriving at a general law. It is the kind of argument commonly used by scientists and by barristers. 'John is a man; John is mortal; therefore men are mortal.'

An inductive argument generally has the following structure: a proposition or statement of the thesis; the evidence presented; the conclusion. Here are some examples of inductive arguments:

Fire burns you when you touch it; Mark has his hand in the fire; therefore Mark will burn his hand.

Water expands when it is frozen; the weather is freezing; therefore it is reasonable to suppose that the pipes may burst.

Regular meals are a requirement of good health; Margaret neglects her meals; so it can be presumed that she will fall ill.

To be effective, both deductive and inductive arguments must be based on proven facts and demonstrable evidence.

Exercises

Examine the following articles, which are examples of the language of argument, and then answer the questions that follow.

Passage 1

Why we dream what we dream

Stephen King, the author of nightmare-inducing horror novels, has a recurring nightmare of his own: he's working in a hot, cramped room, and a madwoman is hiding behind the door, brandishing a scalpel. If he doesn't finish his work, she'll burst into the room. And she does.

King always wakes just before she slashes him. He says he dreams of her when he's scrambling to catch up on his work. 'Consciousness is like an ocean, with different issues living at different levels,' he tells the author Naomi Epel in *Writers Dreaming*. 'Whatever's going on in our lives trickles down and has some sort of influence down there.'

He's right. Dreams, as new research is showing, are often distorted reflections of our daily lives—not necessarily symbolic pictures of our unconscious wishes, as Freud believed, or random nonsensical images caused by brain signals. Many experts now believe our dreams are so closely related to our waking lives that we can use them to help recognise and work out inner conflicts.

Men and women dream differently. Why? 'It's biology and social conditioning,' says Milton Kramer, director of the Sleep Centre at Bethesda Oak Hospital in Cincinnati.

In a study of a thousand dreams, half from each sex, Robert Can de Castle, author of *Our Dreaming Mind,* found that men more often have action dreams involving strangers identified mostly by their occupation. Usually these dreams are set outdoors or in unfamiliar surroundings. Women dream more of emotional one-to-one struggles with loved ones, usually in indoor settings.

When Amy Tan, author of *The Joy Luck Club,* was in her mid-twenties she dreamed she hired a pair of wings for a pittance and took off, flying with other people and having a splendid time. Suddenly she asked herself, How can I fly with these cheap wings? At once she started to fall. She was afraid she was about to die—until she realised that if she'd been flying before the frightening thought came to her, she ought to be able to fly again.

Finally it occurred to her that the wings were not what enabled her to fly: it was her own confidence. Awake, she also saw she wasn't allowing herself to do many things in her life because she lacked the confidence.

Amy Tan's dream was typical of early adulthood, a time when people question confidence and self-esteem. 'Life has stages in which things must be accomplished,' says Rosalind Cartwright, author of *Crisis Dreaming.* 'The issues we grapple with during those stages show up in dreams, and, while asleep, we often update how we're doing in a particular stage.'

Passage 2

The history of life on Earth has been a history of interaction between living things and their surroundings. To a large extent, the physical form and the habits of the Earth's vegetation and its animal life have been moulded by the environment. During the past quarter century the power of man to alter the nature of his world has not only increased in magnitude but has altered in character.

The most alarming of all man's assaults upon the environment is the contamination of air, earth, rivers and sea with dangerous and even lethal materials. This pollution is for the most part irrecoverable: the chain of evil it initiates not only in the world that must support life but in living tissues is for the most part irreversible.

In this now universal contamination of the environment, chemicals are the sinister partners of radiation in changing the very nature of the world—the very nature of its life. Strontium 90, released through nuclear explosions in the air, comes to earth in rain, or drifts down as fallout, lodges in soil, enters into the grass or corn or wheat grown there, and in time takes up its abode in the bones of a human being, there to remain until his death.

Similarly, chemicals sprayed on croplands or forests or gardens lie long in soil, entering into living organisms, passing from one to another in a chain of poison and death. Or they pass mysteriously by underground streams until they combine into new forms that kill vegetation, sicken cattle, and work unknown harm on those who drink from once-pure wells. As Albert Schweitzer has said, 'man can hardly recognise the devils of his own creation.'

[Rachel Carson, *Silent Spring*]

Questions

1. Outline the stages of argument in each article.
2. Identify the reasoning structure used in each case, i.e. whether deductive or inductive.
3. What is the attitude of the writer to the subject in each article?
4. Examine the evidence used by each writer to support their argument. Is this evidence valid? Refer to each article to support your answer.
5. Sum up the main arguments in each article. Would you agree with these arguments? Give reasons for your answer.

The language of persuasion

Persuasive writing is used by writers to win you over to their side. It is a technique often used in advertising and in satirical or political speeches, and it makes use of a variety of devices to achieve its purpose.

Persuasive writing may not depend on facts or logic: instead there is a heavy reliance on emotive language. The techniques used in this style of writing are designed to operate on the level of feeling and emotion, not logic or rational thought. The words that are used are chosen in order to manipulate the emotion and imagination of the reader. Because the persuasive writer aims at manipulating the emotions and feelings of the audience, stress is placed on channelling feelings in a particular direction.

Persuasive writing is not limited to advertising: areas such as business, the media and politics employ persuasive means to achieve their purpose. The audience addressed will generally determine both the content and the quality, together with the type of language used in this type of writing.

Look at the following passages, which are taken from different sources, and then answer the questions that follow.

If you'd like to retire with a million—start taking your own advice.

And if your mind clamps shut at the mere mention of the word 'million', consider this: if you add up your lifetime earnings—past and future—you will see that you will almost certainly earn a fortune in your lifetime. It could add up to a million pounds or more.

The trouble is, like most people you'll earn it—and spend it.

Of course what you could be doing is taking this fortune and turning some of it into another fortune—the one you want to end up with.

Perhaps you think you should entrust you money to an expert. If you do you may be disappointed. The shocking truth is that many professional fund managers are not much good at what they do.

In fact the widely accepted Random Walk theory says that you will beat the pros at picking shares by simply blindfolding yourself and sticking a pin in the share table in your newspaper.

Incredible, but true.

Look at unit trusts. The vast majority underperform the stock market in general over time.

The question is, why pay fat commissions and management fees to have a so-called professional manage your money?

What about seeking advice from a financial adviser—someone who'll give you sound and impartial advice on what best to do with you hard-earned money?

Successful personal investing (SPI) is the much-acclaimed, up-to-the-minute, 'hands-on' self-instruction course in investing and money management that you follow at home, at your own pace—with no pressure.

SPI shows you how to start on the way towards having that million, and being able to tell yourself that you are a millionaire. So, before your mind clamps shut over that word again, why not at least take the opportunity to see for yourself? You can get to look over the first two lessons with no obligation for ten days just by posting the coupon below. And whatever you decide, lesson 1 is yours to keep—FREE!

Why do they schedule meetings for 3:00 in the morning?

Actually, they don't. It only feels that way when you're jet-lagging.

Fortunately, relief is now at hand. It's the Hotel Okura's Jet Lag Plan, designed to get you up on your feet and feeling chipper. It includes a light-box to help put your body's clock back on schedule, a health club work-out and jet bath, relaxation videos, a body sonic massage, your choice of pillows to help you sleep better (we'll even remember your favourite for your next visit), and dinner suggestions for extra energy.

The Jet Lag Plan is only 10,000 yen extra per day, or free for members of the Okura Club International, our special programme for frequent guests. To receive a free brochure, simply send your name and address to our Public Relations Office.

Take the plunge, and don't wait for summer
You won't see coral reefs, shoals of colourful fish, or glamorous film stars, but you will learn to dive at a fraction of the cost.

Weather getting you down? Need something to remind you of the tropics, of beaches and bikinis? Why not learn to scuba-dive?

It's not as daft or as far-fetched as it sounds. Nor as expensive. And come next year you'll have your diving certificate—that coveted bit of paper that says you can swim underwater with heavy metal accessories on your back.

Come next year, when you're diving in the Red Sea, the Great Barrier Reef, or even the wrecks off Scotland, you'll pat yourself on the back for having spent the winter doing something so useful. Unless you decide to take off before then, of course. There are many great winter diving spots: Egypt, Kenya, the Indian Ocean, the Caribbean …

All you need is that bit of paper.

Questions
1. What is the *purpose* of each extract?
2. Pick out *three* examples in each text where the writer appeals to emotion.
3. Who is the intended *audience* in each case?
4. What *techniques* are used in each case to convey the argument? Refer to sensationalism, implication, emotional language, or exaggeration.
5. What type of publication would you consider to be suitable for each passage? Give reasons for you answer.
6. Identify the *facts* in each article.
7. Write a note on the *language* in each extract, paying particular attention to the emotive or rhetorical use of words.

The language of narration
In *narrative* writing the writer is telling a story. There is a definite arrangement of ideas or sequence of events. Narrative writing puts an emphasis on description—describing people, actions and events in detail.

Look at the following examples of narrative writing, then answer the questions that follow.

Passage 1
That morning was bright and clear. There was a noticeable lack of street noise. I had a quick shower, packed my briefcase and dressed. I left at twenty minutes past seven. It took only minutes at most to walk from my villa to the university. In a hurry I could easily make it in five. I left the villa, walking through the long garden that separated it from the street. I stopped as I always did to look at three or four carp which swam in the fish pond. I went to look at some of the creeping plants that were already beginning to spread with some vigour along the wall. I went out through the gate, locking it behind me, and began to walk off in the direction of the university. I had taken, I suppose, no more than twelve steps. I was barely away from the gate and the fence which enclosed the garden when an old Mercedes, hand-painted dark green with a cream roof, pulled up alongside me. The driver's door opened, preventing me from passing on to the narrow street.

Out jumped four men, the driver with a hand pistol, three other young men in their mid-twenties, each with a Kalashnikov in his hand and a hand gun in his belt. I stood and we exchanged silent glances. How long this took I do not know. But I remember looking at them, they looking at me. Then I was pushed quickly into the back seat with two of the Kalashnikov-toting gunmen. The door slammed and the car moved off quickly.

[Brian Keenan, *An Evil Cradling*]

Questions
1. What type of person is the writer? Give reasons for your answer by referring to the extract above.
2. Divide this story into different scenes, and show how each scene develops the action in the story.
3. Pick out *three* details that make this story realistic.
4. Discuss how the writer creates an atmosphere of suspense in the extract above.

Passage 2

Once there lived a lovelorn blacksmith. For years he had loved a local spinster, but he was shy, as most blacksmiths are. The spinster, who eked out a poor existence by boiling and selling toffee, was also lonely, in fact desperate for a husband, but too modest and proud to seek one. With the years the spinster's desperation grew, as did the blacksmith's speechless passion.

Then one day the spinster stole into the church and threw herself down on her knees. 'O Lord!' she prayed, 'please be mindful of me and send me a man to marry!' Now the blacksmith by chance was up in the belfry mending the old church clock. Every breathless word of the spinster's entreaties rose clearly to where he was. When he heard her praying 'Please send me a man' he nearly fell off the roof with excitement. But he kept his head, turned his voice to Jehovah's and boomed, 'Will a blacksmith do?'

'Ern a man's better than nern, dear Lord!' cried the spinster gratefully.

At which the blacksmith ran home, changed into his best, and caught the spinster on her way out of the church. He proposed, and they married, and lived forever contented, and used his forge for boiling her toffee.

[Laurie Lee, *Cider With Rosie*]

Questions

1. Discuss the character of both the woman and the blacksmith in this story.
2. Sum up the main points of this story in three sentences.
3. In your opinion, what is the purpose of this story?
4. What is the climax of this story?

The aesthetic use of language

The emphasis here is on the nature of words and images and on how they function to broaden the imaginative faculty and reveal the richness and beauty underlying ideas. The use of images, the ability to create pictures through striking description, is the significant feature here.

To see how words work to create pictures, it is necessary to examine the nature of imagery.

Imagery

Imagery can be used in prose writing for different reasons:

— **to illustrate a point** (in the following example the writer wishes to point out that African people are good at the art of mimicry; he uses images from animal life to illustrate his argument): 'In the shambas you would sometimes come upon a spurfowl which would run in front of your horse as if her wing was broken and she was terrified of being caught by the dogs. But her wing was not broken, and she was not afraid of the dogs—she would whir up before them the moment she chose—only she had got her brood of young chickens somewhere near by, and she was drawing our attention away from them. Like the spurfowl, the natives might be mimicking a fear of us because of some deeper dread, the nature of which we could not guess.'

— **to evoke atmosphere:** 'As we recline in our comfortable armchairs the silver screen feeds us delicious tales of danger and excitement. Who has not thrilled to the sight of ghost ships whose eerie spectres haunt the waves? Who has not been fascinated by the allure of mermaids and sirens who charm their victims into strange and deadly underwater kingdoms?'

— **to provoke an emotional impact:** 'A fearful man, all in coarse grey, with a great iron on his leg. A man with no hat, and with broken shoes, and with an old rag tied round his head. A man who had been soaked in water, smothered in mud, lamed by stones, cut by flints, stung by nettles, torn by briars, who limped and shivered, glared and growled, whose teeth chattered in his head and who seized me by the chin' [Charles Dickens, *Great Expectations*].

There are different kinds of imagery:

— **simple:** 'For years, horses have been harnessed, ridden, spurred, and whipped.'

— **vivid or clear:** 'He is nearly as tall as a Dublin policeman.'

— **ornate or flowery:** 'tropical islands where luxurious fruits and exotic plants conceal the slopes of sulphurous volcanoes.'

When you see imagery in a comprehension passage, ask yourself the following questions:

- What does it say?
- Why is it used?
- How well does it function in the passage?
- Does it produce 'sound effects'?

The ability to master description and to paint pictures is an important part of the aesthetic use of language.

Descriptive writing

Where narrative writing tells us what people and things *do,* descriptive writing tells us what things are *like.* Descriptive writing

- gives a clear picture
- selects details with great care
- uses precise vocabulary and avoids exaggeration.

The following passage uses a keen sense of detail and a striking power of description.

> The rich colouring of the land was shorn away, or beaten down by wind and rain. On the hills the grey fields were like the faces of spent men; the leaves lay in sodden drifts in the loenens, and the water rose brownly in the wells. The men ran new runlets against the unequivocal storms, patched barns and byres, brerded hedges where the falling leaf revealed gaps, and listened patiently to the indoor needs of the farmwife. The women felt the breasts of fowls, laid fragrant apples in the loft.
>
> Before the boathouse lay bleached rollers, half-buried in the shingle. The two brothers sent the little boat dancing over the shallow leaden waters. Above them to the east a cloud rose up, spreading rapidly on either hand like a sheaf shaken loose. A blue light played swiftly over the low hills of Ards, followed by a distant brattle of thunder. The boat threaded its way between the intervening islets, crept across the sound, and grated on the shingle beach of Pentland's Island.
>
> [Sam Hanna Bell, *December Bride*]

The questions on the comprehension passage may test you in some or all of the following ways:

1. They may test whether you understand the subject and the content of the passage: in other words, do you understand exactly what the writer is saying?
2. Questions can also test your ability to draw conclusions, to follow a line of argument, or to recognise the use of evidence.
3. Some of the questions may also test your assessment of the style or language used in the passage. Questions on style test the ways in which language is used in the passage: they are designed to test your understanding of how the writer expresses the content. In answering questions of this type, you must first of all
   (*a*) identify the feature,
   (*b*) give an example from the passage, and
   (*c*) comment on its effectiveness within the passage, i.e. its effect in communicating the theme.
4. Questions may also test your imaginative response to the passage.

Read the following passages, then look at the questions that follow, which contain an example comment on some of these features.

Passage 1

If we encourage children to take part in adult culture, what conclusions will they draw about us? What does it say about my son that he can spend a morning with three elderly friends of the family and ask as I wave goodbye from the car if they are a *menage à trois*? What kind of values am I—and his devoted restaurant-critic father—really passing on to this boy? I tremble to think—particularly when I recall a conversation we had about a recent car repair bill. £140? Why, that's the price of a good lunch in London!

Some of the excess sophistication is not our doing. We were not to know, when we started this experiment, that the games they would be playing on their expensive new computers were going to be quite so violent, or that sooner or later, if not in their own homes then in the home of a friend or a relative, they would get their hands on X-rated videos.

But the sad truth is that we haven't even been able to turn them into post-hippie altruists. If you don't believe me, try taking four children to a video shop and tell them they have five minutes to agree on a video they all want to watch. Or watch how older boys behave when they have been coerced into letting their younger sisters have ten minutes on their Nintendos. The boys of my acquaintance still act too rough, and the girls play catty tricks on each other while playing School and House.

Another continuing headache: xenophobia. Children who wouldn't dream of judging anyone by their skin will hate, hate, hate countries that destroy their rain-forests or condone the killing of whales. The world is still divided by the good guys and the bad guys. I remember the last election, when I found my eight-year-old daughter in tears in her bed, sobbing, 'Why, oh why, do we have to live in Douglas Hurd country?'

Slowly and reluctantly, we are beginning to discover what everyone else knew all along: that equality is not necessarily educational. As one recovering egalitarian put it, you go along during those happy years when you are teaching them to think independently, but still running the show, because you're bigger and stronger than them, and you realise too late that the point of having some authority over your children is to protect them from doing things that are dangerous and stupid. I have no recourse but to trust my boys, but it's nerve-wracking, because I'm sure they're trustworthy. But trying to get them to obey me without simple safety measures is like trying to walk without arms and legs.

Questions

Questions to test your understanding of the subject or content
1. According to the writer, what prejudices has the modern child?
2. What is the writer saying about the effect of increased responsibility and excessive sophistication on children today?
3. What difficulties does the author claim parents are discovering? Refer to the second-last and last paragraphs in your answer.

Questions to test your ability to draw conclusions or recognise the use of evidence
1. Explain how the writer develops the point made in the third paragraph that 'the sad truth is that we haven't even been able to turn them into post-hippie altruists.'
2. In your opinion, is the writer happy with the behaviour and attitudes of modern children?

Give reasons for your answer.
3. What difficulties does the writer face as a parent based on her encouragement of her children 'to take part in adult culture'?

Questions to test your assessment of the style or language used
1. Comment on the writer's use of quotation in the passage.
2. Pick out three features of style that impressed you.
3. Identify the tone or tones in this passage. How do they contribute to the general impact of the writing?

Passage 2

I asked Captain Hieu, the Vietnamese officer I was assigned to assist, why our base had been established in such a vulnerable spot.

'Very important outpost,' he assured me.

'What is its mission?' I asked

'Very important outpost,' he repeated.

'But why is it here?'

'Outpost is here to protect airfield,' he said, pointing in the direction of a departing helicopter.

'What's the airfield here for?'

'Airfield here to supply outpost.'

This was the reality of Viet Nam. I would spend nearly twenty years, one way or another, grappling with our experience in that country. And over all that time it rarely made much more sense that Hieu's circular reasoning. We're here because we're here because we're here …

During my first patrol I was a quarter of the way back in the column, the customary place for advisers, when I heard several sharp cracks. Incoming fire, the first I had ever experienced. I heard a scream ahead. The men began shooting and running in utter confusion. I repressed my own terror and started to make my way forward.

At the head of the column I saw a crowd of Vietnamese huddled round a groaning soldier, a medic kneeling at his side. In a creek lay another small figure dead. We had taken casualties from attackers who had vanished before we had ever seen them. The whole cycle—silence, shots, confusion, death, and silence again—was over in a couple of minutes.

As night fell we camped on high ground, where we would be less vulnerable to attack. I threw down my pack, my carbine, my helmet damp with cold sweat, and slumped to the ground. I felt drained. The lark was over. The exhilaration of a cocky 25-year-old American had evaporated in a single burst of gunfire. This was not war movies at a Saturday afternoon cinema: it was real, and it was ugly. From then on we were ambushed daily. The entry in my diary for 18 May is significant. 'Contact 0805. 1 VC KIA' (killed in action).

We had been patrolling a gorge fed by a rushing stream. This covered up our noise, and for once we spotted the Viet Cong before they spotted us. For once, we did the ambushing.

We nailed them. A hail of fire dropped several, and the rest fled. We approached gingerly. One man lay motionless on the ground, the first dead Viet Cong I could confirm we had killed. He lay on his back, gazing up at us with sightless eyes. My gaze fixed on his feet. He was wearing sandals cut from an old tyre. This was our fearsome unseen enemy. I felt nothing, certainly not sympathy. I had seen too much suffering and death to care anything about what happened on theirs.

If we came across a village on our march we burned down the thatched huts and destroyed the crops. Why were we doing this?

Ho Chi Min, the North Vietnamese leader, had said the people were like the sea in which his guerrillas swam. Our problem was to distinguish neutral fish from the Viet Cong swimming alongside. We tried to solve the problem by making the whole sea uninhabitable. In the hard logic of war, what difference did it make if you shot your enemy or starved him to death?

I had no qualms about what we were doing. I had been conditioned to believe in the wisdom of my superiors, and to obey. This was counter-insurgency at the cutting edge. Hack down the peasants' crops, thus denying food to the Viet Cong, who were supported by the North Vietnamese, who in turn were backed by Moscow and Peking, who were our mortal enemies in the global struggle between freedom and communism. It all made sense in those days.

Questions

Questions to test your understanding of the content or subject of this passage

1. Why does the writer claim that he had no qualms about what he was doing?
2. Outline four points the writer makes about the American military operation in Viet Nam.
3. What is the significance of the conversation at the beginning of the passage?

Questions to test your ability to follow a line of argument or to draw conclusions

1. Show how the writer reaches the conclusion that the Soviet Union and China were the enemies of the American military in the 'global struggle between freedom and communism.'
2. What does the writer mean by the statement 'We tried to solve the problem by making the whole sea uninhabitable'?
    Show how he succeeded in doing this.
3. Do you think the writer gives a very clear picture of the horror of war? Support your answer by appropriate reference to the passage.
4. The passage finishes with the sentence 'It all made sense in those days.' From reading the passage, written more than twenty years after the events described in it, do you think the writer feels that the events that occurred in Viet Nam make sense? Give reasons for your answer.

Questions to test your analysis of the style

1. Identify *three* different tones in this passage and comment on the function of each one in communicating the points.
2. Do you think this is a well-written passage? Give reasons for your answer.
3. Pick out *three* effective images, and justify your choice in each case.

The summary

Questions may also test your ability to *summarise* the main points of a passage. Summary-writing is an accurate measurement of your ability to understand a passage and to communicate this understanding in writing. A summary tests your ability to choose the main points and to condense them and to organise the material in a logical and coherent manner.

You are required to reduce the material, generally to a specified number of words.

Method of doing a summary

1. Read the passage through several times (three or four times) in order to grasp the gist or central points that are being made. At this stage, check exactly what the writer is saying. How is the writer expressing his or her content? It is important to understand not only what is being said but also how it is being said. In other words, examine the writer's *purpose* in the passage.

2. Don't worry or waste time trying to work out the meaning of difficult words. First get the main ideas of the passage into your head.

3. Notice how the passage is developed, the particular stages through which it moves. In this case note the number of paragraphs (if any). Trace the different stages through which the writer develops his or her thoughts.

4. Work at getting the main points down in the form of a rough draft.

5. Read the passage through again and compare it with your draft. Fill in any gaps or essential points that are missing.

6. Write out your summary in prose form as one main paragraph.

7. Count the number of words and check them against what is asked.

8. Check that all the main points in the original passage are included in your draft.

9. Include all dates, numbers and statistics in the summary.

10. Leave out examples or illustrations unless they are essential.

11. Change direct quotations to indirect quotations, without quotation marks. For example, if the passage contains the quotation '"We are all born to this stage of fools" (Shakespeare)' write instead:

'Shakespeare said that we were all born to this stage of fools.' Notice that the tense changes to the past tense here, and you make use of the word 'that' when reporting speech.

12. Commands and requests must be rephrased. For example: 'The President said, "Stop the war".'—'The President told them to stop the war.' 'The woman asked the girl, "Why are you crying?"'—'The woman asked the girl why she was crying.'

13. Write your summary in the past tense.

14. Make sure to write the number of words at the end of your summary.

Exercise

1. Write a summary of the following article in about sixty words.

With a thorough knowledge of your firm and its products, its markets and marketing policy, your previous advertising, the various constraints imposed, the competition you face, and changes in business background, you can now commence more positive action-problem analysis and determination of your specific advertising objective.

Advertising is a means of achieving an objective. Your firm may have more than one reason for advertising and thus need to run two or more concurrent campaigns. The underlying purpose of these campaigns may also change from time to time with circumstances.

There is a remarkably wide range of reasons for advertising—one well-known analysis contains a check-list of fifty-two advertising tasks! Even the more fundamental reasons are, surprisingly enough, a blind spot to many advertising people, who are so engrossed in the detail of their work that they overlook the need to define clearly the basic purpose of their advertising. Many times, when you enquire about the objective of a proposed advertising campaign, you receive a surprised look and the answer, 'Why, it's to increase sales, of course'—as though you had asked a foolish question. But how are these increased sales to be achieved? 'Increased sales' is not a business objective but only an optimistic hope for the future. If these increased sales are, in fact, to be realised, then there must be a definite objective, for, as you will see later, this will affect the type of advertising campaign, the media used, and its creative content.

[Martyn Davis, *The Effective Use of Advertising Media*]

Sample summary

Advertising is a means of achieving an objective. Your specific advertising policy can be determined with more knowledge of your firm and the competition you face. Many advertisers fail to define a clear purpose. To achieve increased sales a definite objective must be defined, which will affect the content and media used in the advertising campaign. [56 words]

2. Write a summary of the following article in about seventy words.

The Campbell-Bewley group has taken its first sip of the American coffee market, acquiring a Boston café company, Rebecca's Café.

Mr Patrick Campbell, the group's chairman, said yesterday that the decision to buy the company's eleven cafés and its corporate and contract catering business was part of a strategy to introduce the Bewley's brand name to the United States.

The Rebecca's Café name will be maintained, however, and, with the backing of Campbell-Bewley, the chain will expand. Its expected sales in 1997 are about $20 million (£13.5 million), according to Campbell-Bewley. The acquisition cost is believed to be in the region of £5 million.

'We have paid what we consider a good price for it but one that will give us a good return,' Mr Campbell said. He said Rebecca's had established its own reputation, despite aggressive competition from such chains as Starbuck's. 'We see this as a springboard for the American market. The first thing we need to do is get comfortable with Rebecca's. We would hope to open a Bewley's café within the Boston area this year,' he said.

Campbell-Bewley has been seeking an American foothold for the past two years, after establishing eight outlets in England in addition to its twenty-five in Ireland.

The president of Rebecca's Café, Bob Tyack, said that neither he nor his two partners had been seeking to sell the eleven-year-old company, but they had been approached by an investment banker. It had helped that his company's chief financial officer, Conor Creedon, from County Cork, was familiar with the Bewley name.

Because of its size, Rebecca's Café had been frustrated by the limited growth rate it could achieve, Mr Tyack added. It employs three hundred people in nine Boston locations and two locations in nearby Cambridge and Burlington.

[*Irish Times*, 29 August 1997]

Sample summary

Bewley's group has acquired Rebecca's Café, a Boston café company. The name will remain the same. According to the chairman of Campbell-Bewley, expected sales in 1997 will be about $20 million. The acquisition cost is roughly £5 million. Campbell-Bewley has established eight outlets in England, as well as twenty-five in Ireland. Rebecca's Café had a limited growth rate because of its size. It employs three hundred people in nine Boston cafés. [74 words]

Check-list on writing summaries

1. Have you got the required number of words?
2. Is the summary a connected and readable piece of prose?
3. Check for errors in spelling, grammar, and punctuation.

Methods of answering comprehension questions

1. Read first all the questions to be answered. Very often one question can throw light on another.
2. Divide your time between the questions, making sure to note the number of marks allotted to each question.
3. Read the passage through very carefully two or three times in order to understand fully the meaning of what is written. Don't waste time trying to unravel the meaning of difficult or awkward words: the main idea is to get a general idea or gist of the arguments in the passage.
4. It can often help to jot down a title or a heading in order to identify the main theme of the passage.
5. Start on the easiest questions first, and begin to work on a rough draft. Get down notes and ideas related to the question.
6. Read the passage again for each question. If four questions are asked, read it four times. Jot down ideas and points as you go along, all the time organising and forming a rough draft. Read the questions *carefully*. Note the difference between such terms as 'discuss', 'compare', 'contrast', 'criticise'.
7. Write out your answers clearly, factually, and logically. Make your answers as crisp and clear as possible.
8. Use your own words where possible.
9. Keep control of the time: don't let it control you. Dedicate an equal amount of time to each question. Stop writing when your five or ten minutes are up. Leave a space if necessary and come back later if you can. The main thing is to tackle every question and every aspect of every question.
10. Don't waste time trying to puzzle out the answer to a difficult question. Leave it for later. Do the composition, and possibly the answer will come to you.
11. When reading back, read with a purpose. Check that you have answered the actual question. Is your answer logical, relevant, and orderly? Are the examples that are given relevant and useful?

Know how to recognise the kind of tone, and know the reason why it is used.

Know how to identify underlying attitudes, to 'read between the lines.' Know the writer's attitude to the subject in question. Know how to distinguish between a fact and an opinion.

Analyse whether the writer proves the point, and how. This can be done in several different ways: logically, with examples, by means of anecdotes, through facts, comparisons, contrasts, statistics, etc.

Common errors in comprehension answers

1. *Misunderstanding the content:* incorrect facts, or a lack of factual information.
2. *Misunderstanding the questions:* failure to distinguish between terms such as 'How does the writer reach the conclusion that …?' and 'Why does the writer claim that …?' In the first question you are asked about the *method*, the techniques used by the writer, while in the second you are asked for the *reason* underlying the writer's claim.
3. *Not giving reasons for answers* when asked to do so.
4. *Failure to analyse the effect and impact of examples.* Take, for example, a question such as 'Give two examples of the writer's use of effective argument, and justify your choice in each case.' Merely *quoting* two examples, without justifying or showing their use and effect in the passage, will result in a loss of marks.
5. *Badly structured answers,* where minor or irrelevant points are developed and the main point is ignored.
6. *Badly written answers:* answers with faulty grammar or punctuation and weak expression.
7. *Irrelevancies* and information that has no bearing on the question asked: not coming to grips with what is really asked in the question.

Characteristics of well-written answers

1. There must be *a clear analysis and understanding of the content* in the passage.
2. The answers must *focus directly on the questions asked* and make detailed reference to the passage. This is particularly important when the question uses terms such as 'justify your answer' or 'refer to the passage.'
3. You must show *a basic knowledge of the fundamental elements of prose*, for example tone, and structure of sentences
5. Your answers should show clear expression: they should be written in clear, correct English, with good organisation of thought.
6. Answers must be *clear, logical, factual, and precise*.

Vocabulary for comprehension

To answer questions on comprehension you must be aware of the meaning of the following words:

compare: to show the similarities and the differences between things (*compare with:* to make a comparison; *compare to:* to suggest a similarity).

contrast: to show the differences between things.

criticise: to point out mistakes and weaknesses in a balanced way.

define: to give the precise meaning of a concept.

discuss: to explain an item and give details, with examples.

explain: to offer a detailed and exact explanation of an idea or principle.

illustrate: to give examples that demonstrate and prove.

justify: to give the reasons for a position.

prove: to give answers that demonstrate the logical arguments.

state: to express the points, briefly and clearly.

summarise, outline: give only the main points, not details.

trace: to give a description in logical or chronological order of the stages of a process.

Literary terms

You must also have a good understanding of the meaning of the following terms:

alliteration: the repetition of the same initial consonant. 'The day dawns ... dry bedroom air ... a dark exhausted eye, a dry downturning mouth ...'

allusion: a reference. Allusions can be

—**scientific:** 'Darwin suggested in a letter written in 1871 that life arose in a warm little pond'

—**literary:** 'I wondered whether he knew the legend of Diarmaid and Gráinne ...'

—**historical:** 'During the Napoleonic wars the squirearchy were a strong social system in England'

—**political:** 'Was it for this the Wild Geese spread the grey wing on every tide? For this that all the blood was shed?'

—**Biblical or religious:** 'Christ's temptations in the desert are an example to us for all time'

—**mythical:** 'Parnassian islands'; 'no second Troy.'

ambiguity: the use of an expression or word that has a number of possible meanings in such a way that it is difficult to tell which meaning is intended. 'Love is blind'; 'For men were born to pray and save'; 'Fair is foul and foul is fair'. Unintentional ambiguity: 'Woman acts to keep her husband from unemployment.' Ambiguity can also be created by deliberately punning on words that have similar sounds but different meanings.

analogy: a comparison that points out a relationship or similarity between two things. Analogies compare things from different classes: for example, a writer wishing to show the corrupting effect of power could draw an analogy between political power and spiritual power.

assonance: the rhyming of vowel sounds within words: shade, grain, hail ... 'and the watery hazes of the hazel ...'

atmosphere: the feelings or emotions evoked by a scene, by a work of art or music, etc.

balance: the placing of two parts of a sentence, or words within a sentence, in such a way as to be in opposition to one another. 'To make us love our country, our country ought to be lovely'; 'They renounced coercive power, but not the power that rests upon persuasion.'

bias: a prejudice; favouring one side in an argument.

cadence: the rhythmical rising and falling of language in writing or speech.

caricature: the portrayal of a character in which certain characteristics are exaggerated so that the person appears ridiculous.

clause: a division of a sentence containing its own subject and predicate (verb).

cliché: a hackneyed expression so overused as to have lost its impact. 'Each and every one of us'; 'few and far between'; 'it's up for grabs.'

climax: the culminating moment in a poem, play, or piece of prose.

colloquial: belonging to common or ordinary speech; informal language.

connotations: reverberations; what is implied by a word; nuances or suggestions that stem from a word.

cynicism: having little or no faith in human goodness.

diction: the writer's choice of words.

digression: turning aside from the main subject.

ellipsis: the omission of words, usually indicated by *omission points* (…).

emotive: tending to arouse emotion or feelings.

empathy: the complete association of the self with another being.

epigram: a short sentence expressing a witty thought or shrewd comment. 'Too many people expect wonders from democracy, when the most wonderful thing of all is just having it'; 'Genius begins great works; labour alone finishes them.'

euphemism: a mild expression in place of a harsh one. 'He was rough' (a tyrant); 'she's in care' (in a mental home); 'he's down' (depressed).

figurative language: language that contains many *figures of speech*—metaphors, similes, etc. 'He flowed out into a torrent of argument and explanation, very ingenious but impossible to follow. Phrase after phrase rose and turned and went out like a wreath of smoke'; 'He feared he would go mad, or fall ill, yet he could not rest, for if he once let go his fierce hold, the elaborate scaffolding he had so painfully erected would fall asunder.'

idiom, idiomatic expression: an expression peculiar to a certain language, especially one with a meaning that cannot be deduced from the individual words: 'over the moon' (delighted); 'down in the dumps' (depressed), 'a feather in his cap' (a recognised achievement).

implication: something that is hinted at or suggested rather than stated explicitly. 'The bond between the human and the horse ends with the human partner coming out on top, both literally and metaphorically.' The implication here is that the human is superior at every stage to the horse.

inference: a judgment or conclusion derived from a statement. An *implication* is made by a writer; an *inference* is drawn by the reader.

irony: the implication of an attitude or meaning opposite to the one stated. 'Ironically the more we have progressed, the more backward we still remain on many fronts.'

lucid: vivid or clear.

lyrical: literally: like a song; figuratively: enthusiastic, full of praise.

metaphor: making a comparison between two things without using the words 'like' or 'as'. 'Politicians are wedded to the status quo'; 'the very marrow of thought'; 'her eyes are stars.'

mood: the particular feeling or atmosphere created by a piece of writing.

moral: concerned with the good or bad of human behaviour.

oratorical: eloquent.

paradox: a statement that is apparently contradictory but might be true in a way. 'The child is father to the man'; 'tremendous silence'; 'dying generations.'

parenthesis: an aside; a remark inserted into a sentence, like an afterthought. It can be indicated by *commas, dashes*, or *parentheses*, but always in pairs. 'The doctor—he was a little bald man, with gleaming eyes and an excitable manner—rubbed his hands'; 'The average rise and fall of the tide (depending of course on the season) is about three feet.'

pathos: pity, sadness or tenderness created by the writer.

personification: investing inanimate things with human qualities: 'sad Russia'; 'sleeping Jerusalem'; 'his instincts threw up their defences'; 'sullen waterscape'; 'then the idea sauntered up to him, humming happily, and tapped him on the back, wanting to know what all the uproar was about.'

platitude: a trite or commonplace remark, especially when presented as if it is significant. 'He who goes a-borrowing goes a-sorrowing'; 'The team that gets its act together will come out on top at the end of the day.'

polemics: the art of controversial discussion.

précis: a summary.

pun: a play on words that are similar in sound but different in meaning: 'king of every blooming thing' (Kavanagh).

quip: a sharp retort or short sarcastic remark. 'Takes one to know one'; 'Men—can't live with them, can't live without them'; 'It takes two to tango.'

rhetoric: persuasive and impressive speech or writing.

sarcasm: a bitter or wounding remark made at the expense of another.

sardonic: derisive, mocking, or sneering.

satire: the ridiculing of folly. 'The Irish middle classes have long been uncomfortable with the symptoms of Mariolatry in Irish life: Knock and Ballinspittle have seemed to us to be evidence of an embarrassing peasant backwardness. But we have seen in the past week that the need for a single icon of virtue is not confined to the Irish; and in post-Christian England, the figure of Diana, playgirl, adulteress and society star, is surely no less ridiculous as a spiritual assurance than a gable end or moving statue in Ireland' (Kevin Myers, *Irish Times*, 30 August 1997).

simile: the direct comparison of two things, using the words 'like' or 'as'. 'It was as natural as a cat playing with a mouse'; 'It is noble but untameable, like a giraffe'; 'The sea heaves like a mighty animal.'

slang: extremely informal spoken language, generally cultivated by uneducated people in order to create an effect, enjoying a brief burst of popularity before being replaced by a newer fashion. In the written language, slang may be used when it is necessary to convey dialogue accurately, or in certain types of journalism, but it is not generally acceptable in serious writing.

syntax: word order: the arrangement of words according to the established conventions of a language.

tone: the 'tone of voice' of the writer.

verbosity: wordiness; using more words (or longer words) than is necessary.

2
English Grammar

Words do not operate on their own but in groups. We combine words to form sentences; groups of sentences can be combined in paragraphs. A group of paragraphs can constitute an essay or an article, a thesis, or the chapter of a book.

Each word in a sentence carries out a particular function. It is important to know the particular function of each word before embarking on the job of structuring a sentence. This relationship between words in a sentence, the arrangement of words to create meaning, is called *syntax*. Our ability to communicate effectively in language depends on our capacity to manage words—to establish a meaningful relationship between words and to arrange particular words in a suitable context.

Parts of speech

Words must be examined in the context of a particular sentence to find out what function they carry out. A word can perform one function in one sentence and a different function in another.

They live beside a <u>park</u>.
She decided to <u>park</u> the car at the door.

If you fall off that wall you'll <u>break</u> your leg!
The teacher gave us a <u>break</u> between the classes.

The weather had a <u>major</u> effect on sales.
The <u>major</u> lived in the Grange.

Examine the words in the following sentence:
The man and his dog walked slowly.

'the': this is a type of word that makes something *definite*.
'man': this type of word *identifies* a thing (in this case a person).
'and': this word connects the two things referred to ('man' and 'dog').
'his': this type of word tells us *whose* dog is referred to.
'dog': this word also identifies a thing.
'walked': this type of word tells us what the person *did*; it functions as an 'action word'.
'slowly': this type of word describes the *manner* in which an action was performed.

When we classify words in this way according to their function in a sentence, we describe them as belonging to particular *parts of speech*. There are eight principal parts of speech:

- noun
- verb
- pronoun
- adjective
- adverb
- preposition
- conjunction
- interjection.

Nouns

A noun identifies something that is referred to: 'man', 'dog', 'Ireland', 'loneliness'. A group of words can also function as a noun; this is called a *noun phrase*: 'Leaving Certificate', 'Dublin Fire Brigade'.

There are four kinds of nouns:

- common nouns
- proper nouns
- abstract nouns
- collective nouns.

Common nouns

These nouns identify the *kind of thing* something is and generally (though not always) refer to something concrete or physical: 'bicycle', 'father', 'pencil', 'sister', 'woman'.

Proper nouns

These nouns identify a *particular* person, place, or thing: 'John', 'Siobhán', 'Blackrock', 'Canada'. While a common noun identifies or *characterises* a thing, a proper noun *names* it. Proper nouns are distinguished in writing by beginning with a capital letter.

Abstract nouns

These nouns refer to non-material or intangible states or things: 'courage', 'heroism', 'joy', 'grief', 'health', 'happiness'.

Collective nouns

These nouns refer to groups of people or collections of things: 'crew', 'fleet', 'team', 'crowd', 'horde'.

The plural of nouns

The plural of nouns is normally made by adding *s* to the singular:

> day—days
> month—months
> mother—mothers

Nouns ending in *o*, and nouns ending in a *sibilant* (*s*, *x*, or *z*), usually add *es* in the plural:

> potato—potatoes   success—successes
> tomato—tomatoes   box—boxes
> hero—heroes   fizz—fizzes

Nouns ending in *y* preceded by a consonant drop the *y* and add *ies*:

> baby—babies
> country—countries
> fly—flies

But proper nouns just add *s*:

> There are two Marys in my class.

Verbs

A verb is a word that describes an action (including the action of being): the function of the verb is to tell us what the subject *does* or *is* in the particular sentence.

Examine the action in the following sentences in order to find the verbs:

> Can you wait three minutes?

> He did not see the man.
> They are going to Italy.
> The satellite will be seen at midnight.

Tenses of verbs

'Tense' means 'time'. The tense of a verb indicates whether the action takes place in the present, the past, or the future.

> I <u>write</u> every day [present tense].
> I <u>wrote</u> letters yesterday [past tense].
> I <u>will write</u> a chapter tomorrow [future tense].

Continuous tenses show that an action is, was or will be continuing. They are formed by combining the *present participle* of the verb—the form that ends in *ing* ('going', 'eating', 'sleeping', etc.)—with the verb 'be'.

> I <u>am writing</u> every day.
> I <u>was writing</u> letters yesterday.
> I <u>will be writing</u> a chapter tomorrow.

Pronouns

A pronoun is a word used in place of a noun. It carries out the same function as a noun: it identifies a person or thing.

> Mary and Jim have moved house, and <u>they</u> are now very happy.
> The thief tried to escape from the gardaí, but <u>they</u> saw <u>him</u>.
> Bring in your boots and put <u>them</u> away.

Adjectives

An adjective is a word that modifies the meaning of a noun. There are five different kinds of adjectives:

- descriptive adjectives
- possessive adjectives
- demonstrative adjectives
- relative adjectives
- interrogative adjectives.

The definite article ('the') and the indefinite article ('a' or 'an') can be thought of also as special kinds of adjectives.

Descriptive adjectives

These qualify the noun by describing some quality or attribute attached to the person or thing denoted by the noun: 'a blue table', 'twinkling eyes', 'golden stars', 'a pale face'.

Possessive adjectives
Possessive adjectives (not to be confused with *possessive pronouns*) always qualify a noun. They tell us who the owner of the object is: 'my pen', 'her house', 'their books', 'our caravan'.

Demonstrative adjectives
These point out things, just like demonstrative pronouns: 'that question', 'those melons', 'these books'.

Relative adjectives
These are the words 'what', 'which' and 'that' when they are used to introduce relative clauses:

> You can take what money you can find.
> I don't know which book you prefer.
> You can have that one over there.

Interrogative adjectives
These are 'which', 'what' and 'whose' when they introduce questions.

> Which bus will I take?
> What alternatives are there?
> Whose results are these?

Adverbs
Just as an adjective modifies or limits a noun, so an adverb modifies or limits a verb. It can also modify an adjective, or another adverb.

Many adverbs are formed by adding *ly* to an adjective: 'unique—uniquely', 'short—shortly', 'happy—happily'.

> He got an exceptionally good result in his examination. [The adverb 'exceptionally' modifies the adjective 'good'.]
> They left late. [The adverb 'late' modifies the verb 'left'.]
> Those plants are almost fresh. [The adverb 'almost' modifies the adjective 'fresh'.]
> She drove so fast that they nearly crashed. [The adverb 'so' modifies the adverb 'fast'.]

Adverbs may be classified as
- simple
- interrogative
- relative.

Simple adverbs
These indicate *manner, degree, time,* or *place.*

> April came in <u>swiftly</u>. [manner]
> The weather was <u>extremely</u> close. [degree]
> The coach arrived <u>late</u>. [time]
> The pilot landed <u>there</u>. [place]

Interrogative adverbs
These are the words 'how', 'where' and 'why' when used to introduce questions.

> How did she go?
> Where is she going?
> Why did she do that?

Relative adverbs
These are like relative pronouns, because they function as linking words.

> She visited Stratford, <u>where</u> Shakespeare was born.
> Spring is the season <u>when</u> plants begin to blossom.

Remember that 'good' is an adjective, while 'well' is an adverb.

> She has good skills.
> He is doing it well.

Prepositions
Prepositions are words that identify the relative position of something: 'on', 'under', 'over', 'beside', 'with', etc. They relate one word—either a noun or a pronoun—to another word.

> She wrote to me <u>from</u> France.
> He booked a room <u>at</u> the hotel.
> The cat is <u>under</u> the bed.

There is no basis for the assertion that a sentence should not end with a preposition.

> That is the garden we sat in.
> This is the pen he invariably wrote with.

Conjunctions
A conjunction is a *joining* word: it links words or clauses together.

> The family went to Canada, <u>and</u> they will not return.
> I have sent them a letter <u>but</u> have received no reply.

Sentences and phrases

Sentences

A sentence is a group of words that makes complete sense; it is an independent statement and does not need other words to complete its meaning. Every sentence starts with a capital letter and ends with a full stop.

A *sentence fragment* is an incomplete statement, lacking some part of what makes a complete sentence. Sentence fragments are acceptable in certain contexts—in conversation, for example, and as answers to a question. They are wrong only when the writer cannot tell the difference!

> The girl who lost her money. [sentence fragment]
> Feeling awful. [sentence fragment]
> I woke early. [sentence]
> A drugs crisis uncontained will surely grow and spread. [sentence]
> Many thanks for your invitation to lunch. [sentence fragment]

Phrases

A phrase is any sequence of words other than a clause; it generally does not contain a verb.

Punctuation

Punctuation is a vital element in clear writing—and the most neglected. Accurate punctuation is essential in conveying the meaning of a sentence.

The full stop

The full stop marks the end of a sentence. If the sentence is a question, however, you use a question mark instead; if the sentence is an exclamation, use an exclamation mark!

The full stop is also used after abbreviations—

> Co. [County]; Nov. [November]

—but is not required when the abbreviation includes the last letter of the word:

> Dr; Mr; Ltd

nor with groups of initials:

> UNICEF; RTE; PhD.

The comma

The comma has a number of different uses. The principal ones are as follows.

A comma is used to separate independent clauses, i.e. those in which the subject is named:

> The abbey was situated beside the river, and the grounds were extensive.

but not when the second clause shares the first subject:

> The abbey was situated beside the river and had extensive grounds.

A comma is used to separate a *series* of terms.

> He took with him his hunting tackle, gun, leather belt, arrows, and flask.

The same applies to a series of clauses:

> She got off the bus, crossed the road, looked swiftly behind her, and walked across to Main Street.

The last comma in a series should be dropped when any *following* terms or clause *qualify the whole series*.

> She speaks English, Irish, and French.

but

> English, Irish and French are the languages she speaks.

A comma is used to mark off a *parenthesis* (a non-essential element or afterthought) in a sentence.

> This device, constructed last year, works very well.

Note that *parentheses* or *dashes* can also be used for the same purpose, depending on the degree of separation of the parenthesis and the emphasis you wish to give it.

> This device (constructed last year) works very well.
> This device—constructed last year—works very well.

A comma is used to mark off phrases or words in *apposition*.

> Séamus Heaney, the Irish writer, won the Nobel Prize.

A comma is used to mark off the name of a person addressed.

> Milton, thou shouldst be living at this hour.
> Mary, come over here.
> Come over here, Mary.

A comma is used to mark off a *non-defining relative clause*.

> The dancers, who have worked abroad, should get a visa immediately.

Commas are used in introducing direct speech, and following it.

> Then she said, 'I know.'
> 'I've known about it for some time,' he replied.

The semi-colon

A semi-colon creates a greater degree of separation between clauses than a comma.

> I knew he would fail; and he did.
> I've neither father nor mother; I'm poor and of a serious disposition; I'm not pretty.

Semi-colons are used especially to separate clauses that themselves contain commas.

> I studied maths, science, and engineering; I've worked as a fitter, an engineer, a shop assistant, and a salesman; and I've lived in Greece, Turkey, and Spain.

The question mark

A question mark is used after every *direct* question.

> Would you like some tea?
> What day is this?

It is not used in reported speech:

> She asked me if I would like some tea.
> He asked me what day it was.

Nor is it used in *rhetorical questions* (questions to which an answer is not required or expected); these usually have an exclamation mark instead.

The exclamation mark

An exclamation mark is used to identify exclamations and interjections.

> I'm awfully cold!
> How insufferable!
> What a piece of work is man!

An exclamation mark is also generally used instead of a question mark after *rhetorical questions,* i.e. questions to which you do not really expect an answer.

> Do you expect me to go up in that thing!

The apostrophe

The *possessive case* is normally marked by the addition of an apostrophe and *s*.

> the girl's hat
> the boy's coat
> the mother's job

Indefinite pronouns use the apostrophe and *s* to show possession in the normal way.

> one's rights
> somebody else's car

To plural nouns ending in *s*, an apostrophe on its own is added.

> a girls' school
> the pupils' hostel
> the eagles' nest

An apostrophe is also used to show the omission of letters.

> Don't do that. [do not]
> He won't be there. [will not]
> He hasn't come back yet. [has not]
> It's hard to tell. [it is]

Remember that **it's** is a contraction of 'it is,' while **its** is a possessive adjective.

> The cat is licking its fur.
> The world is using up its resources.

Never add an apostrophe to a possessive adjective or possessive pronoun.

> That house is theirs [*not* their's].
> That phone is ours.
> Those records are hers.

The hyphen

A hyphen is used to create compound words, including compound adjectives.

> father-in-law
> down-and-out
> flat-footed
> state-sponsored
> a well-meaning intervention
> a French-speaking Canadian

A hyphen is also used to join most prefixes and suffixes to a word.

> pro-Irish
> anti-war
> north-bound

Quotation marks

Quotation marks—"like this"—are used to mark direct quotations or the actual words that have been spoken. (Sometimes 'single quotation marks' are used instead, as in this book.)

> As Hamlet said, 'To be or not to be: that is the question.'
> She said, 'Let me know tomorrow about that matter.'

Quotation marks are also used to clarify a word or term that should stand apart.

> When you click on 'File', a menu will drop down.
> Please send an application form to everyone who chose 'very interested'.

3
The English Composition

Some of the principal functions of writing can be:
- to tell a story (the *language of narration*)
- to discuss a topic (the *language of argument*)
- to describe or to express oneself imaginatively (the *aesthetic use of language*)
- to inform the reader about some topic (*informative writing*).

The first principle of composition is to foresee and determine the shape of what is to come, and then to pursue that shape.

The process of writing a compositions is a matter of probing ahead and forecasting the general outline or direction of the content. Pre-composition writing is important, therefore, in that it determines what direction the composition is taking and what conclusions will be reached.

The composition must have a beginning, a middle, and a conclusion. The opening states your case: it establishes your stance or your particular commitment to the topic. The middle justifies this stance; and the end reflects on the beginning and the middle.

The composition should be an individual response to the subject.

Pre-composition writing

Pre-composition writing is an indispensable part of the process of composition writing. Remember that a composition must always be written and rewritten. Compositions need to be revised, refined, and rewritten. *Never* hand up the first draft.

Free writing
This is particularly helpful as a warming-up process before the stage of formal writing. The main idea is to put pen to paper and to get going on the writing process immediately.

The purpose of this activity is simply to practise the skill of writing anything and in any order whatever. Simply write about anything you choose and in whatever way you like, not caring about punctuation, spelling, or structure. Write without stopping. Do not stop to plan, organise, or edit.

Brainstorming
This is the process of throwing your imagination into high gear and trying to trigger off as many ideas as possible on a topic.

'Trigger questions' serve a useful function, as they can provide fuel for ideas. Questions such as *why? what? where? how?* and *when?* can generate many different ideas on a topic.

Clustering
'Clustering' of ideas can help to sift your thought and put priority on your content. It helps you to put the most important ideas first. It is the process of developing the relationship between ideas as you record them or jot them down.

Begin by writing your topic on a blank sheet. Draw a circle around it. Write down at random the main ideas around that topic.

Draw a circle around each main idea. Connect each main idea to the topic with a straight line.

Jot down other ideas about the main ideas. Connect them to the subordinate ideas with a line.

In this way you will cluster several ideas around the general topic. The clustering of ideas can help to generate a multitude of ideas that later on can be joined together and interwoven in order to write the composition.

Outlines

An outline is a method of imagining the basic shape, order of sections and structure of argument in the composition. It forms a backbone of the composition.

In the process of constructing an outline, you are breaking the topic down into small stages. Each stage provides the scaffolding that will bring the composition one stage further. The outline is a means of getting organised and overcoming 'writer's block'.

Problems and pitfalls in writing compositions

1. **Choice of titles.** The wide choice of titles can be confusing.
2. **Writer's block and exam paralysis.** The problem of knowing what exactly to write and overcoming writer's block or exam paralysis can be very intimidating. Many pupils are overwhelmed at the process of starting an opening paragraph.
3. **Misinterpreting the title.** This can happen from reading the title carelessly.
4. **Lack of unity or organisation of ideas.** This can occur when a composition is not planned properly. It is shown in obscure argument, woolly and incoherent thought, excessive repetition, and a general lack of direction in the composition.
5. **Content.** Poor content can be reflected in excessive repetition of ideas, digression of thought, or the introduction of irrelevant material.
6. **Repetition.** Repetition can be the result of failure to plan a composition properly. Repeating the same word in sentences or similar sentences in paragraphs only

weakens the structure of the composition.
7. **Faulty style.** Many marks are lost needlessly through carelessness in the mechanics of grammar, spelling, and handwriting, or through a sloppy and untidy style.
8. **Poor timing.** Time can be wasted in mulling over titles or in writing a draft. Give yourself the time required to plan the composition—neither to rush at it without a plan nor to spend too much time thinking about what to write.

Overcoming these problems

1. **Identify your style early on**—whether it is descriptive, factual, or imaginative. The advice from your teacher can be invaluable here. Generally speaking, you will write best on a topic that you are interested in.
2. **Put pen to paper immediately.** Think first about exactly what you want to say; then go and say it in writing. Use writing as a means of working out what you want to say.
3. **Take account of every word** and the possibilities or connotations of each word.
4. **Begin by brainstorming the title.** Then proceed to draw up outlines.
5. **Pre-composition writing** (brainstorming the title and drafting an outline) will help you to draw out ideas on the subject. Think of suitable quotations, or any areas of literature (poetry, drama, fiction) that can be used to develop the content of the composition.
6. **Read your composition aloud if possible,** as it can alert you to unnecessary repetition. Check for repetition not only of words but also of ideas.
7. **Pay attention to detail,** in spelling, handwriting, punctuation, and grammar. Correct all spelling errors, and check that every word you use is the right one.

Features of a good composition

1. The ideas used should be relevant to the subject indicated by the title of the composition.
2. The composition should be structured correctly. Attention must be paid to the basic structure of paragraphs. There must be an overall unity within the composition: every paragraph must relate to the preceding one, and every paragraph must relate to the topic and develop it in some way.
3. There must be correct sentence structure. A good composition should have a variety and strength in sentence structure in order to retain the reader's interest and to communicate the ideas effectively. The language, vocabulary and images used must be relevant and wide-ranging.
4. Care and attention must be paid to the basic mechanics of English: grammar, spelling, and punctuation.
5. The composition must have striking opening and concluding paragraphs, which serve the purpose of conveying an overall unity of impression.

Method of writing a composition

1. Spend time choosing your topic, carefully working out the implications and meanings of each word in the title.
2. If the topic is not already in the form of a question, recast it in question form; this will help you to look at the topic from another angle or angles.
3. Once you have chosen the topic, eliminate all other composition titles from your mind: dedicate yourself fully to that particular title and try to soak yourself in the subject. Be decisive with regard to your topic. For example, in a composition on 'This technological age' you must decide what technology is in question and tackle the issues of positive and negative aspects of this development.
4. Use some of the pre-writing activities to start generating ideas on the topic. Brainstorm the title. Jot down ideas as quickly as you can. Use trigger questions such as *how? why? where? what?* and *who?* on the title to trigger or spark off as many ideas on the subject as possible. You can then expand ideas into sentences, sentences into paragraphs, and paragraphs into longer sections.

Remember before you start to write:

1 Rephrase the title as a question.
2. Brainstorm the topic by using trigger questions.
3. Cluster related ideas.
4. Select material for paragraphs.
5. Write out fully the topic sentence of each paragraph.

Hints on writing a composition

1. **Write every day.** Take a composition from a past Leaving Cert paper and write a paragraph to improve your expression.
2. **Develop the habit of free writing.** This involves writing whatever comes into your mind on any topic. Simply start writing freely; don't worry about grammar, style, or handwriting. The important thing is to put pen to paper in order to overcome writer's block.
3. **Gather information** by listening to good debate programmes on radio or television. Jot down new forms of expression. Read the work of professional writers in books or magazines, and write down phrases or new forms of expression in your notebook. Cultivate your own ideas on the topics raised and on current events: you can do this by having a notebook in which to collect ideas or to record interesting descriptions or anecdotes throughout the year.
4. **Use this material in class compositions** throughout the year.
5. **Understand your title fully.** Otherwise, don't write on it.
6. **Always draw up a rough draft first.** *Never*

write a composition off the top of your head.

7. **Avoid errors made in previous compositions** by learning spellings you have difficulty with and correcting grammatical mistakes.

8. **Identify your own strengths and weaknesses.** Work at eliminating the weaknesses and improving your strong points.

9. **Write simply.** Choose a simple word instead of a more obscure expression. Avoid using clichés, such as 'few and far between,' 'beat around the bush,' 'part and parcel.'

10. **Work at writing interesting opening paragraphs.**

11. **Draw up your own list of quotations and learn them off by heart.**

12. **Do not make general statements without supporting them with clear and specific examples.**

Sentences

Remember that a sentence is a group of words that makes complete sense.

Features of a sentence

1. **Sentences must be clear in their meaning.** The following sentence is an example of one that is ambiguous and confusing.

   The bully attacked the schoolboy with an evil look in his eyes.

   Who exactly has the evil look, the bully or the schoolboy?

2. **Sentences must be correctly punctuated,** otherwise the meaning will be confusing. Look at the difference between these two sentences:

   Not everyone wants to go on a whistle-stop tour around India getting up at dawn packing and unpacking every day.

   Not everyone wants to go on a whistle-stop tour around India, getting up at dawn, packing and unpacking every day.

3. **Every sentence has a subject** (what the

sentence is about) **and a predicate** or verb (what is said about the subject).

The paragraph

A paragraph is very much like a composition in miniature: it must have a beginning, a middle, and a satisfactory conclusion.

Each paragraph should begin with a sentence that relates what comes next to the last point you made and the structure of the composition as a whole.

A paragraph may emphasise a point made earlier by citing further evidence, or it may go on to explore the consequences of a point already made. It can also take a completely new direction towards the subject if necessary.

Each paragraph deals with one section of your subject and makes an important contribution to the subject as a whole. Paragraph follows paragraph in the order of presentation decided in your plan.

The length of a paragraph

A paragraph can be of any length—a single sentence, or a passage of great duration.

Begin each paragraph with a sentence that shows clearly your main idea or one that helps with the transition from the paragraph that went before. Make sure each paragraph develops the flow of thought in your composition.

There are three important things to bear in mind when constructing a paragraph:

1. Every paragraph must have a topic sentence or main idea.

2. Each paragraph must have a unity: all ideas (details, examples, explanations, statistics, etc.) must be related to the main point or topic sentence.

3. A paragraph must have coherence: the ideas must hang together so that the reader can move easily from one point to the next. Take special care with the last sentence of each paragraph, as it is the crucial springboard to the next paragraph.

The introductory and the concluding paragraphs are the most important ones in your composition. The introductory paragraph has two main functions:

- to capture the attention of your reader
- to introduce your material and show your approach or stance to the composition topic.

Opening paragraphs should be short and should focus attention on where your writing is going. The opening paragraph is really a signpost of the route your message is taking.

The concluding paragraph

Your concluding paragraph is your final statement on the composition topic. It is the last impression left on your reader, and therefore it is vitally important.

A conclusion should exude a sense of control. What is important in the conclusion is not *what* one says but *how* one says it.

A good conclusion has two purposes:

- to round off the main ideas of your composition satisfactorily
- to provide an overall unity to your composition.

Avoid conclusions that repeat the main ideas of the composition in exactly the same words. On the other hand, do not go to the other extreme by introducing a completely different approach or new ideas in your conclusion, because this will only frustrate your reader.

One way of giving unity to the composition could be to present both the introduction and the conclusion as a pair: to refer back to the introductory paragraph and develop the anecdote or statistic or simply the point that was made there.

Some phrases that can serve as a way of concluding your composition effectively are: 'To sum up, therefore …' 'In conclusion we can see …' 'Finally it can be taken that …'

Remember that your conclusion must show that you have complete control over your subject.

Check-list for paragraphs

1. What is the purpose of the paragraph?
2. Is there one topic sentence that is easily identifiable?
3. Has the paragraph got clarity of thought, or is it woolly and convoluted?
4. Has the paragraph got substance, i.e. five or six sentences?
5. Is the content unified? Are all examples given relevant to the main or topic sentence?
6. Are the ideas organised correctly? Is there a proper emphasis on the order of ideas in the paragraph?
7. Has the paragraph got coherence? Is there an effective link between all the sentences in the paragraph?
8. What transitional devices are used?
9. Has the paragraph got an effective concluding statement?

Remember!

Each paragraph must begin with a sentence that relates what comes next to the last point you made and the structure of the composition as a whole. All sentences in the paragraph should develop the idea contained in the topic sentence.

Your paragraphs must be structured in the following way:

—**topic sentence:** This makes the main claim of the paragraph and tries to link with what goes before.

Such preoccupations prevented Reverend Mother one day from examining the midday post until late evening.

—**together with subsequent sentences:** these justify or illustrate the claim or idea.

She came to her study desk feeling a little tired, but content with the work of the afternoon. Dusk was advancing, but there was still enough daylight to work by. She laid her restless hands on the pile of letters and allowed her eyes to fall for an indolent second on the pleasant pathway outside with its ivy-niched Stations of the Cross and, beyond, through the gate, on the little black crosses of the convent cemetery.

—**together with the final sentence:** this sums up the paragraph with what will come next.

'Perhaps I shall have to lie there after all,' she thought resignedly. 'Perhaps I shall never see Brussels again—or Father.'

[Kate O'Brien, *The Land of Spices*]

The language of narration

Writing a short story or narrative-style composition

In a narrative-style composition there needs to be a definite arrangement of ideas, and the story usually has a particular point of view. The writer leads the reader along, and there can be a degree of suspense.

When choosing this type of composition, bear in mind that it must be interesting to your reader. An interesting story is original, or at least takes an original approach to an ordinary topic or situation. A good story or narrative composition springs from your own personal experience: it has a flavour of authenticity and truth.

Method of writing a narrative composition or short story

Narrative writing involves telling a story. The structure of a narrative composition can be straightforward and in chronological sequence. The story can be set in the past, the present, or the future.

A story can be told in many different ways. It can be told in dialogue or in the first person or third person.

Examine the following two accounts of the same incident.

> I noticed that there was a similarity between the man's way of eating and a dog's. He snapped up every mouthful quickly and looked around him all the time as if there was danger.

> I had often watched a large dog of ours eating his food; and I now noticed a decided similarity between the dog's way of eating and the man's. The man took strong sharp sudden bites just like the dog. He swallowed, or rather snapped up, every mouthful too soon and too fast; and he looked sideways here and there as he ate, as if he thought there was danger in every direction of somebody's coming to take the pie away.
>
> [Charles Dickens, *Great Expectations*]

The first account is just a reporting of what happened. The second conjures up the action: it shows it happening here and now before our eyes. This is what it means to write at first hand. Only by writing like this can one breathe life into one's work.

The following elements should be borne in mind when you are writing a short story or narrative-style composition:

- plot
- characters
- dialogue
- description
- atmosphere.

Plot

A narrative composition should have a story. This should unfold through a series of events that add up to what is called the plot.

Characters

The characters in a short story or narrative must be real, recognisable figures and not fantasy figures. Characters seem realistic and alive to you as a reader when you are able to realise them with your senses, react to them with your emotions, and follow them with your mind.

Dialogue

The ability to write effective dialogue is another requirement of good narrative writing.

The hallmark of good dialogue is its capacity to evoke relationships between people and to convey conflict in a realistic manner. The use of dialogue in narrative writing can convey realism or show conflict, or give pace and variety to the story.

The main function of dialogue in writing is to reproduce live speech. The use of direct speech can either give a piece of writing variety and excitement or ruin it. Never allow dialogue just to slip into your composition: direct speech must have a purpose or object in a piece of writing.

When you use dialogue, make sure to punctuate it correctly.

- Use quotation marks at the beginning and end of each section of direct speech.

- Separate the dialogue from the narrative by means of commas.
- The first word in every piece of direct speech begins with a capital letter.
- Use a new paragraph every time there is a change of speaker.

The following is an example of very weak dialogue (taken from a composition entitled 'The gang mentality').

> Jack turned to Bulldog and said, 'Why did you not kill him?'
>
> 'I had no butterfly knife,' said Bulldog.
>
> Jack replied, 'Where is the knife my brother handed you yesterday?'
>
> 'I don't know. It was in the holder, but now it's gone.'
>
> Jack shouted, 'Why didn't you tell me this before now?'

This dialogue lacks life and spontaneity. The language fails to show the type of characters and their moods.

Good dialogue must be clear and flow well. It should not need this kind of back-up:

> 'I know it,' he laughed.
>
> 'Don't tell me,' she sighed.
>
> 'They bore me,' he sneered.

Let the speaker's *voice* be angry or sad or ironic. When the writer uses devices such as 'he said,' 'he replied,' 'she laughed,' 'they chanted,' and so on, the rhythmic flow of ideas in the passage can be interrupted.

Another problem with dialogue is correct spacing. A mass of dialogue can interrupt the flow of thought and be jarring to the reader.

The following is a good example of dialogue that expresses anger:

> 'How dare you lie to me!' she screamed gaspingly. 'You saw the hen. I know you saw it! You stopped whistling. You called out. You called out. We were watching you. Isn't that right?' she demanded.

The following extract is taken from the book *Empire of the Sun*. It conveys a vivid picture of character and situation.

> Jim watched the coolies and peasant women staring at the headless bodies. Already the press of tram passengers was pushing them aside, submerging this small death. He turned away, tripping over the charcoal brazier in which a pavement vendor was frying pieces of battered snake. Drops of fat splashed onto the wooden bucket, where a single snake swam, thrashing itself as it leapt at the hissing oil. The vendor lunged at Jim with his hot ladle, trying to cuff his head, but he slipped between the parked rickshaws.
>
> He ran along the blood-smeared tramlines towards the entrance of the depot.
>
> He pushed through the waiting passengers and squeezed himself onto a concrete bench with a group of peasant women carrying chickens in wicker baskets. The women's bodies reeked of sweat and fatigue, but Jim was too exhausted to move. He had walked over two miles along the crowded pavements. He knew that he was being followed by a young Chinese, probably a pedicab tout or a runner, for one of Shanghai's tens of thousands of small-time gangsters. A tall youth with a dead boneless face, oily black hair and leather jacket, he had noticed Jim outside the greyhound stadium. Kidnappings were commonplace in Shanghai: before his parents learnt to trust Yang, they insisted that Jim always drove to school with the governess. He guessed that the youth was interested in his blazer and leather shoes, in his aviator's watch and American fountain pen, which was clipped to his breast pocket.
>
> The youth stepped through the crowd and walked up to Jim, his yellow hands like ferrets. 'American boy?'
>
> 'English. I'm waiting for my chauffeur.'
>
> 'English ... boy. You come now.'
>
> 'No—he's over there.'
>
> The youth reached forward, swearing in Chinese, and seized Jim's wrist. His fingers fumbled at the metal strap, trying to release the watch-clasp. The peasant women ignored him, chickens asleep on their laps. Jim knocked away the youth's hand, and felt fingers grip his forearm.
>
> Inside his leather jacket he had drawn a knife and was about to sever Jim's hand at the wrist.
>
> Jim wrenched his arm away. Before the youth could seize him again, Jim hurled the wicker

basket from the knee of the peasant woman on his right. The youth fell back, flailing with his heels at the squawking bird. The women jumped to their feet and began to scream at him. He ignored them and put away his knife. He followed as Jim ran through the queues of tram passengers, trying to show them the bruised wrist.

A hundred yards from the depot Jim reached the Avenue Joffre.

The youth with the knife was still behind him, skipping and side-stepping through the crowd in his cheap sneakers. In the centre of the Avenue Joffre was the police check-point. Jim knew that neither the Vichy police nor the Japanese soldiers would do anything to help him. They were watching a single-engined bomber that flew low above the racecourse.

Jim joined the crowd of pedestrians moving through the checkpoint. As he guessed, his pursuer had vanished among the beggars and loitering rickshaw coolies on the French side of the barbed wire. Not for the first time, Jim realised that the Japanese, officially his enemies, offered his only protection in Shanghai.

The aesthetic use of language
The art of descriptive writing

Mastering the art of descriptive writing is the essence of good narrative writing. The function of description in a narrative composition is either to form the background or atmosphere of the story or to conjure up images through concentrating on the senses.

Descriptive writing should not attempt to list every detail about the person, place or thing being described: rather it should focus on a number of small, significant details and on describing them with precision.

In good description, all the senses are intimately involved: we hear, see, smell, feel, and taste.

The chief was a fat man with yellow-brown skin who sat under an ancient nim tree in front of his hut, a loose chequered kikoi around his ample belly, naked children and chickens scratching around him in the dusty sand. He wore an embroidered Muslim cap and chewed betel nuts,

occasionally spitting straight sprays of stained rusty saliva at dangerous angles. He was blind from sarcoma. Women with large velvety eyes came and went, some giggling shyly at our strangeness, others made bolder by age and experience. They wore amber or red glass beads around their necks, their heads were covered with thin coloured cloth, in Arab style, with minute silver earrings on their earlobes and rings through their thin Nilotic nostrils.

[Kuki Gallmann, *I Dreamed of Africa*]

When writing description in a short story or narrative, make sure to keep it brief and to blend it in naturally. Because descriptive writing involves giving a clear picture, select details with great care.

The following examples of description are based on a selection of precise and exact details.

The storm came rattling over the marsh in full fury.

The warm wind, which smelt of soda and of waterfowls' guano, blew through his straight fair hair streaked pale by the sun.

He had a narrow, clean-shaven face, with features evenly distributed and an expression of placid acuteness. Tall, lean, loosely and feebly put together, he had an ugly sickly witty charming face furnished but by no means decorated with a straggling moustache and whiskers.

The great still oaks and beeches flung down a shade as dense as that of velvet curtains, and the place was furnished like a room with cushioned seats, rich coloured rugs with the books and papers that lay upon the grass.

[Henry James, *Portrait of a Lady*]

It was late in a dull dark day in January. Huddersfield, far below Roe Head School, was lost in smoky fog. The wide lawns were snow-covered; the beautiful trees under which the pupils sat in summer were bare and weeping. Into this gloomy atmosphere, from the still darker interior of the covered cart which had brought her from Haworth, Charlotte's little figure emerged. She was helped down, and stood there, shrinking into herself from the raw air and from a misery and fear she could not conquer. Her box was lifted out, and the driver rang the doorbell of the school.

[Lynn Reid Banks, *Dark Quartet*]

The effect here stems from a careful selection of small details, which are woven together to form a picture of the arrival of the little girl.

Descriptive writing involves being both selective and specific in the choice of things that it depicts.

Broaden your vocabulary so as to avoid stereotyped descriptions. For example, look at the shape as well as the colour of the eyes:

> narrow, slanting dark eyes
> lively, sharp grey eyes
> large, oval blue eyes

Below are some paragraphs written by pupils in a highly imaginative style and revealing how language can be rich and aesthetic.

Evil is a stronger force than good

It was a humid night and the intense glare of the moon projected itself onto the ice which had begun to accumulate all the way down to Harris Avenue. The entire neighbourhood was sombre and engulfed in an overwhelming silence. I shuffled down the pale pavement, watching closely for any indication of a spot in which I could tumble or fall. Cracks were interwoven artistically on the street like those once drawn on papyrus by the Ancient Egyptians. The echo of passing traffic brushed my ear …

Just after sunrise

The window panes lay dormant, showing no life. The only proof of vitality sprang from the soft rays of sunlight peering through the glass, each vibrant ray claiming a path of dust particles and holding its abode in mid-air. Rays of dust sprinkled and silently hit the ground, not daring to disturb the tranquillity of the primitive chapel, just after sunrise.

What a dazzling and majestic residence the world is seconds after the vibrant sun declares a new and untarnished day!

The giver of all life lavishes its warm and tender rays on all Earth's inhabitants, giving life to inanimate things. The soulful rays are spilt on the highest mountain to the loneliest valley …

The language of argument

Writing a discursive composition

A discursive composition is one in which the writer arrives at a conclusion by means of facts and argument. Some other terms for this type of writing are 'argumentative' and 'controversial' writing.

A good discursive or debate-style composition involves convincing your reader of the validity of your argument, and this can be done through clear logic, sound argument, and the correct organisation of ideas. Argument is at the centre of this type of composition. What is important in a composition of this type is the organisation of facts, together with the proper arrangement of ideas so as to produce a lucid and persuasive argument.

Techniques in writing a discursive composition

1. Identify your audience and the tone or point of view you will use.
2. Develop a controlling idea or stance that will propel you through the composition. This idea will clarify your position on the topic and generally indicate the direction in which your composition is heading.
3. Make sure there is priority in your argument: put the most important ideas first. Give your reader a clear expectation of how your argument will develop and which ideas are more important. For example, in a composition on 'Violence and the media' you might discuss how the media can depict violence and so aggravate the problem.

4. Cultivate the technique of writing persuasively. Treat any arguments against your viewpoint in a balanced way. Give plenty of examples to support your position. Such examples should be woven into the body of your composition in as natural and fluid a way as possible. Gather support in order to ensure a clear focus on your composition and to support your points.

5. Avoid a sensational or exaggerated approach to the subject, such as 'It is time that women stopped being slaves and started to assert their long-overdue rights and began to fight against male dominance.'

6. Avoid a one-sided presentation. You must reflect an awareness of other aspects and other opinions on the topic. Balance of presentation in ideas is an important feature of the discursive composition. Make sure to present your ideas in a detached and objective manner; avoid a subjective or prejudiced approach in a discursive-type composition. A writer of this type of composition must be able to move steadily through conflicting arguments and present a clear, logical conclusion at the end.

7. Never use emotional language when writing a discursive composition. When you have convincing material to offer as evidence, present it as vividly as you can and let your readers draw their own conclusions.

8. Avoid discriminatory language, such as 'male nurse', 'woman doctor', and so on.

9. Clear and concise writing requires the avoidance of jargon and the elimination of redundancy.

The following paragraphs are taken from a discursive-style composition written by a pupil.

A new millennium

If one looks back over the past one hundred years, who would have believed in 1898 that we would be sending people to the moon, and travelling faster than sound? Breaking the speed of light is only the next step, and perhaps in the year 2050 planes will be landing before they have even taken off. But will the technology of this era be our friend or our foe? With the advance of cars, washing machines and the like, life has certainly been made easier in the last few centuries. It has helped humankind to build a more civilised way of life.

Our early ancestors had not yet discovered farming. They had only simple tools and weapons. They did not know how to tame and raise wild animals. The sun was their only source of light. Then they discovered fire and this was, along with the development of the wheel, one of the very first developments in technology.

Higher living standards have resulted from the increased production of goods and services. If one looks at the trends, most people in industrialised countries enjoy a healthier, more comfortable life-style than any other people in history. Better public health practices have ended the plagues that once tormented humankind, such as TB and smallpox. Life expectancy has increased greatly—from approximately fifty years of age to over seventy today; but will the year 2001 boast such advancements, or from now on will we be only going downhill?

Will we continue to experiment without realising the dangers? The dangers of technology were shown recently in a laboratory where chemical warfare is being developed. As a scientist attempted to inject a rabbit with a newly developed chemical he accidentally injected himself and had to go through days of agonising torture before he finally died. Is this what is being planned for us in the new millennium?

Remember always in a discursive composition to work at acquiring a simple and clear expression.

- Group related ideas together.
- Emphasise essential points.
- Always try to write concisely.

The language of information

The language of information—also called *functional writing*—is at the basis of report writing, as well as the writing of instructions, memos, and letters.

The following considerations must be taken into account when you are engaged in this form of writing.

1. What are the reader's expectations? Who is my reader? What job have they?
2. What am I trying to achieve in writing this message or information?
3. What exactly do I need to include in this message to achieve this result from this particular person?

Functional writing tests your ability to use language

- clearly
- appropriately
- concisely.

The style, therefore, should be factual and clear.

Features of functional writing

1. **Clear organisation of information.** All arguments and information must be expressed in a logical and coherent manner.
2. **Relevant content.** There must be no digression from the point and no introduction of useless or irrelevant information.
3. **An appropriate style and expression.** Different situations and circumstances call for different styles of writing. In general, for functional writing the style should be unobtrusive—like a windowpane through which information can be clearly seen.
4. **Short sentences.** The intelligent use of sentence length is an important ingredient of effective style for functional or informative writing. Flexibility and variety in sentence length make writing easier to read. Short sentences can be used to make complex or important information arresting and make it stand out. Generally, long sentences should be avoided.

Features of style

1. **Avoid overlong sentences.**
2. **Use precise and simple vocabulary.**
3. **Avoid jargon, slang, buzz-words, and 'commercialese'.** *Jargon* is the inappropriate use of the terminology of a specialised profession. *Slang* is extremely informal language, generally confined to casual speech, especially among uneducated people. *Buzz-words* are temporarily fashionable expressions, designed to appear like technical language but often with no real meaning and frequently ungrammatical (such as 'ongoing' for 'continuing' or 'continuous'; 'at this point in time' for 'at the present time' or 'now'; 'pro-active' for 'active'; 'nationwide' and 'worldwide' used as adverbs). *Commercialese* is the use of dated and stereotyped formulas of a type once common in business correspondence ('Enclosed herewith' for 'I enclose'; 'I refer to your letter of …' instead of 'Thank you for your letter of …' etc.).
4. **Limit the use of the passive voice.** Use the active form of the verb.
5. **Use concrete words rather than abstract ones.**
6. **Use each word in a way that clearly illustrates its meaning.** For example, does 'Check undercarriage locking-pin' mean remember the information, or record it, or verify that the locking-pin is in place? Remember that words can have different meanings according to their context.
7. **Use factual rather than emotive words.** Use words that are clear, concise, precise, and objective. The word you choose must clearly represent what you want to say. Do not use words figuratively, as many times they can obscure or dim the facts. The literal use of words concentrates the mind on one meaning, whereas a figurative use of words invites the reader to elicit secondary meanings. The raw material of functional writing is

- factual, not emotive;
- informative, not descriptive or narrative.

So an objective and detached tone must be used. Avoid the subjective 'I' as much as possible. Choose words that carry plain, objective meanings; pin down the meaning as closely as possible.

8. **Use the precise number of words.**
9. Use a shorter rather than a longer word.
10. Use a shorter sentence rather than a longer one.

Reports

The differences between a report and other kinds of functional writing are that

(*a*) reports classify, analyse and present material clearly;

(*b*) the subject matter of a report is divided into sections, which are usually further sub-divided.

In writing a report for an examination, you must supply enough details and information to make your report convincing. Your report must also be long enough to show that you can organise material effectively.

When you are writing a report, ask yourself the following questions:

1. What is the purpose of this report?
2. What objectives am I hoping to achieve with this report?
3. What is the theme of the report?
    A report is effective when
    (*a*) it is understood without undue effort;
    (*b*) the findings of the report are
acknowledged to be valid and are acted upon.

Preliminary check-list

1. What would be a suitable title for the report? Giving the report a title can help to establish the main theme or topic being dealt with.
2. What information needs to be included and what needs to be disregarded in the report?
3. Is the report to be a detailed one, or is it to be written in summary form?
4. What resources have I got at my disposal? For example, what equipment have I got? What budget have I been allocated?

5. What time limits am I subject to in producing the report?
6. How will the report be structured?
7. Who will read the report? Assessing exactly who your readers are will determine what particular style you will use. Writing a report for the management of a company will demand a style different from one suitable for a report for your colleagues or for the public.

An information report simply gives give the facts: it does not interpret them or comment on them in any way. An interpretative report, however, gives facts and interprets them for the reader.

An analytical report gives facts, and interprets and comments on them. It goes on to suggest reasons or to explain the significance of these facts. It also draws conclusions or makes recommendations.

Organisation of information in a report

A report will usually have the following elements:

- title
- introduction
- main body of the report, usually divided into sections
- conclusion
- recommendations (where appropriate)
- references (if any were used)
- glossary (where appropriate).

Make liberal use of headings and sub-headings. These will act as signposts, signalling routes and announcing the content of sections.

Sample headings in a report

- Terms of reference
- Introduction
- Work carried out
- Findings
- Conclusions
- Recommendations
- Summary
- Acknowledgments
- References
- Appendixes

Title

The title of a report must inform the reader about what is in it. A good title helps to focus the report. Avoid long-winded titles as far as possible, such as 'A Study to Determine the Usage of School Canteen Facilities at Lunchtime': write instead: 'Report on the Use of the School Canteen'.

Terms of reference

The terms of reference are the detailed instructions given to the writers of the report about what they are to investigate. The terms of reference may also include the date on which the report was commissioned. An official report on the number of pupils taking Irish in the Leaving Certificate might be entitled 'Number of Pupils Undertaking the Leaving Certificate Examination in Irish', while the terms of reference might be something like this:

> At the request of the Minister for Education and Science, the Chief Inspector of the department, Mr Éamann Ó Dálaigh, was instructed on 9 April 1998 to prepare a report on the number of pupils who will sit the Leaving Certificate examination in Irish in 1999.

Introduction

In the introduction you should state fully the problem you are aiming to solve or the aspect of the question you are setting out to investigate. Give the reasons for carrying out this report, together with the time limits, details of those carrying out the investigation, the materials and methods used, and any other relevant details.

Work carried out

This will consist of detailed information on what has been done in order to find information, for example surveys or interviews. Statistics and other data may also have been collected. All accounts of work carried out in gathering the information must be recorded here.

Findings

Under this heading will come the main body of the information you have gathered on the subject.

It is important in this section to organise the information that has been obtained both clearly and well. Understand clearly the relationship between the different parts of the information.

At this stage it is important to distinguish between what information is useful and what can be thrown away.

Conclusions

The conclusions of your report should link your terms of reference with your findings. Conclusions should flow naturally from your evidence and arguments. They should be clear, simple, and objective.

Recommendations

Where *conclusions* refer to the past, *recommendations* point to the future. Recommendations are often best presented as a list. For example, in a report entitled 'Keeping Localities Tidy: Improving the Environment', the recommendations might be presented as follows:

1. Competitions should be organised regularly—for example monthly—to create incentives for improvement.
2. More rubbish bins should be put in areas such as parks and picnic-sites.
3. Youth clubs and other local groups should provide the initiatives by organising a 'tidy town' campaign.

Summary

The summary of a report should reflect the findings, together with comments from the main body of the report. The summary must be a true account of the report and should emphasise any areas requiring special emphasis. A good summary will

- outline the main points of the report by providing a précis of what the recipient is going to read
- provide an outline of the main conclusions, with recommendations, for those recipients who are not going to read any more of the report.

Style of report-writing

The language of reports should be *factual and*

objective. Do not use emotive or ambiguous words. Avoid any tendency to impress: write to express facts, clearly and logically. Reports are generally written in the past tense.

Sample reports
Report on Staff Dissatisfaction at Sligo Distilleries Ltd

1 Terms of reference
On the instructions of the personnel and works director (9 May 1998), to report on staff dissatisfaction and to make recommendations.

2 Introduction
The employees of Sligo Distilleries Ltd have expressed their concern at the management's rejection of the recommendations of the Labour Court for resolving the continuing problems over pay and conditions. Employees are dissatisfied with working conditions and with certain changes in the company. The management wishes to reconsider its policy and to assess the exact grounds for complaint by employees.

3 Procedures
3.1 Questionnaire
A detailed questionnaire on working conditions and changes within the company was circulated to all employees.

3.2 Interviews
All supervisors were interviewed. Twenty other employees, selected at random, were interviewed.

4 Findings
4.1 General
Some of the comments from supervisors indicate a strong sense of grievance among employees. Many feel bitter over loss of earnings over the last two months. Other employees are angry with the company because of the substantial changes in structures and work practices.

4.2 Causes of dissatisfaction
Resentment is felt for the following reasons:

4.2.1 Training
Not enough training time is allocated to informing employees about new technology.

4.2.2 Lack of mobility
Employees are being kept too long in one area or section.

4.2.3 Conditions
1. Not enough equipment has been allocated to dealing with the work load.
2. There is not enough work space for the present number of employees.
3. A backlog of work has accumulated because of the introduction of new technology and changed office procedures.

4.2.4 Pay
1. Wages have not been increased in line with the increase in work load over the last three years.
2. Overtime rates are below the norm.

5 Conclusions
5.1 Training
There is evidence that the complaints about a lack of adequate training are justified.

5.2 Conditions
The present number of workers exceeds the amount of equipment available.

Machines are being repaired on time, but because they are old they break down more often.

There is an increase in the amount of written work, though enough people are available to complete this once the problems with office technology are resolved.

5.3 Wages
Wages are lower than the average available from other employers in the region.

6 Recommendations
1. That a new training programme be

introduced to allow employees to gain knowledge of new machines.

2. That money be allocated in the budget for the provision of new equipment, in accordance with the number of employees.

3. That wages be increased by 6 per cent to bring them into line with present standards.

William O'Brien,
Personnel officer
9 May 1998

Comment

The structure of this report is a standard one. Headings and sub-headings are clearly laid out and numbered, giving a clear indication of the structure and content. The terms of reference are clearly spelt out; the findings are arranged in logical sequence and are clearly outlined by means of sub-headings.

The language is formal and objective. The conclusions spring logically from the preceding points; the recommendations point to realistic areas for improvement.

Final check-list for reports

1. Does the title indicate the nature of the report?
2. Are the objectives of the report clearly stated?
3. Have these objectives been met in the report?
4. Is the language of the report clear? Are there obscure phrases or expressions?
5. Is there evidence of bias, of intemperate language or of emotive terms in the report?
6. Are all the terms that are used clearly defined?
7. Is the report written in the correct tense?
8. Are all the claims made clearly substantiated by fact?
9. Are the conclusions based on evidence?
10. Are the recommendations that are made feasible?

Letters and memos

Every letter carries not only information but an image of the writer and the organisation they work for. It is important to be aware of the power of this image.

There are different kinds of letters; for the most part, however, we think of them as either formal or informal.

Formal letters, which include business letters, demand the ability to choose the appropriate tone and language for the particular occasion. Informal or personal letters are not much written nowadays.

Before you start writing a letter, know what you want to say. Set out your information logically, and organise it into paragraphs. In a letter, paragraphs are signposts to your reader to help them follow your message.

Examinations on the writing of letters and memos are testing

(a) the coherent organisation of information;
(b) the use of appropriate expression;
(c) accepted standards of layout.

The layout of a letter

1. The sender's address is usually written in the top right-hand corner. However, a letter from an organisation or a company will be on a printed letter-heading, which can present the name and address in a variety of ways. Many private individuals have a printed letter-heading also.

2. The name and address of the person the letter is addressed to is usually written on the left-hand side, a little below the printed heading.

3. The date—which can be under the recipient's address or on the opposite side of the sheet—is written out fully, in the form 5 July 1999. All letters must be dated, as they are retained and become a record of the transaction.

4. Any reference number is written either above or below the recipient's address.

5. You can begin a letter with 'Dear sir or madam,' but it is far more acceptable to find out beforehand the name of the person you are writing to; you would then begin 'Dear Mr Murphy,' 'Dear Dr O'Brien,' etc.

6. The first sentence contains the main point

of your letter.

7. You can close your letter with the expression 'Yours sincerely,' 'Yours faithfully,' or 'Yours truly,' according to preference. There is no difference between these terms: they are just standard formulas. Most formal and business letters nowadays have 'Yours sincerely.'

8. Remember:
   - 'Yours' begins with a capital letter;
   - 'sincerely' has an *e*;
   - 'truly' has no *e*.

Characteristics of a letter

1. **A formal and courteous tone.** Delicacy as well as courtesy is required when you are conveying unwelcome information.
2. **Correct layout.** Use the best style, and make it pleasing to the eye.
3. **Correct spelling and punctuation.**
4. **A choice of vocabulary suitable for the person being addressed.**
5. **The absence of clichés.** Use fresh and concise language, free of jargon. Avoid verbose formulas, such as the following:

Dear Mr O'Brien,

Thank you for your letter of 27 April, which we have received. With regard to the matter that you mention in your first paragraph, you will be pleased to know that the filing-cabinets you ordered are now available.

The phrase 'which we have received' is clearly redundant, and the rest of the letter is long-winded.

Dear Mr O'Brien,

Thank you for your letter of 27 April. The filing-cabinets you ordered are now ready.

Generally, both letters and memos involve
- getting the reader's attention
- making a claim
- supporting it—justifying or explaining the claim
- calling for action—indicating what you want the reader to do, what you will do, or both.

Types of letters
Job applications

Use a form of expression that is clear and straightforward. Explain clearly such important details as dates and names.

Even if you are enclosing your CV, mention the reasons why you are suited for this particular job.

Give the times when you are available for interview, and (if possible) include a telephone number.

Some phrases for letter-writing
- I wish to apply for the position of …
- I am applying for the post of …
- In reply to your advertisement of … I would like to apply …
- I am available at any time for interview.
- I wish to apply for the course in …

Letters of complaint

A letter of complaint has to be written with a lot of care, and the control of emotion is essential in order to get the desired result.

When writing a letter of complaint, first make sure that you are complaining to the right person.

Keep letters of complaint short. Focus on the results you want rather than on the incompetence of the person or organisation involved.

Outline your problem clearly, without giving way to anger. Propose a specific solution: suggest something that can be done to remedy the problem. Make sure to keep a record of all contacts.

Here is an example of a letter of complaint:

13 Clonliff Square
Dublin 7

14 November 1997

Mr Seán Graham
Henderson Brothers Ltd
Youghal Road
Cork

Dear Mr Graham,

I am writing to you about the washing-machine that I bought from your firm last month. I am very disappointed with this machine, as it has been out of order since it was bought. The water is not filling up inside the machine; it seems to me that the motor is faulty.

The result of this damage has been enormous inconvenience to the household, as all the dirty clothes have piled up in the last few weeks. I feel that the machine should be replaced, and I would be grateful if you could take immediate action to solve the problem.

Yours sincerely,

Siobhán Murphy

Comment

In writing a letter of complaint, you must give exact details of the transaction carried out. Explain the faults clearly. Ask what action will be taken to rectify the matter. Mention the deadline required.

When writing a letter of complaint, bear in mind the following guidelines:
1. Address the letter to someone who can do something about the problem.
2. Keep the tone polite.
3. State the problem clearly and simply.
4. Give definite details that explain the *who, what, when, where* and *how* of what has happened.
5. Include a photocopy of invoices or receipts, as well as information about prices and any other important details.
6. Suggest a solution.

Answering a letter or complaint

A great deal of tact and sensitivity is needed when answering a letter of complaint. At all times keep the tone courteous, whether you are wrong or not.

Begin by acknowledging the letter and the complaint. Keep your letter clear and factual. Acknowledge the fault if you are to blame, and accept the consequences.

Mention the steps you are taking to rectify the matter, and declare that the problem will not happen again. Conclude with a renewed apology.

Features of a reply to a complaint
- Statement of regret: acknowledge that the letter of complaint has been received.
- Cause of problem: give an account, after an explanation of why it happened.
- Action to be taken: explain whatever action will be taken to remedy the complaint.
- Restatement of apology, together with the hope that good will can be retained.

Letters of condolence

Letters of this type need to be sensitively written. Address the person directly and offer your sympathies sincerely and simply. Mention your availability at any time if the person needs help or support.

Sales letters

Letters of this type are designed to win your reader over, to get them to buy your product.

Start a letter of this type by dramatising a problem. Go on to present your product or service as the solution to this problem.

Speak directly to your reader about how they will benefit from dealing with you. Quote some independent sources of authority, such as the medical profession, to enhance your credibility.

To create a note of urgency, offer a discount or a special offer to prompt the reader to act. Create or include a reference to time, as this will intensify the sense of urgency.

Form letters

Form letters are stereotyped letters that are prepared with standard wording that can be sent to many people. They are designed to suit all routine occasions.

This type of letter can be impersonal, or it can be used as the basis of a more individually tailored letter, in which some paragraphs are standardised and others are customised.

Memos

A *memo* (short for 'memorandum', meaning a reminder) is an internal letter, with a fixed structure and usually written on a printed form, to someone within the same organisation. Memos are usually handwritten.

A good memo should be brief and to the point. It should be unambiguous and clear. It should be relevant and have no digressions.

Memos must be polite and courteous, even when demanding that instant action be taken.

Here are some sample memos:

O'Brien and Flood Ltd

From: John Armstrong, sales director
To: Aisling Griffin, office manager
Subject: Collecting delph from airport
Date: 4 May 1998

Arrangements have been made to collect delph (order no. IL 632) from the airport on Friday at 11 a.m.

From: Mary Downey
To: Head Office
Subject: Returning jeans
Date: 30 April 1999

1. Returning jeans, wrong colour and size, as discussed on phone.
2. Please replace with model specified in order 406613, dated 2 Feb. 1998 (size 14, colour blue).
3. If this is not in stock, please credit this branch.

Operating instructions

A well-written set of instructions begins with a statement of the general aim of the procedure, or an outline of the various steps or stages in the instructions.

1. Choose a sequence for your information. Work from the main points downwards to details, not the other way around.
2. Use the imperative form of the verb.
3. Avoid ambiguity: instructions must be clear-cut and complete.
4. Avoid negative instructions.
5. Be flexible in your organisation of information and layout.

Generally, instructions consist of
- introductory explanations
- information about tools required
- information about materials required
- definitions
- warnings.

Look at the two following sets of instructions on the handling of incoming post, then answer the questions.

Instructions for dealing with incoming post

1. Open all letters. Check for enclosures and place in tray marked Encl.
2. Stamp letters with current date. Place in tray marked L.
3. Cross all drafts and cheques with name of company's bank.
4. Make note of amount in cheques and pass them to cashier.
5. Record all registered letters and addressees in appropriate book.

Instructions for dealing with incoming post

1. All envelopes should be opened completely, so that no enclosure is missed.
2. Enclosures should be placed in the tray labelled "Encl."
3. Letters should be stamped with a date and placed in the tray labelled "L".
4. Check that all bank drafts and cheques are crossed with the name of the company's bank.
5. Make a note of the amount of each cheque, and pass cheques on to the cash department.
6. Registered letters should be recorded in the registered letters book, and a note should be made of who the letter is addressed to.

Check-list for writing instructions

1. Clarity is an indispensable feature of good instructions, so make your statements specific.
2. There must be a logical sequence in the different stages of your instructions.
3. Make sure that the different stages or steps are manageable. Say one thing in each sentence.
4. Put the most important item in each sentence at the beginning.
5. Use the imperative mood of the verb.
6. Use short sentences and short paragraphs.
7. Avoid jargon.

The language of persuasion

A good persuasive writer must be able to express their viewpoint both clearly and logically. A persuasive composition will rely less on fact and argument and more on using opinion and ideas in a convincing and effective fashion.

Method of constructing a persuasive article or composition

1. Know your audience. Know the interests, the knowledge and the motivations of your readers, and adapt your material accordingly. Remember that an article on the dangers of smoking will have little interest to non-smokers, just as a composition on the joys of cooking will probably not interest a group of schoolboys.
2. Adapt your tone and language to the particular reader that you are addressing.
3. Use techniques such as a colourful anecdote or a note of humour to communicate your point more vividly.
4. Do not make sweeping statements or broad generalisations but support your opinions with clear facts. Some examples of sweeping statements are:
   'All teenagers are lazy.'
   'Television corrupts young people.'
   'Books are boring.'

Examine the following article, which is written in a persuasive style on a way of overcoming shyness.

The 43-year-old woman from La Jolla, California, lived in constant fear of strangers, whether at parties with her husband or at school functions with her three children. 'I endured these events', she says, 'by keeping as quiet as possible, not looking anyone in the eye, and just waiting for the hour when I could go home.'

Today this woman has learnt to overcome her shyness, using techniques that are found to be successful in countless cases. She has a circle of friends and is active in the community. She also realises she was not alone in her problem.

There may be no 'cures' for shyness. However, research is uncovering ways in which shy people can overcome their problem so it doesn't take such a toll on their happiness.

Here's the best of the experts' advice:

Use a diary to get to the root of your fears. 'A written record is a cheap, effective therapist,' says Christopher McCullough, a psychotherapist and the author of *Always at Ease*. 'We know more about ourselves than we think, and it is often surprising what comes out when we write down our thoughts and fears.'

Create an un-shy version of yourself, and rehearse your own scenes. A fifty-year-old woman found that her embarrassment vanished when she took a role in a play. Acting became a solution to her shyness.

Simple changes in body language can be most surprising in their immediate results. Shy people send out signals of coldness and withdrawal, often without realising it, says Arthur Wassmer, a psychologist and the author of *Making Contact*. Unfortunately, other people interpret this language as aloofness or conceit and stay away, making the shy person feel even more insecure.

Take small steps. A 35-year-old bookkeeper wanted to take accountancy classes but was too shy. She was afraid she would be called on to speak. First, she walked around the college. Next she signed up for a lecture. She sat at the back and spoke to the person beside her. Eventually she enrolled for a bookkeeping course. Finally she enrolled in the accountancy course and did so well that she was asked to tutor students. When she took on the role of a teacher her shyness went away.

If shy people work at it, most are able to cope with the problem. You're not going to wake up one morning transformed into the life and soul of the party. In fact you may always feel shy inside; but you'll forge ahead and connect with others, and in so doing you'll be refusing to stand on the sidelines of life. That's the real victory.

The use of the anecdotes here lends weight and colour to the arguments.

Exercises

1. Rewrite the following sentences to eliminate unnecessary repetition. (Suggested answers on page 241.)
   (a) Pupils get bored easily in the summer holidays, so pupils should get summer jobs.
   (b) If you cannot see how serious this issue is, I'd seriously think you should consider retiring.
   (c) Life is at best a wonderful experience, but to experience life one must experience happiness and suffering.
   (d) The worst fear has to be the fear of failure, which is a tremendous fear.
   (e) This great story would darken anyone's mind and open anyone's eyes.
   (f) Big cities are overpopulated, overdiseased and so so dirty.
   (g) How can these people know any other way when there's nothing there to teach them another way of life!
   (h) What we've got here is failure: failure to relate, failure to see, failure to communicate—in short failure in life.
   (i) What we don't think of is how long it took them to get there and at what cost.
2. Shorten and increase the vigour of the following sentences, and make any other corrections necessary. (Suggested answers on page 242.)
   (a) I have nothing to offer but blood, toil, sweating, and crying.
   (b) The manager described the department's problems succinctly, clearly, and with candour.

   (c) Reviewing the records daily is as important as to collect accurate information.
   (d) Society has come to the conclusion that law-abiding citizens, who perhaps have a speeding fine at the top of their law-breaking activities, are the exception to the rule in modern society.
   (e) Charles Jarvis is an excellent lecturer, personable conversationalist, and he writes well also.
   (f) Sport has been alive in the world for as long as the history books can tell, and there is no sign of its death.
   (g) People who you might never expect to be interested in soccer could have been washed away by the sea of emotion that swept through Ireland when Ray Houghton scored in the one-nil victory over Italy.
   (h) Life, with its abundance of trials and tribulations, has dealt yet another obstacle that I must overcome, this takes the form of my parents, the bane of my life.
   (i) That night while I was cleaning my room I heard somebody roaring, so I looked out the window; it was the same man throwing stones at everything he saw and roaring at the same time and luckily no-one was outside.
   (j) The amount of young people devoting their lives to youth work and the work and effort that is put in is amazing.
3. Say whether the following groups of words

are whole sentences or sentence fragments.
(Answers on page 242.)

(a) Although it rained.

(b) On the way.

(c) The apostrophe is also used to denote ownership or possession.

(d) You can add the page to a particular folder.

(e) Take a look around.

(f) Happy surfing!

4. Rewrite the following sentences, making them more terse and concise. (Suggested answers on page 242.)

(a) Down through the years I have been graced in contact with a diverse and deep lagoon of people, from every possible race and creed.

(b) Enclosed is a copy of last year's annual report for the fiscal year 1976.

(c) It is my opinion that the co-operation shown by the employees and the co-operation shown by the management was responsible for last year's increase in sales.

(d) At some point in time we must decide on whether or not we are going to build the new addition.

(e) Because all the data is not available, we will withhold making a decision until such time as all the data is accessible.

(f) The power of love is all around and cannot be challenged by any other emotional or physical feeling.

(g) The writer's purpose in writing this passage is to show that the people of society today are very careful to keep the status quo of this society.

(h) The writer's use of statistics, facts and references conveys a clear, persuasive tone.

(i) There was a period of expansion in new areas and then more slowly until it reached a peak in 1998.

Exercises on grammar
(Answers on page 242.)

1. Pick out the nouns in each of the following

sentences and say what kind they are.

(a) Jane went to France with a group of pupils.

(b) The women returned from Madrid in fear.

(c) The team were praised for their courage.

(d) Mrs Smith saw the crowd in Lisbon.

(e) Charity is a strong virtue.

2. Rewrite the following sentences to eliminate all grammatical errors. (Suggested answers on page 243.)

(a) After researching the topic for five months my supervisor cancelled the project.

(b) After being rejected by three companies my employment counsellor suggested I rewrite my CV.

(c) To learn the technique thoroughly the first three exercises must be completed.

(d) Joan is the cleverest of the two.

(e) Entering the golf course the lightning struck.

(f) Their is no hatred among Jack and Mary.

(g) Each of the boys must wear their uniform.

(h) Never before in our great history have we needed the art of conversation to grace our lives more than now.

(i) Is anyone going to be their?

(j) I cannot work like I used to.

3. Rewrite the following sentences, adding apostrophes where necessary to show possession. (Answers on page 243.)

(a) The towns main street is very narrow.

(b) The boys ties are in a bad state.

(c) After yesterdays events I feel very hopeful.

(d) The typist finds Dr Thorntons letters very hard to understand.

(e) Womens rights in this century have been a point of contention.

4. Rewrite the following sentences, adding apostrophes where necessary to show where letters have been omitted. (Answers on page 243.)

(a) Wouldnt it be marvellous to go!

(b) Its not going to rain yet.

(c) Youll find it in the press under the stairs.

(d) Hurry up or well never get there on time.

(e) I didnt say theyre mad.

5. Insert appropriate prepositions in the following sentences.(Answers on page 243.)

(a) You will have to allow … some extra expenses in university.

(b) They carried … their work in spite of the interruptions.

(c) Watch … the sign: I don't want to get lost.

(d) Have you heard … Nora … her return?

(e) She insisted … reading the report.

(f) I'll have to work harder … it, and spend more time … it.

6. Fill in the gaps with appropriate conjunctions.(Answers on page 243.)

(a) Her cat is small … wild.

(b) She was treated with respect … with fear.

(c) The film was funny … simple.

(d) Did you take the train … the bus?

(e) The electrician turned the key … the motor started.

(f) The detectives searched the warehouse … they did not find the file.

Exercises on punctuation

Rewrite the following sentences, putting in the correct punctuation and making any other corrections necessary. (Suggested answers on page 243.)

(a) And now ladies and gentlemen we come to the most interesting exhibit of all.

(b) Your dinner is on the table she shouted all right he replied Im coming now.

(c) He entered the room locked the door took out his papers and seated himself at the desk.

(d) Faith family and football in that order are the most important things in my life but keeping the balance is not easy.

(e) Has she injured you he asked.

(f) Eat more meat otherwise you will regret it.

(g) He said Im going out now and I will be in by nine dont wait up for me.

(h) My younger brother who is a tax inspector knows all about this matter he will advise you best.

(i) Were waiting for the school bus said the children its late again weve made a terrible mistake to wait so long.

Distinguish opinion from evidence in the following sentences

(a) Mother Teresa was one of the best-known and most-loved religious personalities in Christianity. She was well known in Ireland, and in the early seventies her attempt to establish a mission in Belfast ran up against the hostility of the local church establishment.

(b) Harryville, an obscure suburb in Ballymena, may become a watershed in the conflict in Northern Ireland. For the last three months loyalist thugs have waylaid local Catholics on their way to Mass at the weekend.

(c) The French authorities have reacted cautiously to speculation that the bomb outrage in the Paris metro on Tuesday evening was the work of Algerian militants. It is a situation that France, with its large and increasingly restive North African population, is ill equipped to deal with.

(d) There are cities in the world that are always hard to leave, and Prague is definitely one of them.

(e) Camping in the desert is another invigorating change from ordinary life. The Wahiba Sands, a great sand sea inland from Oman's eastern coast, consists of wave after wave of precipitous ridges leading to moonscape plateaus.

Distinguish which of the following deductive arguments are false. State your reasons.

(a) All Europeans eat rice. John is a European. Therefore John eats rice.

(b) All wise men are virtuous. Plato was a wise man. Therefore Plato was virtuous.

(c) All birds have feathers. The sparrow is a bird. Therefore the sparrow has feathers.

(d) All humans will die. Harry is a human. Therefore Harry will die.

Exercises on the paragraph

1. Look at the following sentences, which are in random order. Rewrite them in order to make a coherent paragraph. (Answers on page 243.)

    (a) Poe enjoys cheery subjects like premature burial, plague, the ghastly ruin of an old family, reincarnation, and walling people up in dungeons or vaults.

    (b) What are some of the usual themes of horror fiction?

    (c) A frequent motif is human metamorphosis into animal forms.

    (d) Stoker and King go in for the ugly perversion of vampirism.

    (e) Other odd obsessions are putrefaction, gore, cruelty, torment, sorcery, witchery, demonic possession and madness.

    (f) Mervyn Peake favours degeneracy in labyrinthine castles, foul and cobwebby, slithery and sibilant.

2. The following paragraph has one sentence that breaks the unity. Identify this sentence. (Answer on page 244.)

    The African interior had waited many centuries for the coming of Christianity, and it was not until the late 1800s that missionaries from various European countries followed in the footsteps of explorers like Dr Livingstone. Portugal, Spain, Italy and France took the Catholic faith to the areas they colonised, while Holland and England spread Protestantism. Around 1800 a group of White Fathers were sent by Cardinal Lavigerie from Algeria, which was under French rule, to Buganda in east Africa, a part of what is now Uganda. The missionaries quickly pointed out to Mukabya the error of his ways. The travelling conditions were appalling. They made the journey from Zanzibar on foot. Those who reached Buganda after several months of trekking through the jungle found the situation far from encouraging.

Exercises on pre-composition writing

1. Rephrase the following composition titles as questions:
    The craze for speed
    The beauty of our country
    Road rage
    Relationships
    A good youth club

2. Draft an outline on one of the following topics.
    The seaside in winter
    My kind of music
    The joys of love
    Nothing venture, nothing win

3. Brainstorm *four* of the following topics, and write out a rough draft of the opening paragraph.
    Ireland is still a wonderful country in which to live
    Responsibilities
    An unforgettable character I know well
    Looking through old magazines
    My way
    An unexpected visitor

4. Free-write on one of the following topics.
    Cowardice
    Roads
    Weather—its influence on our lives
    Dieting
    The forgotten war
    Killing time

5. Write an anecdotal opening paragraph on each of the following titles.
    The power of laughter
    Old photographs
    If only …
    Moonlight on the river

6. Write a short story on one of the following topics.
    Leaving home
    A nightmare
    Alone in a forest
    Strangers in the night
    Dreams

7. Write a speech for a debate on one of the following topics.
    (a) City life and country life—the problems

are the same
- (b) Growing up changes your view of the world
- (c) School holidays should be shorter
- (d) Everything nowadays is disposable, even people
- (e) Modern woman has lost her charm

8. Take each of the following opening sentences and write a narrative-style composition.
   - (a) It was late on Saturday night and she was peacefully watching television when suddenly she heard an ear-piercing scream.
   - (b) She moved forward to investigate the noise, when a rough hand gripped her from behind.
   - (c) He struggled wildly, tearing his clothes as he moved in the undergrowth.
   - (d) He stumbled on the worn path, unable to control his flight.
   - (e) When I walked in over the threshold I felt an uncanny sensation that I had been there before.

9. Add words that appeal to the sense of taste, hearing and touch to make the following sentences more specific.
   - (a) Our mother's house needs cleaning.
   - (b) My granny's special pie is tasty.
   - (c) The drive through the valley was relaxing.
   - (d) My uncle painted the front door.
   - (e) The car made a noise as it moved down the street.
   - (f) Her dress was flattering.
   - (g) Peppermint has an interesting taste.
   - (h) The price of crisps is appalling.
   - (i) The noise of the drill drowned the lecturer's voice.

10. Rewrite the following sentences, using active verbs and descriptive adjectives to make the writing more specific and detailed.
    - (a) My house is a mess.
    - (b) The girl rode her bicycle on the footpath.
    - (c) The old woman walked down the lane.

- (d) Our park is very untidy.
- (e) My pet cat can do a number of tricks.
- (f) It is easy to understand why she gets angry.
- (g) My county has many historic sites.
- (h) The dinner we got there was not tasty.
- (i) Our campsite was unappealing.
- (j) There are many professions that interest me.

11. Select a small object—for example an apple, orange, pen, or watch; spend five minutes recording on paper the shape, colour, and size. Make *four* detailed observations about this object.
    Record less prominent features, such as indentations, minor gradations in colour, and the smell, taste, feel and sound of the object.

12. Rewrite the following sentences to include *four* descriptive details and to make the expression more vivid.
    - (a) My father, a butcher, had rough hands.
    - (b) The garden had a nice colour in spring.
    - (c) My old bicycle has an unusual colour.
    - (d) I opened several parcels on my birthday.
    - (e) The animal crawled across the road.

13. Rewrite the following sentences to include a strong focus on description.
    - (a) The girl crawled under the bed.
    - (b) The car moved out from the kerb.
    - (c) Men generally sleep more easily.
    - (d) The garda moved away from the building.
    - (e) Night fell quickly on the land.
    - (f) Darkness crept up silently.
    - (g) Sarah had a short walk.
    - (h) Miriam left the library at four o'clock.
    - (i) The man moved slowly away from the house.
    - (j) The cat remained motionless on the wall.

14. Draft a questionnaire based on the suggestion that television has undermined the literacy level of school-going children. Include a list of specific questions that require short answers but that will reflect the problems involved. Pay attention to

(a) the people who will be answering the questions;

(b) the size of the questionnaire (twenty to thirty questions should be enough);

(c) the issues you want to identify and pinpoint;

(d) possible solutions.

Exercises on letter-writing

1. Write a letter to a newspaper about some issue you feel strongly about.

2. Write a letter of application for a summer job in a restaurant.

3. Write a letter of sympathy to a friend whose mother has died.

4. Write a letter to a friend describing a problem you are having in a relationship.

5. Write a letter of complaint to a local TD about the state of the footpaths in your area.

Exercises on reports

Write a report of 300 to 350 words on the following questions. Define the terms of reference yourself, and do not worry about constructing accurate facts: the important thing to bear in mind is using the correct layout.

(a) As secretary of a foreign-language school, you have been asked to write a report on a trade fair that you attended in Geneva.

(b) You are the personnel manager of a large department store. You have been asked by the managing director to make a report on the number of employees, the quality of their work, and suggestions for improvements.

(c) You are employed as secretary in a secondary school. Prepare an information report on the effects of severe weather during December and January.

(d) You are chief librarian in a university where the facilities cannot provide for the large number of students. Write a report on the library, with recommendations for possible improvements.

(e) You are the secretary of a youth club. You have been offered premises at a low rent, for three years only. Write a report for the committee on the situation of the club and on the need for a new venue.

Exercises on 'loaded' or subjective language

Express the meaning of the following sentences in precise, factual and objective language. (Suggested answers on page 244.)

(a) A soft light spreads across the polished aluminium control panel, illuminating the combined CD, radio and cassette-player in readiness for your decision.

(b) A superb three-year unlimited mileage warranty makes it very, very safe.

(c) Relax and get ready to succumb to the purity of sound as your chosen piece of music envelops you.

(d) Nothing penetrates deeper, while the formula replenishes the shine, root to tip, to bring out your hair's true potential.

(e) The bottom line is that all this technology and expertise puts reliable and more affordable international communication in your hands.

(f) Now wearing heels—even high heels—can be a painless pleasure with these unique new insoles.

(g) It's a personal touch that not only conveys a professional image to your callers but also ensures that all your calls are captured.

(h) The highly acclaimed stylish and sporty Supra combines thrilling performance with the sort of traffic-stopping good looks of a classy sports car.

(i) It's a stupendous award-winning mechanism that utilises a positive electromagnetic charge, which as a result produces about 90 per cent less ozone than other organic drums.

(j) These wide-leg, flat-fronted jeans with authentic styling details are available in many sizes.

Answers to Exercises

Exercise 1 (page 236)
(a) Pupils get bored easily in the summer

holidays, so they should get jobs.

(b) If you cannot see how serious this issue is, I think you should consider retiring.

(c) Life is at best a wonderful experience, though it involves both suffering and happiness.

(d) The worst and most tremendous fear is failure.

(e) This great story would both darken the mind and open one's eyes.

(f) Big cities are dirty, disease-ridden, and overpopulated.

(g) How can these people know anything else when they have nobody to teach them?

(h) What we've got here is failure at every level.

(i) Our society today tends to accept these problems as everyday occurrences, without doing all it can to prevent them.

Exercise 2 (page 236)

(a) I have nothing to offer but blood, sweat, tears, and toil.

(b) The manager described the department's problems succinctly, clearly, and candidly.

(c) It is as important to review the records daily as it is to collect accurate information.

(d) Law-abiding citizens who have a speeding fine are an exception to the rule in modern society.

(e) Charles Jarvis is an excellent lecturer, a personable conversationalist, and a good writer.

(f) Sport has been popular for a long time, and it looks as if this will continue.

(g) People who were never interested in soccer were overjoyed when Ray Houghton scored in the one-nil victory over Italy.

(h) Life has an abundance of obstacles; the greatest one at present is my parents.

(i) While I was cleaning my room that night, I saw the same man throwing stones and shouting at the same time. Luckily, no-one was outside.

(j) The number of young people dedicating their time and skills to youth work is striking.

Exercise 3 (page 236)

(a) Sentence fragment.

(b) Sentence fragment.

(c) Sentence.

(d) Sentence.

(e) Sentence.

(f) Sentence fragment.

Exercise 4 (page 237)

(a) Over the years, I have been enriched by contact with a wide variety of people from different races and creeds.

(b) Enclosed is a copy of the annual report for the fiscal year 1976.

(c) I believe that the co-operation shown by employees and the management was responsible for the increase in sales last year.

(d) We must decide soon whether or not we are going to build the new extension.

(e) We will withhold a decision until we have the necessary information.

(f) Love is universal, and it cannot be challenged by any other emotion.

(g) The writer's purpose in the passage is to show that most people today are careful to maintain the status quo in society.

(h) The sound of horns beeping, the screeching of brakes, the sound of bags, briefcases and boxes clattering, together with the high-pitched noises of people, were to be heard as they made their way down O'Connell Street.

(i) The writer's use of statistics, facts and references is persuasively communicated.

(j) Expansion occurred in new areas; it then slowed down, until it reached a peak in 1998.

Exercises on grammar
Exercise 1 (page 237)

(a) 'Jane': proper noun; 'France': proper noun; 'group': collective noun.

(b) 'Women': common noun; 'Madrid': proper noun; 'fear': abstract noun.

(c) 'Team': collective noun; 'courage': abstract noun.

(d) 'Mrs Smith': proper noun (noun phrase); 'crowd': collective noun; 'Lisbon': proper noun.

(e) 'Charity': abstract noun; 'virtue': common noun.

Exercise 2 (page 237)

(a) After I had researched the topic for five months, my supervisor cancelled the project.

(b) After I had been rejected by three companies, my employment counsellor suggested that I should rewrite my CV.

(c) The first three exercises must be completed in order to learn the technique thoroughly.

(d) John is the cleverer of the two.

(e) As I was entering the golf course, the lightning struck.

(f) There is no hatred between Jack and Mary.

(g) Each of the boys must wear his uniform.

(h) The art of conversation is needed now more than ever before, in order to enrich our lives.

(i) Will anyone be there?

(j) I cannot work as I used to.

Exercise 3 (page 237)

(a) The town's main street is very narrow.

(b) The boys' ties are in a bad state.

(c) After yesterday's events, I feel very hopeful.

(d) The typist finds Dr Thornton's letters very hard to understand.

(e) Women's rights in this century have been a point of contention.

Exercise 4 (page 237)

(a) Wouldn't it be marvellous to go!

(b) It's not going to rain yet.

(c) You'll find it in the press under the stairs.

(d) Hurry up, or we'll never get there on time.

(e) I didn't say they're mad.

Exercise 5 (page 238)

(a) for

(b) out

(c) out ... for

(d) from ... since

(e) on

(f) at ... on

Exercise 6 (page 238)

(a) but

(b) but

(c) but

(d) or

(e) and

(f) but

Exercise on punctuation (page 238)

(a) And now, ladies and gentlemen, we come to the most interesting exhibit of all.

(b) 'Your dinner is on the table!' she shouted. 'All right,' he replied. 'I'm coming now.'

(c) He entered the room, locked the door, took out his papers, and seated himself at the desk.

(d) Faith, family and football—in that order—are the most important things in my life; but keeping the balance is not easy.

(e) 'Has she injured you?' he asked.

(f) Eat more meat; otherwise you will regret it.

(g) He said, 'I'm going out now, and I will be in by nine. Don't wait up for me.'

(h) My younger brother, who is a tax inspector, knows all about this matter. He will advise you best.

(i) 'We're waiting for the school bus,' said the children. 'It's late again. We've made a terrible mistake to wait so long.'

Exercises on the paragraph (page 239)

1. (c)
2. (a)
3. (b)
4. (d)
5. (f)
6. (e)

Exercise 2 (page 239)

The sentence beginning 'The missionaries quickly pointed out to Mukabya ...' breaks the unity in this paragraph.

Exercises on 'loaded' or subjective language (page 241)

(a) There is a CD-player, a radio and a cassette-player inside the aluminium control panel.

(b) A three-year unlimited mileage warranty makes it very safe.

(c) Relax with your favourite music.

(d) This shampoo penetrates deeply and will make your hair shiny.

(e) With this technology you can get cheaper and more reliable communications internationally.

(f) With these insoles you can even wear high heels.

(g) Your calls will be answered in a professional manner.

(h) The Supra is a sports car that operates very well.

(i) It's a mechanism that employs a positive electromagnetic charge, which produces about 90 per cent less ozone than other organic drums.

(j) These jeans, which are wide-leg and flat-fronted, are available in many sizes.